Thinking About Basic Beliefs:

An Introduction to Philosophy

Howard Kahane
University of Maryland
Baltimore County

WADSWORTH PUBLISHING COMPANY
Belmont, California
A Division of Wadsworth, Inc.

Philosophy Editor: Kenneth King
Production Editor: Robin Lockwood
Designer: Hal Lockwood
Copy Editor: Linda Purrington

Cover photograph of dunes and lenticular cloud, Death
Valley, by David Cross.

Printed in the United States of America

1 2 3 4 5 6 7 8 9 10—87 86 85 84 83

ISBN 0-534-01318-X

Library of Congress Cataloging in Publication Data

Kahane, Howard, 1928–
    Thinking about basic beliefs.

    Includes index.
    1. Philosophy—Introductions.   I. Title.
BD21.K33 1983   100   82-21850
ISBN 0-534-01318-X

To my mother and father

Preface

To act without clear understanding, to form habits without investigation,
to follow a path all one's life without knowing where it really leads—
such is the behavior of the multitude. —MENG-TSE

William James used to preach the "will to believe." For my part,
. . . what is wanted is not the will to believe, but the wish to find out,
which is the exact opposite. —BERTRAND RUSSELL

Philosophy is doubt. —MONTAIGNE

The theme of this book is thinking about basic beliefs—those fun-
damentals of our reasoning that may seem so obvious or unquestionable
that we usually take them for granted. Chapter One concerns belief
in God; Chapter Two, belief in free will, determinism, and responsibility; Three, belief in induction (a pattern of reasoning), a physical
world, "other minds," and life after death; Four, moral or ethical
beliefs; and Five, beliefs about social and political institutions and
practices. Chapter Six crosscuts the subject matter by discussing several
recent schools in philosophy, showing how they tend to deal with
some of the beliefs discussed in the first five chapters.

Each chapter contains a systematic discussion of the topics in that
chapter plus relevant short excerpts selected from the great philosophers. The intention is that the two (systematic account and famous
excerpts) together form a more useful tool for today's students than
either one would alone. While the systematic account is complete in
itself, the excerpts from the great philosophers are intended to broaden
the systematic account, and in any event to expose students however
briefly to some of the great writing on the subject. *Extreme* care has
been taken in the selection and editing of these passages; on the whole
only the best known passages are included, and they are edited so as
to ease student comprehension.

A summary at the end of each chapter gives a short resume of the systematic content of that chapter, and is followed by some questions for further thought.

Every effort has been made to make the issues, positions, and arguments in the systematic exposition as clear and concise as possible. Technical material and terms have been kept at a minimum, and those that are included have been carefully explained (key terms appear in their first or most important use in boldface). In addition a running side margin synopsis is included for both the systematic and quoted material, so that it can be more easily located and so that students will more easily grasp the main thrust of things.

The chief problem in teaching an introductory philosophy course is whether to take a systematic or an historical approach. There are obvious virtues and defects in each approach. In particular, there is the problem today's students have in comprehending some of the great works, leading many of us to take a primarily systematic approach. Yet teaching philosophy without having students read anything from Hume, Descartes, Plato, Kant, or any of the classic figures seems less than optimal. This text attempts a particular marriage of the two basic ways of teaching introductory philosophy that some of us have found successful over the years.

Many thanks to my introduction to philosophy students at the University of Pennsylvania, Whitman College, the University of Kansas, Bernard Baruch College (CUNY), and the University of Maryland Baltimore County (UMBC) for their (unwitting) help in the writing of this book. Thanks also to my friends Alan Hausman (Ohio State University), Charles Landesman (Hunter College, CUNY), and Nancy Cavender (College of Marin), and to the publisher's readers: A. Serge Kappler (Southern Methodist University), Lewis M. Schwartz (Lehman College, CUNY), and Alfred MacKay (Oberlin College).

Contents

3   Skepticism and Knowledge   69

CONTENTS

CONTENTS

Introduction

What is the use of studying philosophy if all that it does for you is to enable you to talk with some plausibility about some abstruse questions of logic, etc., and if it does not improve your thinking about the important questions of everyday life. . . ? —LUDWIG WITTGENSTEIN

It seems clear that philosophy somehow is relevant to the important questions human beings deal with in their everyday lives. But it is a matter of great dispute just how philosophy relates to these everyday issues and in particular how philosophy is to be characterized or defined. And the answers philosophers give to the question "what is philosophy" themselves tend to be quite hard to understand without a certain amount of philosophical sophistication or training. That's why the question "what is philosophy" is discussed in this text, to the extent it is discussed, at the end of the book, rather than at the beginning.

Perhaps the best way to come to an understanding of the nature of philosophy is to plunge into some of its basic questions, such as whether there is a God, whether we have freedom of the will, and so on. So this text has selected a few basic topics from the broad field of philosophy to illustrate the philosophic enterprise.

But it has also selected topics in philosophy with an eye to their connection to the problems and disputes that arise in everyday life. An example is the chapters on ethics and social and political philosophy, whose relevance to everyday controversies concerning, say, abortion, fair distribution of wealth, when we're justified in lying, and so on, is obvious.

Although there is no uncontroversial way to characterize philosophy, as we just said, the author does, of course, have his own ideas on the matter, which in fact are somewhat along the lines of the analytic philosophy discussed in Chapter Six. There is no such thing as a completely neutral approach to philosophy, so it is important for the student to note the point of view of the author of any philosophy text.

Even though there is wild disagreement as to the nature of philosophy itself, perhaps one thing can be said about it which most philosophers would accept, that philosophy is the one subject which has no unquestioned assumptions. Philosophers deal with exactly those basic assumptions other disciplines tend to take for granted. For instance, working scientists *use* something called scientific method, but questions *about* scientific method, whether raised by scientists themselves or by peers, are part of the *philosophy* of science.

In other words, philosophers are concerned with our most basic beliefs, accepting nothing without careful examination and proof (or perhaps proof that proof is impossible). This includes even philosophical method itself. Philosophers "keep the books" on everyone, including themselves, on every discipline, including philosophy. It is, therefore, the only self referential or circular discipline (although even that claim is controversial), a fact which, for this writer, gives philosophy a large part, if not of its charm, certainly of its challenge. It is a wonderful activity in which, if we do it well, we succeed in pulling ourselves up by our own bootstraps.

Thinking About Basic Beliefs

It is the heart which experiences God, and not reason. This then is faith: God felt by heart, not by reason.—BLAISE PASCAL

It is expedient that there should be Gods, and as it is expedient, let us believe they exist.
—OVID

If God did not exist, it would be necessary to invent him.—VOLTAIRE

The presence of a superior reasoning power . . . revealed in the incomprehensible universe, forms my idea of God.
—ALBERT EINSTEIN

The name of God is truth.—HINDU PROVERB

Reason unaided by revelation can prove that God exists.   —ROMAN CATHOLIC BALTIMORE CATECHISM (1949 REVISED)

We turn toward God only to obtain the impossible.—ALBERT CAMUS

Archbishop of Paris (to Clemenceau): "Is it really true, Monsieur, you do not believe in God?"
    Clemenceau: "And you, Monsieur?"

One may say with one's lips: "I believe that God is one, and also three"—but no one can believe it, because the words have no sense.
—LEO TOLSTOY

The god of the cannibals will be a cannibal, of the crusaders a crusader, and of the merchants a merchant.—RALPH WALDO EMERSON

Religious values were all considered by the people as equally true; by the philosophers as equally false; and by the magistrates as equally useful.
—GIBBON (on the declining Roman Empire)

Faith, n. Belief without evidence in what is told by one who speaks without knowledge, of things without parallel.—AMBROSE BIERCE (*The Devil's Dictionary*)

That fear first created the gods is perhaps as true as anything so brief on so great a subject.—SANTAYANA

Man is certainly stark mad. He cannot make a flea, and yet he will be making gods by the dozen.—MONTAIGNE

I believe firmly in Divine Providence. Without belief in Providence I think I should go crazy. Without God the world would be a maze without a clue.—WOODROW WILSON

No person who shall deny the being of God, or the truth of the Christian religion, shall be capable of holding any office or place of trust or profit.   —STATE OF NORTH CAROLINA CONSTITUTION (1836)

We have no choice but to be guilty. God is unthinkable if we are innocent.
—ARCHIBALD MACLEISH

A false friend, an unjust judge, a braggart, hypocrite, and tyrant, sincere in hatred, jealous, vain and revengeful, false in promise, honest in curse, suspicious, ignorant, infamous and hideous—such is the God of the Pentateuch.—ROBERT G. INGERSOLL

He was a wise man who originated the idea of God.—EURIPIDES

It is the final proof of God's omnipotence that he need not exist in order to save us.
—PETER DE VRIES

I don't believe in God because I don't believe in Mother Goose.—CLARENCE DARROW

I do not know how to teach philosophy without becoming a disturber of established religion.—SPINOZA (when offered a Heidelberg professorship)

The world would be astonished if it knew how great a proportion of its brightest ornaments, or those most distinguished even in popular estimation for wisdom and virtue, are complete skeptics in religion.—JOHN STUART MILL

William James used to preach the "will to believe." For my part, I should wish to preach the "will to doubt." . . . What is wanted is not the will to believe, but the will to find out, which is the exact opposite.
—BERTRAND RUSSELL

1

God

THE EXISTENCE OF GOD is one of the most controversial issues in philosophy. **Theists** believe that God exists, **atheists** that he doesn't, and **agnostics** that we don't have good reason to believe one way or the other. The thesis of this chapter is that we can't prove either the theistic or atheistic position—belief in God, ultimately, comes down to a matter of *faith*.

Theists, atheists, agnostics.

1. What Do We Mean by the Concept of God?

Let's note first that God and the *idea or concept* of God are two different things. One can exist without the other, just as the idea of Santa Claus can (and does) exist even though Santa Claus does not. So the statements "The concept of Santa Claus exists" and "The concept of God exists" both are true, while the statement "Santa Claus exists" is false. The issue to be discussed in this chapter is whether there is good reason to believe either that the statement "God exists" is true, or that it is false.

God and the idea of God are different. The question is whether God exists.

The Concept of God Is Ambiguous

Notice that the concept of God is **ambiguous,** or in other words, that there is more than one conception of God. In particular, the concept of God differs from society to society and from person to person. Some, for example, think of God as a perfect being who created the universe, while others think of him as something less than perfect (for instance, as jealous and having a chosen people, the way he is described in the

The concept of God is ambiguous, and differs from society to society and person to person.

1

Old Testament). Some conceive of God as being in space, even always at the same place; others conceive of him as immaterial and not located anywhere in particular. The ancient Egyptians, just as the ancient Greeks, thought not of *a* god, but of many gods (examples from the Egyptian animal gods alone are crocodile, wolf, and cat gods, and Taurt, who had the head of a hippo, the back and tail of a crocodile, and the claws of a lion).

The Concept of God Is Vague

The concept of God is vague.

Furthermore, most conceptions of God are **vague;** that is, they are unclear, imprecise, or "fuzzy around the edges." Is God, in your conception, perfect or less than perfect? If perfect, what does that mean? In the Book of Genesis, God is described as having a voice, walking, being retributive (punishing the guilty) and perhaps even vindictive, and as having made mistakes (recall that he repents having created human beings). Can a God be perfect and still make mistakes or be vindictive? Do you conceive of God as existing at some particular place? Is he the sort of entity who has a consciousness and pays attention to prayers? Does God have a sex? And if so is it male, as we imply by referring to him as a "he"? Most people, even believers, have a hard time answering questions of this kind. Yet the less clear our conception of God is, the less content there is in our belief in God. Or to put it the other way around, only to the extent that our idea of God is clear can our belief in God be a belief in *something.*

The less clear our idea of God, the less content in our belief in God.

A Standard Conception of God

A standard Judeo-Christian God, a personal God.

Even though the concepts of God are many and vague, most Jews and Christians, at any rate, have a particular sort of God in mind, even though they differ over detail. They would tend to agree, for instance, that God has much greater power, intelligence, knowledge, and goodness than human beings possess; that he created the universe and can will to do whatever is in his power; that he is a personal God (one who is concerned about individual human welfare, who listens to and, if he so chooses, answers our prayers) as opposed to an impersonal God (one who is not aware of or has no concern for humanity).

Because this idea of God is dominant in Western society, let's use it in our discussion of reasons for believing in God in the rest of Chapter 1 (except where noted otherwise).

2. Are There Good Reasons to Believe God Exists?

Well, is it rational to believe that a standard God exists? Can a good reason or cogent argument be presented in favor of his existence? Some theists say no, and base their belief on **faith;** that is, they believe without evidence or reason. Others, however, believe that arguments can be constructed to prove that a standard God exists.

In fact, all sorts of reasons have been given for believing in God. (Often, the same reasons are given for believing in different, incompatible gods.) Some reasons are easily seen to be unsatisfactory. An example is the argument that there must be a God because people in just about every society believe in him. The widespread nature of a belief surely is not a good reason to accept it. Many false beliefs are or were nearly universal (for example, that the earth is flat). Furthermore, although the belief in some god or other is nearly universal, there is no single god that most people believe in. How could the fact that some people believe in, say, a crocodile god justify belief in a standard Christian God? (Remember, the vast majority of believers in the world do *not* believe in a Christian God.)

Many reasons given for belief in God are easily seen to be defective; for instance, that God exists because belief in him is so widespread.

Lack of Reason to Believe the Contrary

Some believers, noticing that agnostics claim we cannot prove God does not exist, take another tack. They argue that if we can't prove God does not exist, then we're entitled to believe that he does. But atheists could turn this argument around. They could point out that agnostics also claim we cannot prove God *does* exist. So if we can't prove God does exist, we're equally entitled to believe that he does not. Any method of reasoning that allows us to "prove" both sides of an issue surely does not prove either. Absence of proof to the contrary is not a good reason to believe anything. (Are we justified in judging people guilty of a crime simply because we don't have evidence proving them innocent?)

Lack of reason to the contrary is no good reason.

3

Cosmological Arguments

Cosmological arguments are based on need for universe to have a cause.

Several closely related arguments for God's existence are based on the apparent need for the universe as a whole to have a cause. There seem to be three possibilities. Either the universe just "popped into existence" all by itself, or it has always existed, or else it was created—brought into existence by some extremely powerful being or force. Those who believe in God generally find it incredible that the universe could have come into existence all by itself, and equally incredible that it could have already existed for an infinite amount of time. They believe that an extremely powerful being, God, must have brought it into existence. This is one of the most frequent reasons people give for believing in God.

First cause cosmological arguments.

Arguments that try to prove there must be a god because there must be a creator of the universe are said to be **cosmological arguments** for God's existence. Typical are the arguments that try to prove there must be a "first cause" of the universe—namely, God.

The First Cause Argument

Causes are observed in everyday life, but not everything can have a cause.

First cause arguments stem from our everyday observations of the ways in which things and events in everyday life are *caused* to exist or occur. For example, we observe that putting sugar into a cup of coffee causes it to taste sweet, that watering a plant causes it to grow, and that striking a match in the presence of oxygen causes it to burn. However, it seems impossible to explain the existence of everything in terms of cause and effect, because that would mean there would have to be an infinite (or never-ending) series of causes, which seems impossible.

One way these ideas have been used to argue for God's existence is the following:

First cause argument.

1. In everyday life, we find that given things or events are caused by others (as plants are caused to grow by taking in nutrients).
2. But an infinite series of such causes is impossible, because then there would be no first cause, and thus no second, third, and so on.

∴ 3. There must be a first cause: God. *

---

*The symbol ∴ is commonly used to indicate that a conclusion follows. The statements preceding this sign are said to be *premises* of the argument, and the statement that follows the symbol is the conclusion.

Objections to the First Cause Argument

Roughly speaking, we can say that an argument is **cogent** (should persuade us to accept its conclusion) only if it satisfies two conditions:*

1. All its premises are acceptable, or warranted.
2. Its (warranted) premises provide sufficient evidence or reason to justify acceptance of its conclusion (in which case the argument is said to be **valid**).

Cogent arguments must have warranted premises; and be valid.

Many people who reject the first cause argument believe that arguments of its type (often said to be "metaphysical"—see Chapter 6 for more on metaphysics) all suffer from one or both of two defects: Either their premises are just as questionable or unacceptable as their conclusions; or their conclusions do not validly follow from their premises. For instance, one objection raised against the first cause argument is that its second premise is not acceptable (almost everyone accepts its first premise). Mathematicians in particular have argued for the possibility of an infinite series of events or causes on technical grounds, and some philosophers have accepted their reasoning.**

Some reject second premise of first cause argument.

Suppose, however, that we reject the idea that there could be an infinite series of causes, so that both premises of the first cause argument become acceptable. Still, the argument would fail to be *valid*, so that accepting its conclusion would not be justified.

First cause argument isn't valid.

First of all, the argument would prove only that every series of causes has a first or uncaused cause, not that all causes are part of a single series of causes having a single first cause, since it's possible that not all causes are members of a single series of causes. In other words, the argument would prove there are *one or more* uncaused first causes, not that there is just one.

It wouldn't prove just one series of causes.

And second, it would at best prove only that a *first cause* exists, not that the first cause is God. The first cause might instead be the devil (a popular candidate, given the nature of the universe), or even the first instant or event in the history of the universe. And even if the argument proved that the first cause must be *a* god, it wouldn't prove that it has to be *your* God (if you are a believer) or a god who fits a standard Christian, Jewish, or Muslim picture of God. It might

It wouldn't prove a first cause is God.

---

*A third (disputed) condition, not pertinent in this case, is that we use all available relevant information.
**See, for instance, Hans Reichenbach, *The Rise of Scientific Philosophy* (Berkeley, Calif.: University of California Press, 1951), pp. 207–8.

5

be any one of the thousands of different gods human beings believe in, or perhaps one that no human being has ever thought of. In fact, the first cause argument allows the possibility that there once was a god who created the universe (or perhaps even many gods), but that now *God is dead.*

Perhaps God is dead.

What Is the Cause of God's Existence?

In addition to the two objections just raised against the first cause argument, there is a general objection to all kinds of cosmological proofs of God's existence. Recall that the force of a cosmological argument rests on the idea that it is incredible to think the universe just popped into existence all by itself. In other words, it seems to many believers that such a grand thing as the universe requires a being who is at least as grand as the being who created it.

If the universe has to have a creator, then . . .

But this line of reasoning only gets us into trouble. If the universe requires a god to account for its existence, what of the existence of God himself? Again, either God has always existed, or he just popped into existence, or else he too must have a cause. Yet it is just as incredible to think that God has always existed, or that God just popped into existence, as it is to think of the universe as having done so. So the very reasoning that leads us to propose a god as the cause of the universe should lead us to propose a supergod as the cause of God. And, or course, that supergod also needs a cause, Super-Super-god, and so on to infinity.

. . . the creator has to have a creator, and so on.

Thus, no matter how we twist or turn, what we end up with is equally incredible. It is just as incredible to believe in an uncaused god as in an uncaused universe, and just as incredible to believe in an infinite series of causes as in an infinite series of gods.

Any answer will seem incredible.

To summarize, we can challenge cosmological arguments for God's existence in at least three important ways. First, we can challenge the idea that an infinite series of causes is not possible. Second, we can question the validity of the conclusion that there is just one first cause and that that first cause is God. Third, we can point out that any god proposed to account for the existence of the universe is just as much in need of a cause as the universe itself, so that the argument proves the existence of an infinite series of gods if it proves the existence of even one.

Summary of objections to cosmological arguments.

Cosmological arguments try to account for the existence of the universe by postulating a creator. Some others argue for a god to account not for the universe as a whole but only for certain of its features, such as the existence of goodness, or the fact that the universe is orderly rather than chaotic.

The Argument from Design

The **argument from design** (also known as the **teleological argument**) takes off from the fact that the universe contains all sorts of patterns or orderliness, as different as the intricate patterns of snowflakes, the law of universal gravitation, and the marvelously complex human body. Some kinds of order (for instance, the order in the mechanism of a wristwatch, or in the construction of a beaver dam) are accounted for by humans or other animals. But much order cannot be accounted for in this way; for example, the order in crystals or in the constant melting point of each different kind of element. The argument from design postulates a god to account for these otherwise unexplained types of order. Here is a version of the argument from design:

The argument from design is based on the observation of many kinds of order in the universe.

1. There is order in the universe.
2. But order cannot exist without design (that is, without a designer).
∴ 3. There must be a designer: God.

The argument from design.

The psychological pulling power of the argument from design is clear. The bewilderingly wonderful intricacy of something like the human body seems to cry out for a designer—a being who figured out how it would work and who then put it together. Nor does a theory of evolution satisfy this need, since the details of such a theory depend on the laws of physics and chemistry, which themselves exhibit marvelous orderliness. Yet the argument from design has serious, indeed fatal, flaws.

The argument from design satisfies a need.

Objections to the Argument from Design

The most obvious objection is that at best the argument from design proves only that there is a designer (orderer or architect) and not a standard God, just as the first cause argument at best proves only that there is a first cause. The designer, of course, need not be a standard God; again it could just as well be the devil, many gods, some other god, or perhaps a deceased god.

The argument from design proves only a designer, not a creator.

7

Cosmological arguments are just one type proposed to prove God exists. Another is the ontological argument. Here is the kernel of that argument as proposed by St. Anselm (1033–1109), Archbishop of Canterbury, with a reply by the monk Gaunilon (translated by S. N. Dean).

St. Anselm: THE ONTOLOGICAL ARGUMENT

. . . I do not seek to understand that I may believe, but I believe in order to understand. For this I also believe—that unless I believed, I should not understand. . . .

And so, Lord, do thou, who dost give understanding to faith, give me, so far as thou knowest it to be profitable, to understand that thou art as we believe; and that thou art that which we believe. And, indeed, we believe that thou art a being than which nothing greater can be conceived. Or is there no such nature, since the fool hath said in his heart, there is no God? (Ps. 14:1) But at any rate, this very fool, when he hears of this being of which I speak—a being than which nothing greater can be conceived— understands what he hears, and what he understands is in his understanding; although he does not understand it to exist.

God is the greatest conceivable entity.

For, it is one thing for an object to be in the understanding, and another to understand that the object exists. When a painter first conceives of what he will afterwards perform, he has it in his understanding, but he does not yet understand it to be, because he has not yet performed it. But after he has made the painting, he both has it in his understanding, and he understands it to exist, because he has made it.

Even the fool admits that God exists in the understanding.

Hence, even the fool is convinced that something exists in the understanding, at least, than which nothing greater can be conceived. For, when he hears of this, he understands it. And whatever is understood, exists in the understanding. And assuredly that, than which nothing greater can be conceived, cannot exist in the understanding alone: then it can be conceived to exist in reality; which is greater.

But the greatest conceivable entity can't exist in the understanding alone, because then something greater could be conceived.

Therefore, if that, than which nothing greater can be conceived, exists in the understanding alone, the very being, than which nothing greater can be conceived, is one, than which a greater can be conceived. But obviously this is impossible. Hence, there is no doubt that there exists a being, than which nothing greater can be conceived, and it exists both in the understanding and in reality.

And it assuredly exists so truly, that it cannot be conceived not to exist. For, it is possible to conceive of a being which cannot be conceived not to exist; and this is greater than one which can be conceived not to exist. Hence, if that, than which nothing greater can be conceived, can be conceived not to exist, it is not that, than which nothing greater can be conceived. But this is an irreconcilable contradiction. There is, then, so truly a being than which nothing greater can be conceived to exist, that it cannot even be conceived not to exist; and this being thou art, O Lord, our God.

So if the greatest conceivable being existed only in the understanding, a greater could be conceived as existing also in reality.

Gaunilon's Reply: IN BEHALF OF THE FOOL

The fool might make this reply: This being is said to be in my understanding already, only because I understand what is said. Now could it not with equal justice be said that I have in my understanding all manner of unreal objects, having absolutely no existence in themselves, because I understand these things if one speaks of them, whatever they may be? . . .

Gaunilon's reply: I have in my understanding all sorts of unreal objects.

For example: it is said that somewhere in the ocean is an island, which, because of the difficulty, or rather the impossibility, of discovering what does not exist, is called the lost island. And they say that this island has an inestimable wealth of all manner of riches and delicacies in greater abundance than is told of the Islands of the Blest; and that having no owner or inhabitant, it is more excellent than all other countries, which are inhabited by mankind, in the abundance with which it is stored.

For example, I have an idea of an imaginary perfect island.

Now if someone should tell me that there is such an island, I should easily understand his words, in which there is no difficulty. But suppose he went on to say, as if by a logical inference: "You can no longer doubt that this island which is more excellent than all lands exists somewhere, since you have no doubt that it is in your understanding. And since it is more excellent not to be in the understanding alone, but to exist both in the understanding and in reality, for this reason it must exist. For if it does not exist, any land which really exists will be more excellent than it; and so the island already understood by you to be more excellent will not be more excellent."

I can't argue that this island must exist in reality as well as in my understanding because otherwise a greater can be conceived.

If a man should try to prove to me by such reasoning that this island truly exists, and that its existence should no longer be doubted, either I should believe that he was jesting, or I know not which I ought to regard as the greater fool: myself, supposing that I should allow this proof; or him, if he should suppose that he had established with any certainty the existence of this island. For he ought to show first that the hypothetical excellence of this island exists as a real and indubitable fact, and in no wise as any unreal object, or one whose existence is uncertain, in my understanding.

If someone tried to prove this, I should think he jests. (Similarly for St. Anselm's proof of God's existence.)

Why can't order exist without an orderer?

But the argument from design doesn't even prove that much, because its second premise (that order cannot exist without an orderer) is doubtful, to say the least. Why assume that order cannot exist without an orderer?

It is sometimes claimed that we can argue for the existence of a designer or orderer by a method called *induction*. (More will be said about induction in Chapter 3.) Many things that exhibit order (wristwatches, for example) turn out to have been deliberately put together by human or animal orderers. We've seen many watches that we know are of human design but have never seen one that, when we checked, proved not to have been so designed. Therefore, if we now discover a wristwatch in the sand on a deserted beach, we assume (by induction) that it too is of human design.

It's sometimes said we can use induction to prove the existence of an orderer.

Snowflakes, the laws of nature, and the human body also exhibit order (although, of course, we have never seen a designer, human or otherwise, designing them). We know, of course, that human beings (or other animals) cannot have ordered them, so we conclude by induction that some nonanimal orderer, namely God, must have done so.

But we can't prove an orderer by induction.

But such a conclusion is not warranted. When we conclude by induction that a wristwatch found in the sand didn't put itself together or come together accidentally, and thus must have been designed by human beings, we're on safe ground. Our argument looks like this:

1. Many wristwatches have been observed, and all those which have been examined are of human design.
∴ 2. This wristwatch must have been designed by human beings.

We might even argue in a more general and thus more powerful way, as follows:

1. Many mechanical devices have been observed, and all those which have been examined are of human design.
∴ 2. This mechanical device (which happens to be a wristwatch) must have been designed by human beings.

But now observe how much more general an argument would have to be to lead us to a designer of snowflakes, laws of nature, or human beings:

10

1. Many orderly things have been observed, and all those which have been examined have been found to be designed by a designer.
∴ 2. This orderly thing (which happens to be a snowflake, a law of nature, or a human being) must have been designed by a designer.

Clearly, this argument is defective, because its premise is so obviously false. There are a great many orderly things for which we have failed to find a designer or orderer—snowflakes, rainbows, crystals, and human beings are just a few. (If there is a god who designed all of these things, then to observe the designer of snowflakes at work we would have to catch God in the act of fashioning them out of H_2O, or perhaps catch him in the act of designing the laws of physics that result in H_2O arranging itself into snowflakes.)

The premise of a strong enough induction is defective.

The point is that things exhibiting order seem to fall into two distinct classes: those we (or other animals) have ordered; and those we have not. We have checked and found many items in the first class that are of human design. But we have never found a designer for even a single member of the second class. Hence, we aren't entitled to conclude by induction that *all* order implies an orderer or designer, so the argument from design cannot be supported by inductive reasoning. If we are to accept it, we must do so without reason; that is, on faith.

We've not found an orderer for most kinds of order.

Pascal's Wager

The great French mathematician and philosopher, Blaise Pascal (1623–1662), argued for belief in God in a somewhat different manner:

"God is, or He is not." . . . What will you wager? According to reason, you can do neither the one thing nor the other; according to reason you can defend neither of the propositions . . . but you must wager. [What of] your happiness? Let us weigh the gain and loss in wagering that God is . . . If you gain [win the wager], you gain all; if you lose, you lose nothing. Wager, then, without hesitation that He is. *

Pascal's Wager.

---

*Blaise Pascal, *Pensées*, Everyman's Library (1958).

11

We must bet. If God doesn't exist, no matter. But if he does, we gain by betting he exists and lose all by betting he doesn't.

The point of Pascal's Wager seems to be this: we must wager (believe) either that God exists or that he does not. If God does not exist, it makes little difference how we bet. But if he does exist, we gain a great deal—in particular, great happiness after life—if we believe he does, and we lose a great deal if we believe he doesn't. So the smart or prudent person will bet (believe) that God does exist.

Objections to Pascal's Wager

Objections: (1) We don't have to bet.

First of all, Pascal is wrong in his belief that we must wager either for or against God's existence. We may choose to stay on the sidelines, as the agnostic does. Of course, we then may lose the prize, if there is a prize, for betting incorrectly. But Pascal can't prove there is such a prize.

(2) Since there are lots of possible gods, why bet on any particular one?

Second, the wager isn't as simple as Pascal thought, because there are indefinitely many possible creators. The standard Christian God on whom Pascal wagered is only one of them. So the number of possibilities to bet on is many more than two, and the reasonable gamblers have no way to choose, even if they want to choose some god or other. Put another way, if Pascal's Wager makes sense, it would be just as reasonable to bet on a sun or moon god as on the God of the Jews, Christians, or Muslims.

(3) We don't know how God will treat those who accept the wager.

And finally, there is no proof or reason for supposing that if we wager on the God that actually exists we will gain a benefit. For we can't assume without reason that God rewards believers or punishes nonbelievers. (Indeed, in the last analysis Pascal himself appealed to revelation or faith.) On the contrary, the intuitions of many of us are

He might think the wagerers hypocritical.

all the other way around, perhaps because when we try to imagine ourselves in God's shoes, we see that we would be inclined to regard belief based on Pascal's Wager as hypocritical. God, if he exists, could well be more impressed with the honesty of those who fail to believe (wager) in the absence of evidence than with those who believe because they think it is prudent to do so.

3. Do Miracles or Mystical Experiences Prove God Exists?

Should we accept reports of miracles?

If experiences of God were as common as of rainbows or lightning, no one would bother to argue for God's existence, any more than they do for the existence of rainbows or lightning. Should those of us who have not had God revealed to us directly accept the reports of those who claim mystical or miraculous revelation?

Reasons for Doubting Reports of Miracles

Although some of the reports of religious miracles or mystical experiences clearly involve fraud, many others do not. Why not accept them, then, as evidence of a divine presence? Here are some of the reasons that have been suggested for doubting the divine nature of the alleged miraculous experiences.

Reasons for doubting reports of miracles.

1. Many alleged miracles could be the result of psychological deception. People often "see" things that aren't there to be seen (scientists once "saw" canals on Mars), or see reality distorted by wishful thinking (sports fans see close plays in favor of the home team; crime victims "identify" innocent suspects). Hardly anyone believes reports of sightings of fairies or goblins, even when upstanding, sober, honest citizens make them. Why then believe similar reports of religious miracles?

Psychological deception is always possible.

2. We've known how to produce mystical experiences for a long time, by means of drugs, fasting, meditation, and so on. The fact that we can produce them almost at will (think of the medicine man who just has to eat peyote or the mushroom *Amanita muscaria*) casts doubt on their "otherworldly" nature.

We've known how to produce miracles for a long time

3. What seems miraculous at one time or place often is explained in another. Lodestones (magnets), eclipses, sudden cures (or illnesses), electricity, and airplanes are just a few examples of ordinary things (to we who understand them) that have been believed to be miraculous. It may be, therefore, that some of the alleged religious miracles (the manna provided to the Hebrews in the wilderness, or their crossing the Sea of Reeds on dry land) have perfectly ordinary explanations.

What seems miraculous at one time is explained in another.

4. Those who believe in other religions or other kinds of gods support their belief by appeals to alleged miracles that are equally plausible as the Judeo-Christian ones. Why, then, accept miracles supporting one god but not the others? (The answer to this given by most students is that they were brought up in the Christian, or Jewish, or Mohammedan religion, but is that a *good* reason?)

Equally plausible experiences support the existence of other gods.

5. Finally, it should be noted that alleged miraculous or mystical experiences at best would prove only that God exists *with a certain*

St. Thomas Aquinas (1225–1274), perhaps the most celebrated Catholic theologian, gave "five ways" to prove God exists.

St. Thomas Aquinas: THE FIVE WAYS*

The first way. Things in motion are moved by other things, for motion is reduction from potentiality to actuality.

The first and more manifest way is the argument from motion. It is certain, and evident to our senses, that in the world some things are in motion. Now whatever is in motion is put in motion by another, for nothing can be in motion except it is in potentiality to that towards which it is in motion; whereas a thing moves inasmuch as it is in act [actuality]. For motion is nothing else than the reduction of something from potentiality to actuality, except by something in a state of actuality. Thus that which is actually hot, as fire, makes wood, which is potentially hot, to be actually hot, and thereby moves and changes it. Now it is not possible that the same thing should be at once in actuality and potentiality in the same respect, but only in different respects. For what is actually hot cannot simultaneously be potentially hot; but it is simultaneously potentially cold. It is therefore impossible that in the same respect and in the same way a thing should be both mover and moved, i.e., that it should move itself. Therefore, whatever is in motion must be put in motion by another. If that by which it is put in motion be itself put in motion, then this also must needs be put in motion by another, and that by another again. But this cannot go on to infinity, because then there would be no first mover, and, consequently, no other mover; seeing that subsequent movers move only inasmuch as they are put in motion by the first mover; as the staff moves only because it is put in motion by the hand. Therefore, it is necessary to arrive at a first mover, put in motion by no other; and this everyone understands to be God.

Nothing can be actual and potential at the same time in the same respect. So nothing can be self-moved. But an infinity of movers is impossible, because then there would be no first mover, thus no second mover, etc. So, there must be a first mover: God.

The second way. Nothing is the (efficient) cause of itself, and an infinity of causes is impossible, so there must be a first cause: God.

The second way is from the nature of efficient cause. In the world of sense we find there is an order of efficient causes. There is no case known (neither is it, indeed, possible) in which a thing is found to be the efficient cause of itself; for so it would be prior to itself, which is impossible. Now in efficient causes it is not possible to go on to infinity, because in all efficient causes following in order, the first is the cause of the intermediate cause, and the intermediate is the cause of the ultimate cause, whether the intermediate cause be several, or one only. Now to take away the cause is to take away the effect. Therefore, if there be no first cause among efficient causes, there will be no ultimate, nor any intermediate cause. But if in efficient causes it is possible to go on to infinity, there will be no first efficient cause, neither will there be an ultimate effect, nor any intermediate efficient causes; all of which is plainly false. Therefore it is necessary to admit a first efficient cause, to which everyone gives the name of God.

The third way is taken from possibility and necessity, and runs thus. We find in nature things that are possible to be and not to be, since they are found to be generated, and to corrupt, and consequently, they are possible to be and not to be. But it is impossible for these always to exist, for that which is possible not to be at some time is not. Therefore, if everything is possible not to be, then at one time there could have been nothing in existence, because that which does not exist only begins to exist by something already existing. Therefore, if at one time nothing was in existence, it would have been impossible for anything to have begun to exist; and thus even now nothing would be in existence—which is absurd. Therefore, not all beings are merely possible, but there must exist something the existence of which is necessary. But every necessary thing either has its necessity caused by another, or not. Now it is impossible to go on to infinity in necessary things which have their necessity caused by another, as has been already proved in regard to efficient causes. Therefore we cannot but admit the existence of some being having of itself its own necessity, and not receiving it from another, but rather causing in others their necessity. . . .

St. Thomas's third way. If a time were possible when nothing existed, it would be impossible for anything to have begun to exist. So something must exist necessarily, namely God.

The fourth way is taken from the gradation to be found in things. Among beings there are some more and some less good, true, noble, and the like. But "more" and "less" are predicated of different things, according as they resemble in their different ways something which is the maximum . . . so that there is something which is truest, something best, something noblest, and, consequently, something which is uttermost being; for those things that are greatest in truth are greatest in being; . . . Now the maximum in any genus is the cause of all in that genus; as fire, which is the maximum of heat, is the cause of all hot things. Therefore there must also be something which is to all beings the cause of their being, goodness, and every other perfection; and this we call God.

The fourth way. The maximum in a genus is the cause of all in the genus, so there must be a maximum good that causes all good, namely God.

The fifth way is taken from the governance of the world. We see that things which lack intelligence, such as natural bodies, act for an end, and this is evident from their acting always, or nearly always, in the same way, so as to obtain the best result. Hence it is plain that not fortuitously, but designedly, do they achieve their end. Now whatever lacks intelligence cannot move towards an end, unless it be directed by some being endowed with knowledge and intelligence . . . Therefore some intelligent being exists by whom all natural things are directed to their end; and this being we call God.

The fifth way. Things in nature act toward an end. They do so not by accident but by design. So there must be a designer, namely God.

Mystical or miraculous experiences at best only make God's existence probable.

degree of probability. This is so because the reasoning from the experience of the alleged miracle to the existence of God would have to be what is called *inductive* reasoning (discussed a bit in Chapter 3), and one feature of inductive reasoning is that at best it gives us conclusions that are only probable. Yet most believers believe with absolute conviction, with certainty, with no doubt whatsoever; their belief can't be justified by any kind of inductive reasoning from alleged miraculous or mystical experiences.

4. Doesn't the Bible Prove God Exists?

It is fallacious for non-believers to accept the Bible's word that God exists.

Many believers try to convince doubting friends that God exists by citing biblical chapter and verse to that effect. But appeals of this kind are not satisfactory. After all, only those who already believe God exists have good reason to accept the Bible's word on this extremely controversial question. Anyone else who accepted the Bible on this point would be guilty of the fallacy of *begging the question* by presupposing (in a disguised form) the very point at issue (whether God exists).

If the Bible told us things its writers couldn't have known in an ordinary way, that would count as evidence of its divine origin. But it doesn't.

One way to get around this difficulty is to give some other reason, completely independent of any belief in God, for concluding that the Bible is indeed divinely inspired. For example, if the Bible told us about things that the people who wrote it down couldn't have known in the ordinary course of their lives (say, that there are bacteria, viruses, koala bears, or pandas) or revealed facts about physics or chemistry (say, that stars are masses of very hot gases such as the sun, and come clustered in galaxies), that would count as evidence of its divine origin. But in fact the Bible seems to contain no such information. Some believers do indeed cite references to lost cities later rediscovered from biblical clues as proof of the Bible's divine nature. But these are exactly the sorts of things ordinary people in those days could have known without special divine guidance. So they aren't good evidence for the divine inspiration of the Bible.

Taken Literally, the Bible Contains Contradictions

Worse, the Bible seems to many atheists and agnostics to be not at all the kind of document a Christian-style God would have inspired.

16

For one thing, when the Bible is taken literally, or at least taken to state facts about history or the nature of the world,* it contains gross contradictions, hardly a mark of divine inspiration. The book of Genesis, for example, starts out with two very different and contradictory accounts of the order of creation, the first in Genesis 1, the second right after in Genesis 2, stemming from two separate but related myths current in those days. Here is a rough comparison of these two contradictory orderings of the events of creation:**

Taken literally, the Bible is contradictory, a mark against its divine origin.

Genesis 1	Genesis 2
Heaven	Earth
Earth	Heaven
Light	Mist (rain)
Firmament	Man
Dry Land	Trees
Grasses and Trees	Rivers
Luminaries (sun, moon, stars)	Beasts and Cattle
Sea Beasts	Birds
Birds	Woman
Cattle, Creeping Things, Beasts	
Man and Woman	

The Bible gives two different and contradictory accounts of the creation.

Of course, the objection that the Bible contains gross contradictions is relevant only for those who take the Bible more or less literally (as do Fundamentalists and many Catholics). But many Christians and Jews believe the Bible has to be interpreted. Their problem is to determine how God intends us to interpret the Bible, a very difficult question over which theologians massively disagree. We have to be careful, then, in accepting one interpretation rather than another. (That's one point of the old saying that scripture can be quoted for the Devil's own purpose.) Doubters believe there are no sufficient

Those who think the Bible has to be interpreted have no way to choose one interpretation over others.

---

*The idea of taking the Bible literally is very complicated, but roughly it means taking the Bible to say that Christ rose from the dead and is the son of God, that God gave Moses the Ten Commandments, that Jesus said more or less what he is quoted as saying, and so on. It also means taking metaphoric or figurative uses of language in their usual senses, so that, for example, the reference to a camel and the eye of a needle is not about camels and needles, but states that the rich have no chance of getting into Heaven when they die.

**Excerpts from *Hebrew Myths: The Book of Genesis* by Robert Graves and Raphael Patai. Copyright © 1963, 1964 by International Authors NV. Reprinted by permission of Doubleday & Company, Inc., and the authors.

17

Here is the pragmatist William James (1842–1910) with a novel argument for believing in God.

William James: THE WILL TO BELIEVE*

We must decide by passion when we can't decide a genuine option by reason. To decide not to decide risks losing truth as much as deciding.

. . . I have brought with me tonight . . . a defense of our right to adopt a believing attitude in religious matters, in spite of the fact that our merely logical intellect may not have been coerced. . . . The thesis I defend is, briefly stated, this: *Our passional nature not only lawfully may, but must, decide an option between propositions, whenever it is a genuine option that cannot by its nature be decided on intellectual grounds; for to say, under such circumstances, "Do not decide, but leave the question open," is itself a passional decision—just like deciding yes or no—and is attended with the same risk of losing the truth.* . . . [Religion] says that the best things are the more eternal things, the overlapping things, the things in the universe that throw the last stone, so to speak, and say the final word. "Perfection is eternal,"—this phrase of Charles Secrétan seems a good way of putting this first affirmation of religion, which obviously cannot yet be verified scientifically at all.

Religion says the best things are the eternal things—"the final word," and we're better off believing it.

The second affirmation of religion is that we are better off even now if we believe her first affirmation to be true.

Now, let us consider what the logical elements of this situation are *in case the religious hypothesis in both its branches be really true.* . . . We see, first, that religion offers itself as a *momentous* option. We are supposed to gain, even now, by our belief, and to lose by our non-belief, a certain vital good. Secondly, religion is a *forced* option, so far as that good goes. We cannot escape the issue by remaining sceptical and waiting for more light, because, although we do avoid error in that way *if religion be untrue,* we lose the good, *if it be true,* just as certainly as if we positively chose to disbelieve. . . . Scepticism, then, is not avoidance of option; it is option of a certain particular kind of risk. *Better risk loss of truth than chance of error,*—that is your faith-vetoers exact position. . . . To preach scepticism to us as a duty until "sufficient evidence" for religion be found, is tantamount therefore to telling us, when in the presence of the religious hypothesis, that to yield to our fear of its being error is wiser and better than to yield to our hope that it may be true. It is not intellect against all passions, then; it is only intellect with one passion laying down its law. And by what, forsooth, is the supreme wisdom of this passion warranted? Dupery for dupery, what proof is there that dupery

Religion offers us a momentous, forced, option. We're supposed to gain by belief and lose by our nonbelief.

*From "The Will to Believe," New World, June 1896.

through hope is so much worse than dupery through fear? I, for one, can see no proof; and I simply refuse obedience to the scientist's command to imitate his kind of option, in a case where my own stake is important enough to give me the right to choose my own form of risk. If religion be true and the evidence for it be still insufficient, I do not wish, by putting your extinguisher upon my nature . . . to forfeit my sole chance in life of getting upon the winning side,—that chance depending, of course, on my willingness to run the risk of acting as if my passional need of taking the world religiously might be prophetic and right. . . . One who should shut himself up in snarling logicality and try to make the gods extort his recognition willy-nilly, or not get it at all, might cut himself off forever from his only opportunity of making the gods' acquaintance. This feeling, forced on us we know not whence, that by obstinately believing that there are gods (although not to do so would be so easy both for our logic and our life) we are doing the universe the deepest service we can, seems part of the living essence of the religious hypothesis. If the hypothesis *were* true in all its parts, including this one, then pure intellectualism, with its veto on our making willing advances, would be an absurdity; and some participation of our sympathetic nature would be logically required. I, therefore, for one, cannot see my way to accepting the agnostic rules for truth-seeking, or wilfully agree to keep my willing nature out of the game. I cannot do so for this plain reason, that *a rule of thinking which would absolutely prevent me from acknowledging certain kinds of truth if those kinds of truth were really there, would be an irrational rule.* That for me is the long and short of the formal logic of the situation, no matter what the kinds of truth might materially be. . . . Let me end by a quotation from [Fitz-James] Stephen. In all important transactions of life we have to take a leap in the dark. . . . If we decide to leave the riddles unanswered, that is a choice; if we waver in our answer, that, too, is a choice: but whatever choice we make, we make it at our peril. If a man chooses to turn his back altogether on God and the future, no one can prevent him; no one can show beyond reasonable doubt that he is mistaken. If a man thinks otherwise and acts as he thinks, I do not see that any one can prove that *he* is mistaken. Each must act as he thinks best; and if he is wrong, so much the worse for him. We stand on a mountain pass in the midst of whirling snow and blinding mist, through which we get glimpses now and then of paths which may be deceptive. If we stand still we shall be frozen to death. If we take the wrong road we shall be dashed to pieces. We do not certainly know whether there is any right one. What must we do? "Be strong and of a good courage. Act for the best, hope for the best, and take what comes. . . . If death ends all, we cannot meet death better."

Skeptics say it's better to risk loss of truth than error. But fear of error is just one passion. Why should it override others? Why is dupery through hope worse than dupery through fear?

I, for one, don't wish to forfeit my one chance to win in life.

A rule that prevents me from gaining great truth is an irrational rule.

criteria for choosing one interpretation over others, so that we can't be sure the one we choose is divinely inspired.

Biblical Stories Reflect the Myths of Their Times

Finally, it should be noted that the stories in the Bible did not arise in a vacuum; they reflect the mythology of their approximate times and places. There thus is the question why we should accept these particular myths as divinely inspired, indeed these particular versions of myths, rather than others (a question just like the one as to why we should accept the reports of Christian miracles and not those supporting the existence of other gods). For example, the Genesis version of the Flood story is just one of several different variations told in ancient times. Here is an ancient Greek version (cited by Graves and Patai, in *Hebrew Myths*):

Since biblical stories reflect myths current in biblical times, why believe they're divinely inspired?

Example: The ancient Greek version of the Flood myth.

Disgusted by the cannibalism of the impious Pelasgians, Almighty Zeus let loose a great flood on earth, meaning to wipe out the whole race of man; but Deucalion, King of Phthia, warned by his father, Prometheus the Titan, . . . built an ark, victualed it, and went aboard with his wife Pyrrha. . . . Then the South Wind blew, rain fell and rivers roared down to the sea which . . . washed away every city of coast and plain; until the entire world was flooded, but for a few mountain tops, and all mortal creatures seemed to have been lost, except Deucalion and Pyrrha. The ark floated about for nine days until, at last, the waters subsided, and it came to rest on Mount Parnassus or, some tell, on Mount Aetna; or Mount Athos; or Mount Orthyrys in Thessaly. It is said that Deucalion was reassured by a dove which he had sent on an exploratory flight. Disembarking in safety, they offered a sacrifice to Father Zeus, the preserver of fugitives, and went down to pray at the Goddess Themis's shrine beside the River Cephissus. . . . They pleaded humbly that mankind should be renewed, and Zeus . . . sent Hermes to assure them that whatever request they might make would be granted forthwith. Themis appeared in person, saying: "Shroud your heads, and throw the bones of your mother behind you." Deucalion and Pyrrha . . . decided that the Goddess meant mother Earth. . . . Therefore . . . they picked up rocks and threw them over their shoulders; these became either men or women. . . . Thus mankind was renewed, and ever since "a people" (*laos*) and "a stone" (*laas*) have been much the same word in many languages. Yet the flood proved of little avail; for some Pelasgians who had taken refuge on Mount Parnassus revived the cannibalistic abominations which had prompted Zeus's vengeance. *

5. Can We Prove God Does Not Exist?

So far we have dealt with reasons for believing that God exists; and we've concluded that there are no good reasons for believing this. Well, then, are there good reasons for believing God does not exist? Yes and no.

Can we prove God does not exist?

Proving a thing does not exist is different from proving it does. If something exists, it may be observed, or leave causal signs of its existence; what does not exist cannot be observed, and has no causal consequences.

It's harder to prove something does not exist than that it does.

Still, we can have good reason to think that certain kinds of things do not exist. Santa Claus is a good example. Children can become reasonably sure that Santa Claus does not exist by performing "experiments" (making relevant observations) that prove his nonexistence. Santa is the kind of entity who, if he exists, can be "caught in the act" of fulfilling his role (because our conception of him is such that a thing cannot be Santa Claus if it does not play a certain role, for instance, the role of gift giver to children on Christmas). A doubting child who stays up all night on December 24 and fails to catch Santa in the act gains important evidence against his existence.

Still, we can have good reason to believe some things don't exist; for example, Santa Claus.

Now suppose a doubting child wants to prove that God does not exist. What experiments should he perform? What observations should he make? Unfortunately, God is conceived of differently from Santa Claus. If a person prays to God, for instance, and his prayer is not answered, this is not good evidence against the existence of a standard God, for such a God is not conceived of as a being who answers *all* prayers, or even the prayers of those who are true believers. The Santa story says that if a child is good, Santa will deliver presents; scriptures (for most Christians) say that if you believe in God and repent your sins now, God may or may not answer your prayers now, but he *will* reward you after death. If there is no God and no life after death, the crucial experiment proving this would have to be made, per impossible, after death. Thus, if there is no standard God, his nonexistence can't be proved (the Catch-22 in most conceptions of God), although if he does exist and cares to reveal himself now, before death, then his existence can be proved.

But how can we prove God does not exist? If there is no God, and no life after death, the experience proving he doesn't exist would be impossible.

21

The Problem of Evil

Still, there is one kind of God, a perfect God, whose existence can be disproved because of the existence of evil.

But atheists do have good evidence (good reasons) for denying the existence of a particular kind of god; namely, one who is conceived to be absolutely perfect (as, for instance, St. Anselm and many other theologians conceive of him). For the existence of evil in the universe would appear to be inconsistent with the existence of a perfect creator, who, if he creates at all, must create a perfect world. (Why a perfect God would choose to create a universe in the first place is an interesting theological problem—why he would choose to create *this* all too imperfect world, it can be argued, is an insoluble one.)

The Argument from Evil

The argument from evil: If evil exists, any creator could not be perfect.

The argument from evil proceeds as follows:

1. If evil exists, then the creator (if any) is not perfect (that is, he is either not all-powerful and thus not able to do away with all evil, or not all-knowing and thus not aware of the evil, or not perfectly good and thus not interested in doing away with the evil).
2. Evil exists.
∴ 3. The creator (if any) is not perfect.

This argument is much more powerful than the one (just considered) about the absence of evidence for God's existence, because this one is based on a great deal of positive evidence; namely, the evidence of vast amounts of evil in this universe. For the idea of a perfect creator does seem to imply that whatever he creates will be perfect. Evidence that this universe is very imperfect indeed is thus evidence, in fact very good evidence, that it was not created by a perfect being.

God Brings Good Out of Evil

Theists have tried to counter the argument from evil in several ways. One is to argue, as St. Thomas does, that "He would not allow any evil to exist in His works, unless His omnipotence and goodness were such as to bring good even out of evil." But it seems to many of us that it would be even better of him to bring good solely out of *nothing* (or out of other goods) rather than out of evil. And anyway, St.

Thomas never proved that all or even most evil is connected with the production of good, an idea that seems false to everyday experiences of life and suffering (not that some evil—for example, the pain of practicing and training hard—does not often produce good).

Some argue, as Christian Scientists do, that evil is only "in the mind," and that no *real* evil exists in the world. The trouble is that (unjustified) *pain* is for us the ultimate evil, even if it is just "in the mind." Anyway, our mental experiences are just as much a part of the universe as anything else.

Others argue that only the *illusion* of pain exists, not real pain. The trouble this time is that illusory pain (whatever that might be) would drive us up the wall just as much as the genuine article (because it would *be* the genuine article) and thus would be just as evil as real pain.

Replies to argument from evil: (1) God brings good out of evil. Reply to reply: Better to bring good out of nothing. But lots of evil produces no great good anyway.

Reply (2): Evil exists only in the mind, or as an illusion. Reply to reply: Mental or illusory pain is evil, and part of the universe.

Some Evil May Be Necessary

Another reply to the argument from evil is that some evil is necessary even in the "best of all possible worlds" in order to increase the amount of pleasure (good). It serves as a warning (the pain of a broken leg, for example, warns us not to walk on it) or helps us to get maximum satisfaction out of good (bad weather, for instance, helps us to appreciate good weather).

The trouble with this reply is that most evil has nothing to do either with warning us of still greater evil or with increasing our enjoyment of the good. Those suffering the terror and pain of terminal cancer, or of death by slow torture, are not being warned of some greater evil, nor is their appreciation of good increased.

Furthermore, the fact that we need warnings at all, or need bad experiences to better appreciate good ones, proves that *we* are not by any means perfect creatures in a perfect world. For such creatures would never break legs and would not need bad weather to better enjoy good (as presumably residents in heaven do not).

Reply (3): Some evil is necessary, e.g., to warn of a broken leg.

Reply to reply: Most pain is not necessary, e.g., pain of terminal cancer.

In a perfect world, legs don't break, and we need no warnings.

We Know Only a Small Part of the Universe.

Another reply to the argument from evil is that we experience only a tiny portion of the universe, just a small "time slice" of the whole.

Reply (4): We see only a small part of the whole picture. Reply to reply: But any evil is more than is necessary.

Perhaps the world has a Hollywood ending and we suffer now so that future generations (or we, in an afterlife) can be supremely happy.

But even the tiniest amount of evil is more than a perfect creator needs to allow—endless bliss later does not eliminate flaws in his work now. And anyway, would a perfect God let one person's happiness depend on another's suffering?

Evil May Result from Our Free Wills

Reply (5): Free will is a good. God can't be blamed if he gives us free will and we choose to do evil.

Finally, there is what may be the most popular reply to the argument from evil: God wanted to give us *free will*, because freedom constitutes a good, yet in doing so he had to accept the evil that free human beings choose to bring about. So it isn't the perfect creator who is responsible for the evil in the world; it's we evil mortals who deserve the blame.

Replies to reply: If placed in a better world, we'd choose less evil.

There are several reasons why this reply is not acceptable. First, if God had given us free wills but placed us in a *better world*, we would choose to do evil much less often. Many a good person has been forced to lie, steal, or kill to get food for starving children when a flood, drought, or typhoon resulted in great famine.

Much evil is due to lack of intelligence or information.

Second, much human evil is due to ignorance or lack of intelligence. A perfect God would make us more intelligent and better informed, so that we would not choose evil out of stupidity or ignorance.

Having free will does not imply ever choosing evil.

Third, a being who has free will is not therefore *forced* to choose evil, not even once in a lifetime. There is nothing in the concept of a free will requiring that some free choices be evil ones. * (Theists who deny this fail to notice that they themselves generally conceive of those in heaven, or at least of God himself, as having free will but never choosing to do evil.)

Most evil doesn't result from human choices, e.g., diseases and droughts.

Finally, and of great importance, most evil does not result from evil human choices. The millions who have died in volcanic eruptions, hurricanes, blizzards, or earthquakes did not choose their fate, nor did others evilly choose it for them. They were victims of natural forces, as were those who suffered from epilepsy, congenital blindness, tuberculosis, or sickle-cell anemia. Similarly, people do not choose to

---

*If it did, that would mean all of us *must* sin in our lifetimes. That a good God would then require us to repent of these God-guaranteed sins (as many Christian theologians believe) strikes nonbelievers as odd, to say the least.

One of the best-known defenses against the argument from evil was given by the German philosopher and mathematician Gottfried Wilhelm Leibniz (1646–1716).

G. W. Leibniz: GOD AND EVIL: A POSITIVE VIEW*

It follows from the supreme perfection of God that in producing the universe He chose the best possible plan, containing the greatest variety together with the greatest order; the best arranged situation, place, and time; the greatest effect produced by the simplest means; the most power, the most knowledge, the most happiness and goodness in created things of which the universe admitted. For as all possible things have a claim to existence in the understanding of God in proportion to their perfections, the result of all these claims must be the most perfect actual world which is possible. Otherwise it would not be possible to explain why things have happened as they have rather than otherwise. . . .

Since God is perfect, he created the best possible universe. If not, there would be no reason why things are this way rather than that.

The ultimate reason of the reality both of essences and of existences in a Unity must certainly be greater, higher, and prior to the world itself, since through it alone not only the existent things, which the world contains, but also the things that are possible have their reality. It cannot be found except in one single source, because of the interconnection of all these things with one another. It is evident that from this source existent things are continually issuing and being produced, and have been produced, since it is not clear why one state of the world rather than another, yesterday's state rather than today's should flow from the world itself. It is also evident how God acts not only physically but also freely; and how there lies in Him not only the efficient but also the final cause; and how from Him proceeds the reason not only of the greatness or potency that there is in the mechanism for the universe as now established, but also of the goodness or wisdom involved in the establishing of it . . . it should be pointed out that it follows from what has been said not only that the world is the most perfect physically, or, if you prefer it, metaphysically, or in other words that the series of things will be forthcoming which in actual fact affords the greatest quantity of reality, but also that the world should be the most perfect morally, because true moral perfection is physical perfection in minds themselves. . . .

The cause of the world must be higher and prior to the world.

God is the cause of the world, and its greatness and morality stem from him. So the world must be perfect, both physically and morally.

But, you will say, we find in the world the very opposite of this. Often the worst of sufferings fall upon the best men; the innocent (I speak not only

*From G. W. Leibniz, *Philosophical Writings*, Everyman's Library. Reprinted by permission of J. M. Dent & Sons Ltd., London.

But the world seems just the opposite of this. Yet it is evident a priori (by just reason alone) that the world is perfect.

of the brutes, but of men also) are afflicted, and are slain even with tortures; indeed the world, especially if we look at the government of the human race, seems rather a confused chaos than an affair ordained by some supreme wisdom. So it appears at first sight, I allow: but on deeper examination it must be agreed that the opposite is the case. It is evident *a priori* from those very principles which I have adduced that without doubt there is secured in the world the highest perfection that there could possibly be of all things, and therefore of mind.

We have only experienced a small part of the universe, like someone seeing only part of a picture, and yet make rash judgments about the whole world. The whole world may be the most beautiful possible even though small parts seem ugly when viewed alone.

And indeed it is unreasonable, as the lawyers say, to give a judgment without inspecting the whole law. We have knowledge of a tiny part of that eternity which stretches out immeasurably. For how small a thing is the memory of a few thousand years which history hands down to us! And yet out of so little experience we rashly make judgments about the immeasurable and the eternal . . . Look at the most lovely picture, and then cover it up leaving uncovered only a tiny scrap of it. What else will you see there, even if you look as closely as possible, and the more so as you look from nearer and nearer at hand, but a kind of confused medley of colours, without selection, without art! And yet when you remove the covering, and look upon the whole picture from the proper place, you will see that what previously seemed to you to have been aimlessly smeared on the canvas was in fact accomplished with the highest art by the author of the work. What happens to the eyes in painting is equally experienced by ears in music. The greatest composers frequently mingle discords with harmonious chords so that the listener may be stimulated and pricked as it were, and may become eager to know what is going to happen; presently when all is restored to order he feels so much the more content. In the same way we may take pleasure in small dangers, or in the experience of ills, from the very sense or proof

We need some bitter to maximize enjoyment of the sweet.

they give us of our own power or felicity. . . . On the same principle it has an insipid effect if we always eat sweet things; sharp, acid, and even bitter things should be mixed in to stimulate the taste. He who has not tasted what is bitter has not earned what is sweet, nor will he appreciate it. This is the very law of enjoyment, the positive pleasure does not come from an even course; such things produce weariness, and make men dull, not joyful.

What I have said, however, about the possibility of a part being disturbed without upsetting the harmony of the whole must not be interpreted to mean that no account is taken of the parts; or that it is sufficient for the whole world to be completed at all points, even though it should turn out that the human race was wretched, and that there was in the universe no care for justice and no account was taken of us—as is maintained by some people whose judgment about the sum of things is ill-grounded. For the truth is that, just as in a well-regulated commonwealth care is taken that as far as possible things shall be to the interest of the individual, in the same way the universe would not be sufficiently perfect unless, as far as can be done without upsetting the universal harmony, the good of individual people is considered. Of this there could be established no better measure than the very law of justice itself, which dictates that each should have a part in the perfection of the universe and in his own happiness in proportion to his own virtue and to the extent to which his will is directed towards the common good; by which is fulfilled what we call the charity and love of God, in which alone, according to the judgment of wise theologians also, stands the whole force and power of the Christian religion. Nor ought it to seem remarkable that all this deference should be paid to minds in the universe, since they bear the closest resemblance to the image of the supreme Author, and their relation to Him is not that of machines to their artificer (like the rest of the world) but rather that of citizens to their prince. . . .

But the universe would not be perfect unless individual justice is considered, and it is— happiness is proportional to virtue.

As for the afflictions of men, and especially of good men, we must hold ourselves assured that they contribute to the greater good of those who suffer them; and this is true not only theologically, but physically also, just as a grain of wheat cast into the earth must suffer before it bears fruit. And in general it is true to say that afflictions are for the time being evil, but in effect good, since they are short cuts to a greater perfection. . . .

The afflictions of good men are explained as contributing to their greater good.

Further, we realize that there is a perpetual and a most free progress of the whole universe in fulfillment of the universal beauty and perfection of the works of God, so that it is always advancing towards a greater development.

And the world is always advancing toward greater good.

To the objection that may perhaps be offered that if this were so the world would long ago have become a paradise, the answer is at hand: although many substances have already come to great perfection, yet owing to the infinite divisibility of what is continuous, there always remain in the abyss of things parts that are asleep, and these need to be awakened and to be driven forward into something greater and better—in a word, to a better development. Hence this progress does not ever come to an end.

But because reality is infinitely divisible, progress toward perfection is never reached—it is never ending.

be eaten alive by crocodiles, bitten by poisonous snakes, stung by poisonous insects, attacked by viruses, or itched silly by fungus infections. (There is, further, the incredible amount of animal suffering not brought about by human choice.) Because there are thousands of ills of this kind that human beings are subject to which are not the result of any free human choices, it seems clear that those who believe in a perfect God cannot defend that belief by arguing that all evil results from free human choices.

Conclusion: Evil counts against existence of perfect God.

It seems sensible, therefore, to conclude that anything even close to a perfect God does not exist. This says nothing, of course, against the existence of a less than perfect God. It's certainly possible that a creator exists, say, of the kind depicted in the Old Testament.

6. Faith and Reason

There has never been agreement concerning proofs and evidence for God's existence.

It is a striking fact about the arguments and evidence presented to prove the existence of God that there has never been anything close to universal agreement concerning the validity of any particular item. It isn't just that believers accept and doubters doubt. Among believers themselves, certainly among theologians and philosophers, there is no agreement about which proofs are valid or which evidence authentic. Philosophers are notorious for rejecting the famous proofs of their predecessors only to invent new ones of their own. *

Both Sides Have the Same Evidence

All sides know all the evidence, yet intelligent people disagree.

Furthermore, it isn't that believers know some secret proof nonbelievers haven't yet heard of, or that nonbelievers have a secret disproof. And it surely isn't that believers have just carelessly overlooked the

---

*Immanuel Kant is a good example, because his refutation of the ontological argument is celebrated. Roughly, Kant argued that (1) it is our duty to promote the *summum bonum* (the supreme good); (2) this presupposes the possibility of achieving the *summum bonum*; but (3) it can't be achieved in this life since it requires us to be *holy* (always choose the morally right), something impossible for us in this life; so (4) there must be an immortal afterlife in which the *summum bonum* is to be achieved; and therefore (5) God must exist "as the necessary condition of the possibility of the *summum bonum*."

invalidity of their arguments. If it were any of these, the issue would have been settled hundreds or thousands of years ago. No, all the cards are on the table for everyone to see, yet intelligent human beings disagree over them.

This significant fact suggests that belief in God is not a matter of arguments, evidence, or proof, but of *faith*. Those who don't have faith find the proofs unconvincing, while those whose faith (psychologically) requires argument seem able to find one that satisfies them. (Of course, not all who have faith need proofs to support it.)

Belief in God is a matter of faith, not arguments, reasons, or evidence.

More will be said about faith in Chapter 3. But two things should be said now. First, there is no mystery about belief based on faith. Faith is just belief that is not based on evidence, reasons, or arguments. That some people have faith while others don't seems to result from psychological differences, not differences in evidence or brainpower.

Faith is belief not based on evidence, reasons, or arguments, and has psychological origins.

Although Not Provable, Faith in God Has Psychological Benefits

Furthermore, while faith alone cannot give purpose or meaning to an otherwise purposeless life, there can be no doubt that religious faith gives great comfort to believers, perhaps by helping to "fortify and direct" their lives, by strengthening their will and desire, or (in modern psychological terms) by reducing depression and anxiety resulting from the terrifying nature of life and the human predicament. In any event, it makes the great show of human life seem more worthwhile to many believers. That nonbelievers are not helped in this way should not blind them to the fact that believers do gain psychological benefit from their belief. Of course, gaining psychological benefit from belief in God does not give us good evidence, or good *reason*, for believing in him, any more than it gives weak people who are comforted by the belief that they are strong good reason for their belief.*

Still, faith in God seems to give believers great psychological benefit. Of course, that isn't a good reason for believing.

---

*The point is connected to the theory of truth proposed by William James. James defined the *true* as that which it is most profitable to believe. Adopting James's definition would force us to say that the weak people just referred to truly believe they are strong if, as may well sometimes be the case, it is more profitable for them to believe they are strong than that they are weak.

The Danish theologian Søren Kierkegaard (1813–1855) has had perhaps more influence on twentieth-century Protestant theologians than any other modern writer. Here are excerpts from his Concluding Unscientific Postscript.

Søren Kierkegaard: **THE ETERNAL HAPPINESS PROMISED BY CHRISTIANITY***

How can I get the happiness promised by Christianity?

Faith doesn't result from scientific inquiry, because that loses the passion which is the condition of faith.

An objective approach loses the passion that is the condition of faith; passion and certainty don't go together.

It's easier to have faith given that the world is imperfect than if it were perfect. In the eternal afterlife, faith can't exist.

Suppose opponents prove what they will about the scriptures. This proves nothing against belief in Christ—he still

The objective problem consists of an inquiry into the truth of Christianity. The subjective problem concerns the relationship of the individual to Christianity. To put it quite simply: How may I, Johannes Climacus [Kierkegaard], participate in the happiness promised by Christianity? . . .

Everything being assumed in order with respect to the Scriptures—what follows? Has anyone who previously did not have faith been brought a single step nearer to its acquisition? No, not a single step. Faith does not result simply from a scientific inquiry; it does not come directly at all. On the contrary, in this objectivity one tends to lose that infinite personal interestedness in passion which is the condition of faith, the *ubique et musquam* in which faith can come into being. Has anyone who previously had faith gained anything with respect to its strength and power? No, not in the least. Rather is it the case that in this voluminous knowledge, this certainty that lurks at the door of faith and threatens to devour it, he is in so dangerous a situation that he will need to put forth much effort in great fear and trembling, lest he fall a victim to the temptation to confuse knowledge with faith. While faith has hitherto had a profitable schoolmaster in the existing uncertainty, it would have in the new certainty its most dangerous enemy. For if passion is eliminated, faith no longer exists, and certainty and passion do not go together. Whoever believes that there is a God and an over-ruling providence finds it easier to preserve his faith, easier to acquire something that definitely is faith and not an illusion, in an imperfect world where passion is kept alive, than in an absolutely perfect world. In such a world faith is . . . unthinkable.

I assume now the opposite, that the opponents have succeeded in proving what they desire about the Scriptures, with a certainty transcending the most ardent wish of the most passionate hostility—what then? Have the opponents thereby abolished Christianity? By no means. Has the believer been harmed? By no means, not in the least. Has the opponent made good a right to be relieved of responsibility for not being a believer? By no means. Because these books are not written by these authors . . . are not inspired it does not

*Søren Kierkegaard, *Concluding Unscientific Postscript*, trans. David F. Swenson and Walter Lowrie. Copyright 1941 © 1969 by Princeton University Press. Excerpts, 4.5 pp., reprinted by permission of Princeton University Press.

follow . . . that Christ has not existed. In so far, the believer is equally free to assume it. . . .

Here is the crux of the matter, and I come back to the case of the learned theology. For whose sake is it that the proof is sought? Faith does not need it: aye, it must even regard the proof as its enemy. But when faith begins to feel embarrassed and ashamed, like a young woman for whom her love is no longer sufficient, but who secretly feels ashamed of her lover and must therefore have it established that there is something remarkable about him—when faith thus begins to lose its passion, when faith begins to cease to be faith, then a proof becomes necessary so as to command respect from the side of unbelief. . . . Philosophy teaches that the way is to become objective, while Christianity teaches that the way is to become subjective, i.e., to become a subject in truth . . . Christianity wishes to intensify passion to its highest pitch; but passion is subjectivity, and does not exist objectively. . . .

The task of becoming subjective, then, may be presumed to be the highest task, and one that is proposed to every human being; just as, correspondingly, the highest reward, an eternal happiness exists only for those who are subjective; or rather, comes into being for the individual who becomes subjective.

When the question of truth is raised in an objective manner, reflection is directed objectively to the truth, as an object to which the knower is related. Reflection is not focused upon the relationship, however, but upon the question of whether it is the truth to which the knower is related. If only the object to which he is related is the truth, the subject is accounted to be in the truth. When the question of the truth is raised subjectively, reflection is directed subjectively to the nature of the individual's relationship; if only the mode of this relationship is in the truth, the individual is in the truth even if he should happen to be thus related to what is not true. Let us take as an example the knowledge of God. Objectively, reflection is directed to the problem of whether this object is the true God: subjectively, reflection is directed to the question whether the individual is related to a something in such a manner that his relationship is in truth a God-relationship. . . . The existing individual who chooses to pursue the objective way enters upon the entire approximation-process by which it is proposed to bring God to light objectively. But this is in all eternity impossible, because God is a subject, and therefore exists only for subjectivity in inwardness. The objective accent falls on WHAT is said, the subjective accent on HOW it is said. This distinction holds even in the aesthetic realm, and receives definite expression in the principle that what is in itself true may in the mouth of such and such a person become untrue. . . . Objectively the interest is focused merely on the thought-content, subjectively on the inwardness.

may have existed.

Proof is faith's enemy. When faith begins to lose its passion, proof becomes necessary. Philosophy teaches objectivity, Christianity subjectivity; because passion is subjectivity.

Becoming subjective is the highest task; the highest reward is for the subjective.

Thinking of God objectively, we ask whether the object is the true God; thinking of him subjectively, we ask whether the individual is related to God in the truth; whether his relationship "is in truth a God relationship."

Objectivity fails. God is a subject, and exists only for subjectivity in inwardness.

Objective interest is in what is

said, subjective in how it is said. This inward "how" is the "passion of the infinite," which is truth. The truth is an objective uncertainty of the most passionate inwardness. Faith is the contradiction between inward passion and objective uncertainty. I can't grasp God objectively, so I must believe. The more objective security, the less inwardness. Religious absurdity repels the individual. Socrates rooted faith in objective uncertainty. Now there is certainty—that objectively belief in God is absurd. Faith holds fast to it in the passion of inwardness. Suppose we want faith by means of an objective inquiry. As we inquire, it becomes more probable until we're ready to believe it. But then it's not possible to believe it.

At its maximum this inward "how" is the passion of the infinite, and the passion of the infinite is the truth. But the passion of the infinite is precisely subjectivity, and thus subjectivity becomes the truth. . . . Only in subjectivity is there decisiveness, to seek factor and not its content, for its content is precisely itself. In this manner subjectivity and the subjective "how" constitute the truth. . . Here is such a definition of truth: An objective uncertainty held fast in an appropriation-process of the most passionate inwardness is the truth, the highest truth attainable for an existing individual. . . .

But the above definition of truth is an equivalent expression for faith. Without risk there is no faith. Faith is precisely the contradiction between the infinite passion of the individual's inwardness and the objective uncertainty. If I am capable of grasping God objectively, I do not believe, but precisely because I cannot do this I must believe. . . . Without risk there is no faith, and the greater the risk the greater the faith; the more objective security the less inwardness (for inwardness is precisely subjectivity), and the less objective security the more profound the possible inwardness. When the paradox is paradoxical in itself, it repels the individual by virtue of its absurdity, and the corresponding passion of the inwardness is faith.

When Socrates believed that there was a God, he held fast to the objective uncertainty with the whole passion of his inwardness, and it is precisely in this contradiction and in this risk, that [his] faith is rooted. Now it is otherwise. Instead of the objective uncertainty, there is here a certainty, namely, that objectively it is absurd; and this absurdity, held fast in the passion of inwardness, is faith. The Socratic ignorance is as a witty jest in comparison with the earnestness of facing the absurd; and the Socratic existential inwardness is as Greek light-mindedness in comparison with the grave strenuosity of faith. The absurd is precisely by its objective repulsion the measure of the intensity of faith in inwardness. Suppose a man who wishes to acquire faith; let the comedy begin. He wishes to have faith, but he wishes also to safeguard himself by means of an objective inquiry and its approximation-process. What happens? With the help of the approximation-process the absurd becomes something different; it becomes probable, it becomes increasingly probable, it becomes extremely and emphatically probable. Now he is ready to believe it, and he ventures to claim for himself that he does not believe as shoemakers and tailors and simple folk believe, but only after long deliberation. Now he is ready to believe it; and lo, now it has become precisely impossible to believe it. Anything that is almost probable, or probable, or extremely and emphatically probable, is something he can almost know, or as good as know, or extremely and emphatically almost know—but it is impossible to believe. . . .

Now listen to the English philosopher Bertrand Russell (1872–1970) on science and the existence of God.

Bertrand Russell: **THE SCIENTIFIC OUTLOOK***

Evolutionary Theology. Evolution, when it was new, was regarded as hostile to religion, and is still so considered by fundamentalists. But a whole school of apologists has grown up who see in evolution evidence of a Divine Plan slowly unfolding through the ages. . . . From a cosmic point of view, life is a very unimportant phenomenon: very few stars have planets; very few planets can support life. Life, even on the earth, belongs to only a very small proportion of the matter close to the earth's surface. During the greater part of the past existence of the earth, it was too hot to support life; during the greater part of its future existence, it will be too cold. It is by no means impossible that there is, at this moment, no life anywhere in the universe except on earth; but even if, taking a very liberal estimate, we suppose that there are scattered through space some hundred thousand other planets on which life exists, it must still be admitted that living matter makes rather a poor show if considered as the purpose of the whole creation. There are some old gentlemen who are fond of prosy anecdotes leading at last to a "point"; imagine an anecdote longer than any you have ever heard, and the "point" shorter, and you will have a fair picture of the activities of the Creator according to the biologists. Moreover, the "point" of the anecdote, even when it is reached, appears hardly worthy of so long a preface. I am willing to admit that there is merit in the tail of the fox, the song of the thrush, or the horns of the ibex. But it is not to these things that the evolutionary theologian points with pride: it is to the soul of man. Unfortunately, there is no impartial arbiter to decide on the merits of the human race; but for my part, when I consider their poison gases, their researches into bacteriological warfare, their meannesses, cruelties and oppressions, I find them, considered as the crowning gem of the creation, somewhat lacking in lustre.

Is there anything in the process of evolution that demands the hypothesis of a purpose? This is the crucial question. . . . I am . . . quite unable to see why an intelligent Creator should have the purpose which we must attribute to Him if He has really designed all that happens in the world of organic life. Nor does the progress of scientific investigation afford any evidence that

When new, evolution was regarded an an enemy of religion. But now some take it to be evidence of a divine plan. However, life on earth hardly seems the point of the universe.

And when life finally is reached, it hardly seems worth the effort, considering the evil nature of mankind.

The crux: Does evolution require purpose? Hard to imagine God having a purpose for it. Science can explain life.

*Reprinted from *The Scientific Outlook* by Bertrand Russell, by permission of W. W. Norton & Company, Inc. Copyright 1931 by Bertrand Russell. Copyright renewed 1959 by Bertrand Russell. Permission also granted by George Allen & Unwin Ltd.

the behaviour of living matter is governed by anything other than laws of physics and chemistry.

Reproduction seems explainable on mechanistic grounds.

Or take again reproduction, which though not universal throughout the animal kingdom, is nevertheless one of its most interesting peculiarities. There is now nothing in this process that can rightly be called mysterious. I do not mean to say that it is all fully understood, but that mechanistic principles have explained enough of it to make it probable that, given time, they will explain the whole. . . .

Some, like Lloyd Morgan, believe a divine purpose must lie behind evolution, because otherwise we can't explain "emergent" properties, such as the fluidity of H_2O, or the emergence of mind in physical bodies.

One of the best statements of the point of view of a religiously minded biologist is to be found in Lloyd Morgan's *Emergent Evolution* (1923) and *Life, Mind and Spirit* (1926). Lloyd Morgan believes that there is a Divine Purpose underlying the course of evolution, more particularly of what he calls "emergent evolution." The definition of emergent evolution, if I understand it rightly, is as follows: it sometimes happens that a collection of objects arranged in a suitable pattern will have a new property which does not belong to the objects singly, and which cannot, so far as we can see, be deduced from their several properties together with the way in which they are arranged. He considers that there are examples of the same kind of thing even in the inorganic realm. The atom, the molecule, and the crystal will all have properties which, if I understand Lloyd Morgan aright, he regards as not deducible from the properties of their constituents. The same holds in a higher degree of living organisms, and most of all with those higher organisms which possess what are called minds. Our minds, he would say, are, it is true, associated with the physical organism, but are not deducible from the properties of that organism considered as an arrangement of atoms in space. "Emergent evolution," he says, "is from first to last a revelation and manifestation of that which I speak of as Divine Purpose." Again he says: "Some of us, and I for one, end with a concept of activity, under acknowledgment, as part and parcel of Divine Purpose.". . .

But Lloyd Morgan gives no reasons for his view. For aught Russell knows, there may be a God who chooses the terrible evils.

It would be easier to deal with this view if any reasons were advanced in its favour, but so far as I have been able to discover from Professor Lloyd Morgan's pages he considers that the doctrine is its own recommendation and does not need to be demonstrated by appeals to the mere understanding. I do not pretend to know whether Professor Lloyd Morgan's opinion is false. For aught I know to the contrary, there may be a Being of infinite power who chooses that children should die of meningitis, and older people of cancer; these things occur, and occur as the result of evolution. If, therefore, evolution embodies a Divine Plan, these occurrences must also have been planned. I have been informed that suffering is sent as a purification for sin, but I find it difficult to think that a child of four or five years can be sunk in such black depths of iniquity as to deserve the punishment that befalls not a few of the children whom our optimistic divines might see any day, if they choose, suffering torments in children's hospitals. Again, I am told that though the child himself may not have sinned very deeply, he deserves to suffer on account of his parent's wickedness. I can only repeat that if this is the Divine sense of justice it differs from mine, and that I think mine superior. If indeed the world in which we live has been produced in accordance with a Plan, we shall have to reckon Nero a saint in comparison with the Author of that Plan. Fortunately, however, the evidence of Divine Purpose is non-existent; so at least one must infer from the fact that no evidence is adduced by those who believe in it. We are, therefore, spared the necessity for that attitude of impotent hatred which every brave and humane man would otherwise be called upon to adopt towards the Almighty Tyrant. . . .

If this is the divine sense of justice, it differs from Russell's. But no evidence is given, so we are spared the need to have "impotent hatred" toward the almighty tyrant.

We have reviewed . . . a number of different apologies for religion on the part of eminent men of science. We have seen that Eddington and Jeans contradict each other, and that both contradict the biological theologians, but all agree that in the last resort science should abdicate before what is called the religious consciousness. This attitude is regarded by themselves and by their admirers as more optimistic than that of the uncompromising rationalist. It is, in fact, quite the opposite: it is the outcome of discouragement and loss of faith. Time was when religion was believed with wholehearted fervour, when men went on crusades and burned each other at the stake because of the intensity of their convictions. After the wars of religion, theology gradually lost this intense hold on men's minds. So far as anything has taken its place, its place has been taken by science. In the name of science we revolutionize industry, undermine family morals, enslave coloured races, and skilfully exterminate each other with poison gases. Some men of science do not altogether like these uses to which science is being put. In terror and dismay they try to find refuge in the superstitions of an earlier day.

Those who believe science should bow to faith think themselves more optimistic than nonbelievers. But it's the opposite. It is for some a loss of faith in science, perhaps because of some of the uses to which science has been put, leading them to religious belief.

But it is not by going backward that we shall find an issue from our troubles. No slothful relapses into infantile fantasies will direct the new power which men have derived from science into the right channels; nor will philosophic scepticism as to the foundations arrest the course of scientific technique in the world of affairs. Men need a faith which is robust and real, not timid and halfhearted. Science is in its essence nothing but the systematic pursuit of knowledge, and knowledge, whatever ill-uses bad men may make of it, is in its essence good. To lose faith in knowledge is to lose faith in the best of man's capacities; and therefore I repeat unhesitatingly that the unyielding rationalist has a better faith and a more unbending optimism than any of the timid seekers after the childish comforts of a less adult age.

Science is just the systematic pursuit of knowledge. And knowledge itself, however used, is good. To lose faith in knowledge is to lose faith in mankind's best capacities.

Summary of Chapter 1

1. *Atheists* believe there is no God; *theists* that there is; and *agnostics* that there isn't good reason to believe either way.

2. The concept or idea of God and (if he exists) God himself are two different things. The concept of God surely exists. The question is whether God exists.

3. The concept of God is *ambiguous*—there are many different conceptions of God. People at different times and places have conceived of him quite differently, examples being the Judeo-Christian God, the ancient Greek gods, sun and moon gods, and the various animal gods worshipped around the world.

4. The various conceptions of God also tend to be quite *vague*—they tend to be unclear, imprecise, or fuzzy around the edges. The less clear a belief is, the less it is a belief in *something*. Still, there is a conception common to most believers in a standard Judeo-Christian God, which is generally what we have in mind when referring to God in this chapter.

5. The fact that people in all societies believe in some god or other is not a good reason to believe in any god in particular, for one thing because all sorts of false beliefs have been more or less universal and for another because the fact that some believe in a cat god, or sun god, hardly is a good reason to believe in a Christian or Muslim God.

6. The argument that we're entitled to believe God exists because we can't prove he doesn't exist is defective. Inability to prove something never justifies believing the opposite. If it were, people could argue that God does not exist because we can't prove that he does.

7. *Cosmological* arguments for God's existence are based on the apparent need for the universe as a whole to have a cause. An example is the *first cause* argument:

    a. In everyday life we find given things or events caused by others.
    b. But an infinite series of such causes is impossible.
∴ c. There must be a first cause: God.

    Objections raised to this argument are:

    a. Its second premise is questionable.
    b. The causes observed in daily life could trace back through many different series to many different first causes.

c. Even if it proved the existence of a single first cause, the argument wouldn't prove that that first cause is a god, and certainly wouldn't prove it is the Christian God. The first cause could be a devil, Zoroaster, or just the first instant in time.

d. If the reasoning behind a first cause argument, or any cosmological argument, were valid—that is, if something as immense, complicated, or wonderful as the universe *had* to have a cause, or maker—then God too would have to have a cause, Supergod, who in turn would have to have a cause, Super-Supergod, and so on. But no one believes in an infinity of Gods each causing another.

8. The *argument from design* stems from the fact that the universe contains all sorts of patterns or orders, only a small portion of which are of human design:

    a. There is order in the universe.
    b. But order cannot exist without design.
∴ c. There must be an orderer or designer: God.

Objections raised to this argument are:

a. At best, this proves only the existence of an orderer or designer, not the existence of a creator, or God. The orderer could be the devil; there could be many orderers; or a god who did the ordering could now be dead.

b. There isn't any good reason for accepting the second premise of the argument. In particular, we can't reason from the fact that the order brought about by human beings (or other animals) has an orderer to the conclusion that all other kinds of order, such as the laws of nature, also must have been brought about by some orderer or designer.

9. According to *Pascal's Wager*, either God exists or he doesn't, and we must decide (wager) one way or the other. If we weigh the gains and losses and then wager that God exists, and he does, we gain a great deal; but if he doesn't, we lose nothing. So we should wager that he exists, because we have a great deal to gain and nothing to lose.

Pascal's argument has been objected to because:

a. He seems to be wrong in arguing that neutrality (agnosticism) is the same as disbelief (atheism).

b. There are all sorts of possible creators, and Pascal gives us no way to decide which one to believe in, yet the reward may well come only if we believe in the one who actually exists (thus, if the Jewish God exists, then idol worshippers—and Christians?—are in trouble).

c. Pascal offers no proof or reason (outside of Christian revelation) for believing that a wager on the right God—the one that actually exists—will yield the benefits he claims. God may well think of belief on such a basis as hypocritical and punish those who believe for this reason while rewarding honest doubters.

10. People often cite miracles or mystical experiences to justify belief in God. Against this idea, it has been argued that:

a. Alleged miraculous or mystical experiences may be the result of psychological deception.

b. The knowledge needed to produce mystical experiences or visions has always been widespread and the means readily available (fasting, mushrooms), which casts doubt on their "otherworldly" nature.

c. What seems miraculous at one time or place often is explained and understood in another (such as lodestones and lightning).

d. Equally plausible, equally attested-to miracles and visions are alleged in support of many radically different sorts of gods, making acceptance of the miracles supporting one's own god (while rejecting the others) hard to defend on rational grounds.

e. Even acceptable evidence of a miracle or genuinely mystical experience at best makes the existence of any particular God only probable, yet true believers aim at absolute, 100 percent faith, which can't be achieved in this way.

11. Furthermore, we can't appeal to the Bible as a divinely inspired document:

a. We can't argue that God exists because it says so in the Bible, for that would beg the question and so be fallacious.

b. Taken literally, the Bible contains gross contradictions (for example, two different accounts of the creation).

c. It tells us no incontrovertible facts that were not generally known at the times when the Bible was written down.

d. It contains versions of myths that existed in other, equally plausible variations in those days (such as the Flood story).

12. Can we prove God does *not* exist? No, we can't. But some argue that the *argument from evil* proves that a perfect creator doesn't exist. The argument

states that if evil exists, the creator can't be perfect, and evil does exist, so the creator can't be perfect.

Believers have replied that: (1) God's greatness even brings good out of evil (reply to this reply: better yet to bring good out of nothing); (2) evils, such as pain are merely mental or illusory, not real (reply: any sort of pain is an evil); (3) some evil is necessary, for instance as a warning (reply: no warnings are needed in a perfect world); (4) we see only a small slice of the universe (reply: no part of a perfect world would have evil); and (5) God gave us free will—a good—and it's our fault if we choose evil (replies: we'd do much less evil in a better world; or if we knew more or were smarter; having free will doesn't mean we ever have to choose evil; and most evil is not the result of human choices).

13. Because the arguments, reasons, and proofs of God's existence that convince one rational person notoriously fail to convince others, it seems plausible to suppose that acceptance of a "proof" that God exists results from psychological rather than logical considerations, and that in the last analysis genuine belief in God is based on faith alone. That some people have faith while others don't seems to be a matter of psychological need, not of reasoning, evidence, or intelligence. Faith gives comfort to believers, helps them face the difficulties and terrors of life, and makes life seem more worthwhile somehow. Yet this isn't a good *reason*, or logical justification for believing.

Questions for Further Thought

1. If you believe in God, what do you think God is like? (If you also believe in a devil, what is he or she like?)

2. If you don't believe in God, what (if anything) might convince you? If you do believe, what (if anything) might convince you to stop believing?

3. St. Thomas Aquinas argued that the possibility of evil is required so that more good will be possible:

> If there were no death of other animals, there would be no life for the lion; if there were no persecution from tyrants, there would be no occasion for the heroic suffering of the martyrs.

He also argued,

> As Augustine says: *Since God is the highest good, He would not allow any evil to exist in His works, unless His omnipotence and goodness were such as to bring good even out of evil.* This is part of the infinite goodness of God, that he should allow evil to exist, and out of it produce good.

What do you think of these passages, in particular with respect to their solving the problem of evil?

4. A recent theological writer, John Hick, has argued that some evil is necessary to carry out God's intent in creating the world:

> Christianity . . . has never supposed that God's purpose in the creation of the world was to construct a paradise. . . . The world is seen, instead, as a place of "soul making" in which free beings grappling with the tasks and challenges of their existence in a common environment, may become "children of God" and "heirs of eternal life." For suppose . . . that this world were a paradise from which all possibility of pain and suffering were excluded. . . . It is evident that our present ethical concepts would have no meaning in it. If, for example, the notion of harming someone is an essential element in the concept of a wrong action, in our hedonistic paradise there could be no wrong actions—nor any right. . . . Courage and fortitude would have no point in an environment in which there is . . . no danger or difficulty.

How does his idea about this being a soul-building world strike you?

5. David Hume argued that if our experiences in this life on the earth are relevant, they indicate that the creator of this world, if there is one, would seem to be indifferent with respect to human good and evil, because he gives us one or the other without any apparent pattern. Do you think the earthly evidence supports his view?

6. Hume also held that in the argument from design we argue by induction from experiences of this world to something beyond it and beyond those experiences, something we can't legitimately do. Do you think Hume would win or lose on this point in a debate with a severe critic?

7. What do you think of the following passage—Hume against belief in miracles:

> No testimony is sufficient to establish a miracle, unless the testimony be of such a kind that its falsehood would be more miraculous than the fact which it endeavors to establish.

8. If you believe in God as a matter of faith, how would you try to persuade a very good friend of the good news?

9. What do you think of William James's argument in favor of faith in God presented in the James reading in Chapter 1?

10. What argument, evidence, or reason do you think is the best for proving God exists (even if you don't believe it really proves this)? How would you best defend it against the strongest attacks you can think of?

11. How would you answer an exam question that asked you to defend the existence of a perfect God against the attack of an atheist who appeals to

the argument from evil? (It's interesting and useful to ask and try to answer such questions whether you believe in God or not.)

12. Many believers argue that life would be purposeless if God did not exist—"a tale told by an idiot, full of sound and fury, signifying nothing." Belief in God, they say, gives life purpose or meaning. But some atheists and agnostics say that a life directed by God's purposes would be like the life of a rabbit in an elaborate rabbit hutch, God being the hutch keeper. How does this analogy strike you? Is a life lived to satisfy God's purposes better than one led to satisfy our own? (Or do the two coincide?)

13. Some people argue that belief in God is just a holdover from the days when we had no scientific answers to the great questions about life, such as how it all got started and how it has unfolded. Now, they say, we have scientific answers to more and more of these questions, for instance, in the theory of evolution and in particular in the theory of the "big bang" origin of the universe. What do you think of this argument?

This also is clearly defined in the teaching of the Church, that every rational soul is possessed of free will and volition; that it has a struggle to maintain with the devil and his angels, and opposing influences, because they strive to burden it with sins.
—ORIGEN: *De Principiis*, Proem. 5

Without our faith in free will the earth would be the scene not only of the most horrible nonsense but also of the most intolerable boredom.—ARTHUR SCHNITZLER

Only two possibilities exist: either one must believe in determinism and regard free will as a subjective illusion, or one must become a mystic and regard the discovery of natural laws as a meaningless intellectual game. Metaphysicians of the old schools have proclaimed one or the other of these doctrines, but ordinary people have always accepted the dual nature of the world.—MAX BORN

I confess that mankind has a free will, but it is to milk kine, to build houses, etc., and no further.—MARTIN LUTHER

I can either will myself to sleep until 10:30 A.M. and get my ass beat, or I can will myself to get up at 6:00 A.M. and become President.—JIMMY CARTER

Whatever befalls you was preordained for you from eternity.—MARCUS AURELIUS

Among mortals there is no man free . . . he is slave to riches or else to fortune.
—EURIPIDES

Freedom in general may be defined as the absence of obstacles to the realization of desires.—BERTRAND RUSSELL

If we grant freedom to man, then there is an end to the omniscience of God; for if the Divinity knows how I shall act, I must act so perforce.—GOETHE

No man has ever escaped his destiny.
—HOMER

This is one of man's oldest riddles. How can the independence of human volition be harmonized with the fact that we are integral parts of a universe which is subject to the rigid order of Nature's laws?—SIR ARTHUR EDDINGTON

We are forced to fall back on fatalism as an explanation of irrational events, that is to say, of events the rationality of which we do not understand.—TOLSTOY

If a man referred to his brother or to his cat as "an ingenious mechanism," we should know that he was either a fool or a physiologist. No one in practice treats himself or his fellowman or his pet animals as machines; but scientists who have never made a study of Speculative Philosophy seem often to think it their duty to hold in theory what no one outside a lunatic asylum would accept in practice.
—C. D. BROAD

Men are deceived because they think themselves free . . . and the sole reason for thinking so is that they are conscious of their own actions, and ignorant of the causes by which those actions are determined.—SPINOZA

Nor is it possible to explain directly, how the deity can be the mediate cause of all the actions of men, without being the author of sin and moral turpitude.—DAVID HUME

2

Free Will, Determinism, and Moral Responsibility

ACCORDING TO A TRALFAMADORIAN extraterrestrial being in Kurt Vonnegut, Jr.'s book *Slaughterhouse Five*, Tralfamadorians have traveled to the ends of the universe and only on earth is there talk of free will. Perhaps. But there is a great deal of such talk here on earth.

1. Free Will versus Determinism

The problem of free will versus determinism arises because of an apparent contradiction between two plausible ideas. The first is the idea that human beings are free to do or not do whatever they choose (within limits, of course—no one believes we can fly just by choosing to do so). This is the idea that human beings have **freedom of the will**—or **free will,** for short. The second is the idea, mentioned in Chapter 1, that everything that happens in this universe is caused, or determined, by prior events or circumstances. Those who accept this idea are said to believe in the principle of **determinism,** and are called **determinists.** (Those who deny this second idea are said to be **indeterminists.**)

The problem: apparent conflict between belief in free wills and in determinism.

These two ideas are often thought to conflict because it seems as though we can't have free wills—our choices can't be free—if they are determined by past events or circumstances.

If our choices are determined, how can we have free wills?

43

2. Are We Ever Responsible for Our Actions?

Can we all be morally blameless because we don't have free choices?

Furthermore, some have argued that if everything we do is determined by what has happened in the past, so that our choices are never free, then we aren't morally responsible for any of our actions, because then we don't freely choose to do them. Can this be right?

Hard Determinism, Soft Determinism, and Libertarianism

Hard determinists: Determinism is true, so moral responsibility is senseless. Libertarians: Determinism is false, so moral responsibility makes sense. Soft determinists: Determinism and free will are compatible, so moral responsibility makes sense.

In the history of philosophy, there have been essentially three different sorts of answers proposed to this question. One is to bite the bullet and agree that determinism is true and so moral responsibility makes no sense. This view is generally called **hard determinism,** and those who accept it are called **hard determinists.** A second view is that it does indeed make sense to hold people morally accountable for their actions, because determinism is wrong and we do after all have free wills. This view is often called **libertarianism,** and its champions **libertarians.** And finally, a third view is that we don't contradict ourselves in accepting both determinism and freedom of the will, so that we can be held morally accountable for our free choices even though they are determined. This last view is generally called **soft determinism,** and its advocates are called **soft determinists.**

3. Hard Determinism

Hard determinists: (1) determinism is true; (2) determined actions are not free; (3) we're responsible only for free actions.

On examination, hard determinism turns out to rest on three principles:

1. the principle of determinism—that everything that happens has a cause;
2. the principle that if an action is determined, then it isn't free (the person couldn't really have chosen not to do it); and
3. the principle that a person is morally accountable only for free actions.

Arguments for Hard Determinism

Points (2) and (3) seem obvious to hard determinists (and libertarians).

Hard determinists have tended to believe that the second and third of the assumptions needed to support their position are obvious (so do libertarians). It seems obvious to them that actions determined, say, by heredity and environment cannot be freely chosen actions, and equally obvious that people are only responsible for actions they have freely chosen. So hard determinists have concentrated their fire on the first principle—that determinism is true. Their arguments are very powerful.

In the first place, the evidence for determinism in general from everyday life seems overwhelmingly strong. When we put sugar into coffee, we expect the coffee to taste sweet, and would be very surprised if it didn't. When we take a walk, the ground always supports us—we don't slowly sink into the earth. Nor does gravity ever fail—we never float gently up to the stars. When astronauts go into outer space, thousands of pieces of equipment have to work exactly right millions of times—"exactly right" meaning exactly as predicted by scientific theories about the laws of nature, which explain how things are determined to happen.

Evidence from everyday life strongly supports determinism.

The truth is that we can't make a move without relying on at least something working as it has in the past. Thus, every experience we ever have seems to support the general thesis that everything that happens in this universe is caused or determined by what has happened in the past.

But the main issue between hard determinists and their opponents is not over determinism or causality in general. The question concerns just one narrow range of events or circumstances in the universe, namely, human choices and actions, in particular, moral choices and actions. Are our actions free (undetermined)? Are our choices free? Is there sufficient "loose play" in the laws governing the universe to allow room for these things? Determinists say *no*, and the evidence seems strongly in their favor.

The issue is over human choices, not whether determinism rules elsewhere.

For one thing, in daily life we constantly make predictions about what people will do. Of course, we can't predict with anything like 100 percent accuracy, but perceptive people, at any rate, do get passably good at the job. They label people *trustworthy, selfish, unprincipled, outgoing, aggressive, hostile,* and all the rest with a modest success that's hard to explain if our actions and choices are not determined.

We predict human choices well in daily life; how do we explain this if we have free will?

Furthermore, we know from daily life how easily we can change our mental states and abilities by taking drugs. That's the point of the widespread use of alcohol, marijuana, caffeine, nicotine, aspirin, Valium, and the other mind alterers—we alter our perceptions, release our inhibitions, or get rid of pain. In the case of alcohol, we often weaken moral will or resolve, for instance, the resolve to refrain from

We can change mental states in general, willings in particular, thus supporting determinism.

45

immoral sexual relations. All this speaks in favor of the determinist's viewpoint and against the idea of free (uncaused) wills.

Science has good reason to believe all human bodily motions are determined. So how can the will be free?

In addition, there is the crucial evidence from science. Scientists assume that the laws of nature they have discovered apply to *all* things in the universe, including the tiny particles that make up the human brain and nervous system. When we choose to do something—say, squeeze an index finger around the trigger of a loaded gun aimed at an enemy—electrical impulses must travel from the brain to relevant muscles in the body. There is an immense amount of scientific evidence (and *no* convincing counterevidence) that these electrical impulses are caused by other impulses in the brain, which ultimately are caused by chemical interactions somewhere in the body (for instance, in the various glands that secrete hormones and in the retina of the eye). The notion of a free (uncaused) will thus seems to contradict some very well established scientific principles.*

Indeterminists, just like everyone else, act as though determinism were true.

Finally, it should be noted that indeterminists, just like everybody else, act in everyday life as though they did in fact believe that determinism were true. In particular, they anticipate the moral choices of others in the same way as everyone else. And they assume that things such as moral exhortation, moral training, and moral education will be effective, although the very point of moral training is to influence the student's moral decisions. If people really make their moral decisions free from causal forces, how is it that moral training has any effect?

The Argument against Hard Determinism

As we have seen, hard determinism rests on three principles. We can't refute it by rejecting the first of these principles (the principle of determinism), as we just argued. To refute it, then, we must attack the second or third (but hardly anyone picks on the third). As we shall see, this is exactly how soft determinists refute hard determinism. But lying behind this refutation is a very strong desire to hold people

Ultimate reason for rejecting hard determinism: the strength of our desire to hold

---

*Until recently, the social scientists and biologists who study human nature have not been nearly as successful as their counterparts in the physical sciences. But the recent trend has been toward greater success, especially in biology, with no reason other than wishful thinking to believe it will be reversed, and all sorts of reasons for thinking it will accelerate. (Recent evidence, for instance, strongly suggests that mental depression is associated with an imbalance of one of several chemicals in the brain.)

accountable for their actions and choices, and a very strong need to admire and reward those who sacrifice for their duty and to hate and punish the devil's work. And that, ultimately, is the basic reason for rejecting hard determinism. (Whatever some philosophers may claim, the truth seems to be that when we morally judge others, we don't *care* whether our moral choices are determined or not—again, witness the everyday behavior of everyone, including hard determinists.)

each other accountable for our actions.

4. Libertarianism

In contrast to hard determinists, **libertarians** (often called **indeterminists**) deny that determinism is true. **Libertarianism** is the view that moral choices are in general free; that is, uncaused (or self-caused), and that therefore we are justified in holding people morally accountable for their actions. This is another way of saying that determinism is false, so there is freedom of the will, and therefore morality does indeed make sense.

Libertarianism: Determinism is false; we have free will; so moral responsibility makes sense.

Of course, libertarians realize that we can't choose to do just anything—we can't simply will ourselves to have superhuman powers. But we're usually free, they claim, in typical moral situations in which we can choose either to do or not do evil, which is what counts in justifying the practice of morality.

Reasons for Accepting Libertarianism

There are two basic reasons why libertarianism is so popular. The first is the belief that otherwise we are not justified in holding people responsible for their actions. (Libertarians thus agree with hard determinists that if our moral choices are determined, they are not free.)

Libertarianism is required to make sense of morality.

We Feel Free

The second important reason why libertarians believe that we have free (uncaused) wills is that it feels as though we are free. When we choose, say, to lie, we generally feel that we could have chosen not to lie, that our choice was not forced on us by what has happened to us in the past. We feel, in other words, that there were genuinely alternative paths open to us.

47

Here is an excerpt by the Dutch philosopher Baruch Spinoza (1632–1677), one of the few important Jewish philosophers in Western philosophy, in which he defends determinism.

Baruch Spinoza: IN FAVOR OF DETERMINISM*

Freedom is acting by the necessity of one's own nature.

I say that a thing is free, which exists and acts solely by the necessity of its own nature. Thus also God understands Himself and all things freely, because it follows solely from the necessity of His nature, that He should understand all things. You see I do not place freedom in free decision, but in free necessity. However, let us descend to created things, which are all determined by external causes to exist and operate in a given determinate manner. In order that this may be clearly understood, let us conceive a very simple thing. For instance, a stone receives from the impulsion of an external cause, a certain quantity of motion, by virtue of which it continues to move after the impulsion given by the external cause has ceased. The permanence of the stone's motion is constrained, not necessary, because it must be defined by the impulsion of an external cause. What is true of the stone is true of any individual . . . inasmuch as every individual thing is necessarily determined by some external cause to operate in a fixed and determinate manner.

Just as a stone's motion is constrained by external causes, so every individual is determined by external causes.

Further conceive, I beg, that a stone, while continuing in motion, should be capable of thinking and knowing, that it is endeavouring, as far as it can, to continue to move. Such a stone, being conscious merely of its own endeavour and not at all indifferent, would believe itself to be completely free, and would think that it continued in motion solely because of its own wish. This is that human freedom, which all boast that they possess, and which consists solely in the fact, that men are conscious of their own desire, but are ignorant of the causes whereby that desire has been determined. Thus . . . a drunken man thinks, that from the free decision of his mind he speaks words, which afterwards, when sober, he would like to have left unsaid. As this misconception is innate in all men, it is not easily conquered. For, although experience abundantly shows that men can do anything rather than check their desires, and that very often, when a prey to conflicting emotions, they see the better course and follow the worse, they yet believe themselves to be free; because in some cases their desire for a thing is slight, and can easily be overruled by the recollection of something else. . . .

If stones were conscious, they'd believe they were free and moved by their own choice. People who boast of human freedom are aware of their own desires but not of the causes of those desires.

*Translated by R. H. M. Elwes. (The two concluding paragraphs are from Spinoza's *Principles of Cartesian Philosophy*, translated by Harry E. Wedeck, Philosophical Library, New York, 1961.)

For when [your friend] says, with Descartes, that he who is constrained by no external cause is free, if by being constrained he means acting against one's will, I grant that we are in some cases quite unrestrained, and in this respect possess free will. But if by constrained he means acting necessarily, although not against one's will (as I have explained above), I deny that we are in any instance free.

We're not free to act necessarily, although not against our will.

But your friend asserts that *we may employ our reason absolutely, that is, in complete freedom;* and is, I think, a little too confident on the point. *For who,* he says, *could deny, without contradicting his own consciousness, that I can think with my thoughts, that I wish or do not wish to write?*

As a matter of fact . . . deny that I can by any absolute power of thought think, that I wish or do not wish to write. I appeal to the consciousness . . . that in dreams he has not the power of thinking that he wishes, or does not wish to write; and that, when he dreams that he wishes to write, he has not the power not to dream that he wishes to write. I think he must also have experienced, that the mind is not always equally capable of thinking of the same object, but according as the body is more capable for the image of this or that object being excited in it, so is the mind more capable of thinking of the same object.

Some think we have the power to think what we wish, but we don't—think of dreams, where we can't choose our thoughts.

When he further adds, that the causes for his applying his mind to writing have led him, but not constrained him to write, he merely means . . . [that] causes, which at other times would not have constrained him, have constrained him in this case, . . . necessarily to wish to write.

Without freedom, sins aren't excusable.

What he finally adds, that *if this were granted, all wickedness would be excusable,* I meet with the question, What then? Wicked men are not less to be feared, and are not less harmful, when they are wicked from necessity.

In a word, I should like your friend, who makes these objections, to tell me, how he reconciles the human virtue, which he says arises from the free decision of the mind, with God's pre-ordainment of the universe. If, with Descartes, he confesses his inability to do so, he is endeavouring to direct against me the weapon which has already pierced himself. But in vain. . . .

There is no way to reconcile free will with God's preordaining the universe.

It will again be asked: Why then are the wicked punished? For they act according to their own nature and the divine decree.

I reply that it is also in accordance with the divine decree that they should be punished: and if only those whom we imagine as sinning by virtue of their own freedom were to be punished, why do men try to exterminate poisonous serpents? For they sin only in accordance with their own nature, and cannot do otherwise.

The wicked are punished, because that's the divine decree.

Arguments against Libertarianism

But some feelings are misleading. Unfortunately, both of these libertarian defenses are defective. Take the second—that we have a feeling of freedom. Even if this were true (and some determinists also think it is), it wouldn't prove that we do in fact have free will, because many feelings are misleading (for instance, the feeling that the air is colder than the water on a chilly day at the beach). Merely feeling free is thus not sufficient reason for believing that we are in fact free.

And we don't feel free from cause. But it would count as *evidence* that we are free, just as feeling, say, that we've broken a bone counts as evidence that we've done so. Well, don't we feel free when we choose to do this rather than that? Yes, of course. But not in the relevant sense of *freedom from cause,* for a cause isn't the sort of thing that can be felt! So the absence of a cause can't be felt either.

We don't feel cause of a knee jerk. Why think we feel absence of causes? Take a case where everyone would agree that no free choice is involved—say, a reflex action like a knee jerk. When the doctor hits a patient's knee in just the right place and his leg flies up, he doesn't experience the cause of this leg motion—he simply experiences the movement of the leg. In cases of this kind, the motion of our body certainly is caused, but we don't feel that cause. Why then should we believe we can experience the *absence* of a cause? Yet if we are to experience a choice as free, we have to experience it as uncaused, we have to experience the absence of a cause. And this we can't do. (If you think otherwise, ask yourself what causes—as opposed to willings—feel like.*)

We do feel free from compulsion. It's true that choices may feel *compelled* (forced) or *uncompelled* (not forced). But, as we shall see when discussing soft determinism, being compelled is quite different from being caused, and being free from compulsion much different from being free from causation.

We Aren't Responsible for Uncaused Actions

Now let's consider the second important argument for libertarianism—that only libertarianism makes sense of the idea of moral responsibility. Suppose Smith decides to rob the Third National Bank of Sheboykosh

---

*By way of analogy, we see the water in the pot boil away and feel the heat of the flame, but we don't see the heat cause the water to boil. If we could experience causes, scientists wouldn't have to bother constructing theories about causal connections; they'd just see (or hear, or taste) them.

and that no one forced him to do it (so that no compulsion is involved). To be consistent, libertarians have to say that we are justified in holding Smith morally accountable for his action only if it was uncaused, even by his own motives, desires, or goals.*

The trouble is that libertarians have things backward. It makes sense to hold a person morally responsible only for choices resulting at least in part from that person's having wants or desires that he tried to satisfy by making those choices! This startling reversal of the libertarian claim is crucially important. To see its force, imagine that you are free in the libertarian sense. That is, imagine your choices are not caused, even by your desires, motives, or goals. Suppose you're walking down Main Street when suddenly you whip out a pistol and murder someone in cold blood. If asked why you did such a horrible thing, what could you reply? Only that you don't have any idea why you chose to do it, because if you did know why, you would know what motivated you to do it, and thus know (in part) what caused you to do it. (Some would say that your desire was not the cause of the action but rather an effect of the same physiological process that caused that action.)

To grasp the point, imagine you say you murdered because you wanted to show you could escape from the ordinary constraints on human actions, wanted to break the rule against murder just to show you could do it (as some people streaked nude a few years ago just to prove they could do it). Then your desire to prove the point would be (part of) the cause of your action. For the murder to be a truly free action, no desires of this or any other kind can have caused your choice. Thus, if asked why you did the act, you would have to reply that you had no reason at all, you just chose to do it.

So if libertarianism were correct, what you chose to do could not be caused by your character, or result from any of your desires, motives, or values. It could not be caused by jealousy, your desire to prove a point, revenge, or anything else. It thus could not have any real connection to *you*, or who you are. So if your choices were truly uncaused, it would be a mistake to praise, blame, reward, or punish you for what you chose to do, which is just the reverse of what libertarians claim.

Libertarians are wrong to believe we're only morally responsible for uncaused choices. The reverse is true.

You would have no reason to do an uncaused act.

If you kill to prove your free will, your desire to prove it is a cause.

Truly uncaused actions would have nothing to do with our desires, goals, motives; with who we are.

---

*Or else, they have to say that we can freely choose our own motives, desires or goals, an option discussed soon.

Can We Freely Choose Our Desires and Motives?

Confronted with objections of this kind, some libertarians agree that what we will is influenced by our desires and motives, but argue that we can freely choose our own desires and motives, or at least decide which ones to act on.

Evidence shows our desires and motives are caused.

But is this right? First, as argued before, all the evidence seems to indicate that our desires and motives are just as caused as anything else. And second, if we really were free to choose things such as desires, there would be no reason to choose one desire rather than another. We would have no more reason to desire love than hate, apple pie than poison, revenge than children, or life than death.

But if they weren't, we'd have no way to choose them.

Example to show our choices can't be free from causes.

To see that this is so, imagine that you are free to choose your own desires, goals, and motives—not on the basis of the ones you now have, but starting from scratch. Let's say you choose some Set A of desires rather than some other Set B. Suppose Set A contains the desire to murder your grandmother and that you in fact do so. If asked why you desired to do such a horrible thing, what could you reply? Only that you don't have any idea why you chose that desire, because if you did know why, you would know what *motivated* you to do it, and we are assuming that you started from scratch, that is, chose without having any prior desires or motives. So if you were totally free to choose your own desires and motives, free even from the desires and motives you in fact now have, the desires you chose would have no connection whatever with you, as argued before. (It won't do to say that you could freely choose your own desires on the basis of the desires you already have, because then the allegedly "freely chosen" new desires would in fact stem from the old ones and not from your free choice.)

Can We Choose to Resist Our Desires and Motives?

It's often said we can't choose our desires, but we can exert willpower and resist them.

Confronted with objections of this kind, some libertarians agree that what we will is influenced by our desires and motives and that we can't choose our desires and motives independently of the ones we already have. But they argue that we can freely choose to *resist acting on* our immoral motives and desires by exerting *willpower* (or more willpower), and thus we are morally accountable for actions taken to satisfy those desires. (For instance, it is commonly said that we can't rid ourselves of the desires of the flesh, but we can control these desires if we try hard enough.)

But everyday experience as well as psychological theory indicates that the amount of willpower we can exert in resisting the temptation to do a particular immoral action depends on the relative strength of the desire to commit the evil deed compared to the desire to do the morally right thing. For instance, whether Smith will resist the temptation to have sex with a friend's (willing) wife or not depends on the strength of his desire to do so compared to his desire to be loyal to his friend or to avoid what he believes to be wrong. We can no more freely choose the strengths of our desires than we can freely choose the desires themselves.

But how much effort we can exert depends on the strength of our desire to exert it, and we can't choose that.

Think for a moment what it would be like to choose the strengths of our desires. Suppose Smith's desire for sex is twice the strength of his desire to be loyal to his friend, and that he chooses to double the strength of his desire to be loyal. If asked *why* he chose to increase the strength of his desire to be loyal, what could he say? Only that he has no idea why he chose this. In particular, he couldn't appeal to any motive or desire to do so, because we're assuming he *freely* chose to increase his desire, which means that he chose to do so without a motive or desire causing him to do so.

Example of what it would be like if we could choose our own desires.

Or suppose he chose to double his willpower, that is, chose to resist twice as hard the temptation to sin. Again, if asked why he chose to do so, what could he reply? He couldn't appeal to any motive or desire to try harder, because we're assuming he freely chose to try harder.

We're stuck with the conclusion that our choices and actions must stem from our desire and motives, or, more accurately, from our character. We can, of course, choose to get rid of, or strengthen, a particular desire, but only on the basis of our other desires and motives. Otherwise, our doing so would have no connection with who we are— it would come as a bolt from the blue—and we certainly would not bear any responsibility for having done so.

Conclusion: Our choices and actions result from our character. We can change part of it, but only on basis of the other part.

It seems, then, that libertarianism is not satisfactory.

5. Soft Determinism

It looks as though we've backed ourselves into a corner. We have to reject hard determinism because it denies the validity of moral responsibility. But we also have to reject libertarianism, because if it were true we would never be justified in holding people morally accountable for their actions.

This excerpt is from Existentialism *by French philosopher Jean Paul Sartre (1905–1979). He argues in a somewhat novel way that determinism is false and that human beings are free in what they do and therefore are responsible for their actions.*

Jean Paul Sartre: ON FREE WILL*

Existentialists believe human existence precedes human essence.

There are two kinds of existentialists; first, those who are Christian, . . . and on the other hand the atheistic existentialists, among whom I class . . . myself. What they have in common is that they think that existence precedes essence, or, if you prefer, that subjectivity must be the starting point.

But for other things, essence precedes existence. E.g., a paper-cutter's essence exists in worker's mind before he makes it.

Just what does that mean? Let us consider some object that is manufactured, for example, a book or a paper-cutter: here is an object which has been made by an artisan whose inspiration came from a concept. He referred to the concept of what a paper-cutter is and likewise to a known method of production, which is part of the concept, something which is, by and large, a routine. Thus, the paper-cutter is at once an object produced in a certain way and, on the other hand, one having a specific use; and one can not postulate a man who produces a paper-cutter but does not know what it is used for. Therefore, let us say that, for the paper-cutter, essence—that is, the ensemble of both the production routines and the properties which enable it to be both produced and defined—precedes existence. Thus, the presence of the paper-cutter or book in front of me is determined. Therefore, we have here a technical view of the world whereby it can be said that production precedes existence.

A religious person can believe human essence exists in God's mind before human existence.

When we conceive God as the Creator, He is generally thought of as a superior sort of artisan. . . . He knows exactly what He is creating. Thus, the concept of man in the mind of God is comparable to the concept of paper-cutter in the mind of the manufacturer, and, following certain techniques and a conception, God produces man, just as the artisan, following a definition and a technique, makes a paper-cutter. Thus, the individual man is the realisation of a certain concept in the divine intelligence. . . .

But if there is no God, then human essence can't precede

Atheistic existentialism, which I represent, is more coherent. It states that if God does not exist, there is at least one being in whom existence precedes essence, a being who exists before he can be defined by any concept,

---

and that this being is man, or, as Heidegger says, human reality. What is meant here by saying that existence precedes essence? It means that, first of all, man exists, turns up, appears on the scene, and only afterwards defines himself. If man, as the existentialist conceives him, is indefinable, it is because at first he is nothing. Only afterward will he be something, and he himself will have made what he will be. Thus, there is no human nature, since there is no God to conceive it. Not only is man what he conceives himself to be, but he is also only what he wills himself to be after this thrust toward existence.

existence. Man therefore exists first and then defines himself; there is no human nature because there is no God to define it.

Man is nothing else but what he makes of himself. Such is the first principle of existentialism. It is also what is called subjectivity, the name we are labeled with when charges are brought against us. But what do we mean by this, if not that man has a greater dignity than a stone or table? For we mean that man first exists, that is, that man first of all is the being who hurls himself toward a future and who is conscious of imagining himself as being in the future. Man is at the start a plan which is aware of itself, rather than a patch of moss, a piece of garbage, or a cauliflower. . . .

People are what they make themselves. This is subjectivity. "Man is at the start a plan which is aware of itself."

But if existence really does precede essence, man is responsible for what he is. Thus, existentialism's first move is to make every man aware of what he is and to make the full responsibility of his existence rest on him. . . .

Man is responsible for what he is.

The existentialist . . . thinks it very distressing that God does not exist, because all possibility of finding values in a heaven of ideas disappears along with Him; there can no longer be an *a priori* good, since there is no infinite and perfect consciousness to think it. Nowhere is it written that the good exists, that we must be honest, that we must not lie; because the fact is we are on a plane where there are only men. Dostoievsky said, "If God didn't exist, every thing would be possible." That is the very starting point of existentialism. Indeed, everything is permissible if God does not exist, and as a result man is forlorn, because neither within him nor without does he find anything to cling to. He can't start making excuses for himself.

No God implies no a priori good. "If God does not exist, everything is possible." And permissible.

If existence really does precede essence, there is no explaining things away by reference to a fixed and given human nature. In other words, there is no determinism, man is free, man is freedom. On the other hand, if God does not exist, we find no values or commands to turn to which legitimize our conduct. So, in the bright realm of values, we have no excuse behind us, no justification before us. We are alone, with no excuses.

There is no fixed human nature, so no determinism. Man is free. We're also alone, with no excuses. We're condemned to be free, because we are responsible for our actions.

That is the idea I shall try to convey when I say that man is condemned to be free. Condemned, because he did not create himself, yet, in other respects is free; because, once thrown into the world, he is responsible for everything he does. . . .

Mistake to call choices free if uncaused.

The trouble is in our definition of freedom. We said before that we would call choices *free* if they are uncaused. But there is another, more useful, conception of free choice. To illustrate it, imagine Privates Smith and Jones on sentry duty during wartime, Smith after 72 hours awake in battle, Jones after a nice rest. Suppose Smith tries his best to stay awake, while Jones deliberately goes to sleep, say, as a lark.

Free acts are uncompelled acts, not uncaused acts.

It seems in this case that we should blame Jones for falling asleep, but not Smith, because Jones could have stayed awake if he had wanted to, while Smith could not have although he in fact did want to. Jones should be judged guilty because he wanted to do the nasty deed, while Smith should be judged innocent, or at least excused, because he

We act freely when we do what we want to, when not compelled.

wanted to do his duty and stay awake, and he tried his best to do so. We can say that Jones's falling asleep was a **free** act, because it wasn't *compelled*—he wasn't forced to go to sleep "against his will." But Smith's falling asleep was not free, because he was compelled by bodily fatigue to do what he desperately did not want to do, namely, to fall asleep.

Soft determinism: A free will is an uncompelled will.

Soft determinists take lack of *compulsion* to be the criterion of freedom of choice, not lack of a cause. Roughly speaking, they hold that people act freely when they do what they want and choose to do, and do not act freely when what they do is forced or compelled. In other words, according to soft determinists, a **free will** is just an uncompelled will.

Internal and External Compulsion

Two kinds of compulsion: internal and external.

Compulsive actions divide into two types, *internal* and *external*, depending on where the compulsive force originates. The sentry who tries his best to stay awake but falls asleep anyway is a victim of **internal compulsion,** because physiological forces within his body cause him to sleep. Children locked in their rooms by parents are victims of **external compulsion,** because the forces constraining their behavior are external to their bodies. Soft determinists argue that lack of compulsion, and not lack of cause, is the mark of a free act. All acts are caused, but only some are compelled.

Determined Actions Can Be Free

Soft determinists deny that actions

Recall now the three principles that lead to *hard* determinism, namely, that (1) determinism is true, so that all our choices and actions are

56

determined by past circumstances; (2) actions determined by past circumstances can't be free; and (3) we're morally accountable only for free actions. It should be clear now that soft determinists accept principles (1) and (3) but reject principle (2). They point out that in daily life the criterion of free choice is not that the choice be uncaused but rather that the choice be uncompelled, unforced, so that the person does what he or she wants and chooses to do. Soft determinists thus "save" the idea of moral responsibility and solve the problem of free will versus determinism by arguing that the freedom needed to justify the practice of holding people morally responsible for their actions is not freedom from determinism, which we never have, but freedom from compulsion, freedom to do what we want to do, which we have quite often.

caused by the past can't be free.

The relevant freedom for moral responsibility is thus freedom from compulsion, not from cause.

Reasons for Accepting Soft Determinism

The basic reason for accepting soft determinism is that it seems to solve the problem without violating any strongly held intuitions. Unlike libertarianism, soft determinism is consistent with the well-supported determinist thesis that everything has a cause. Unlike hard determinism, it's consistent with the idea that we're justified in holding people morally accountable for most of their actions. Furthermore, it tells us roughly which actions we're responsible for (the uncompelled ones) and which we aren't (the compelled ones), and gives us a criterion for deciding in particular cases (actions we want to do are uncompelled, or free, actions we don't want to do but do anyway are compelled, or unfree). And it does so in a way that roughly conforms to our everyday practice. For on the whole, compelled actions are excused in everyday life, and we're held responsible only for uncompelled ones.

Soft determinism seems to solve the problem: It's consistent with determinism, with the idea of holding people accountable for most actions, and with most everyday practice.

Difficulties with Soft Determinism

There are two basic problems with soft determinism. First, as soft determinists themselves would insist, the criterion for determining whether choices are free or compelled needs to be refined. We said that, roughly speaking, actions are free when the actors do what they want to do, and are compelled otherwise, and that a person is responsible only for free actions. Consider then the following kinds of cases:

Soft determinist criterion needs refining.

57

Can it handle klepto case? 1. An immensely wealthy Park Avenue matron steals a diamond stickpin from Cartier Jewelers, on Fifth Avenue. She has no use for the pin and later will regret having taken it. But at the time, for whatever reason, she can't resist the temptation to steal it—her desire to steal it is stronger than her desire not to—so she chooses to do so. Still, it is often said that such a person is mentally ill, a kleptomaniac acting compulsively, and thus not responsible for her action. Yet on the criterion of compulsion presented here, her action has to be classified as free.

Or torture victim example? 2. A prisoner of war gives secrets to the enemy after being severely tortured. He wants to reveal the secrets and chooses to do so (to avoid further torture). It is generally supposed that he shouldn't be blamed for doing so, because almost everybody gives in to torture sooner or later. Yet he does freely choose to reveal the secrets according to the criterion of freedom we've provided here.

Or insanity case? 3. An insane asylum inmate kills another inmate in a fight over a sex partner. The inmate wants to kill and chooses to kill, yet most of us would say that he isn't responsible, because insane.

Or fit of passion example? 4. A husband who has sacrificed a great deal for his wife and marriage catches her in bed with another man and murders her in a fit of passion. At the time, he wants to kill her and chooses to do so—no one forces him to. Yet some would argue that he should not be blamed for his act, because he was not free to control his rage under such circumstances.

Or posthypnotic suggestion case? 5. Under posthypnotic suggestion, Smith murders his grandmother. He loves his grandmother and ordinarily would not dream of harming her. Still, he does want to kill her at the moment of decision. Thus, the act seems to be free according to the soft determinist's criterion of freedom, although most of us would say that Smith was not a true free agent.

Or compulsive drug-taking case? 6. Jones innocently acquired the morphine habit when he was given repeated large doses to help him endure the pain from battle injuries. Now he is ruining his life trying to feed that habit. Although it's true that he wants to break the habit, it also is true that when he gives in and takes the drug he wants to take it (his desire for the drug is stronger than his desire to break the habit) and chooses to take it. Most of us would say that his taking the drug is compelled, yet on the criterion presented here it seems to be free.

Compulsion Is Not the Only Defense

Obviously, we can't be sure that soft determinism solves the problem until we know how to deal with cases such as the ones just given. Different soft determinists deal with these cases in different ways. One way is to note that freedom from compulsion is not the only criterion for moral responsibility. Children, for instance, are often excused for freely choosing wrong actions adults are blamed for. So are insane people. The point is that such people somehow lack moral standing, perhaps because they can't be expected to know the moral nature of their acts (like the three-year-old who pushes her baby sister out of the crib) or to know the consequences of their actions (the insane person who accidentally sets a house on fire) or to have the will to act on that knowledge (the schizophrenic patient who won't get out of bed). *

Some of the preceding problems solved by appeal to other principles; for example, being a child or insane.

We Need a Better Criterion of True Desire

Another way to deal with the problem is to argue that sometimes what we want and choose at a given moment—say, in the heat of passion, as in Case 4, above—is not what we really wanted to do; witness the regret later on at having done it. In this view, the relative strengths of our various desires over some longer period of time determine our true desires at a given time. Thus, compelled actions sometimes result when our strongest desires at a given moment conflict with our strongest desires over the long run. An example is a drug addict's desire at a given moment to take the drug even though on the whole his strongest desire is to kick the habit.

Soft determinists need a better criterion of true desire.

Many Still Find Determinism and Moral Responsibility Incompatible

The point of philosophical inquiry is to see how things seem to us *after* we've heard the arguments, especially those on the other side.

---

*Those who accept the idea that moral obligations are contractual (see Chapter 4 for more on this) might want to say that the insane and children are not capable of entering in to fair contractual arrangements and thus are not capable of having moral obligations.

The English philosopher Thomas Hobbes (1588–1679) was perhaps the first modern writer to put the soft determinist position into reasonably clear form.

Thomas Hobbes: **LIBERTY AND NECESSITY**

Quick actions follow thoughts of the good or evil expected to result.

First I conceive, that when it cometh into a man's mind to do or not to do some certain action, if he have no time to *deliberate*, the doing it or abstaining *necessarily* follow the present thought he hath of the *good* or *evil* consequence thereof to himself. As for example, in sudden *anger*, the *action* shall follow the thought of *revenge*; in sudden *fear*, the thought of *escape*. Also when a man hath time to *deliberate*, but deliberates not, because never anything appeared that could make him doubt of the consequence, the *action* follows his opinion of the *goodness* or *harm* of it. These actions I call *voluntary*,

These quick actions are voluntary, because they follow the "last appetite."

my Lord, if I understand him aright that calls them *spontaneous*. I call them *voluntary*, because those *actions* that follow immediately the *last* appetite, are *voluntary*, and here where is one only appetite, that one is the last. Besides, I see it is reasonable to punish a *rash* action, which could not be justly done by man to man, unless the same were *voluntary*. For no *action* of a man can be said to be without *deliberation*, though never so sudden, because it is supposed he had time to *deliberate* all the precedent time of his life, whether he should do that kind of action or not. . . .

Deliberate actions follow thoughts about the consequences, good or evil.

Secondly, I conceive when a man *deliberates* whether he shall do a thing or not do it, that he does nothing else but consider whether it be better for himself to do it or not to do it. And to *consider* an action, is to imagine the *consequences* of it both *good* and *evil*. From whence is to be inferred, that *deliberation* is nothing else but *alternate* imagination of the *good* and *evil* sequels of an *action*, or, which is the same thing, alternate *hope* and *fear*, or alternate *appetite* to do or quit the action of which he *deliberateth*.

In deliberation, the last of the succession of desires is called the will.

Thirdly, I conceive that in all *deliberations*, that is to say, in all alternate *succession* of contrary *appetites*, the last is that which we call the *will*, and is immediately before the doing of the action, or next before the doing of it become impossible. All other *appetites* to do, and to quit, that come upon a man during his deliberations, are called *intentions* and *inclinations*, but not *wills*, there being but one *will*. . . .

Actions done after deliberation are voluntary, and the doer is free.

Fourthly, I conceive that those *actions*, which a man is said to do upon *deliberation*, are said to be *voluntary*, and done upon *choice* and *election*, so that *voluntary* action, and action proceeding from *election* is the same thing; and that of a *voluntary agent*, it is all one to say, he is *free*, and to say, he hath not made an end of *deliberating*.

Fifthly, I conceive *liberty* to be rightly defined in this manner: *Liberty is the absence of all the impediments to action that are not contained in the nature and intrinsical quality of the agent.* As for example, the water is said to descend *freely,* or to have *liberty* to descend by the channel of the river, because there is no impediment that way, but not across, because the banks are impediments. And though the water cannot ascend, yet men never say it wants the *liberty* to ascend, but the *faculty* or *power,* because the impediment is in the nature of the water, and intrinsical. So also we say, he that is tied, wants the *liberty* to go, because the impediment is not in him, but in his bonds. . . .

Liberty (freedom) is the absence of impediments aside from the doer's nature.

Sixthly, I conceive that nothing taketh beginning from *itself,* but from the *action* of some other immediate *agent* without itself. And that therefore, when first a man hath an *appetite* or *will* to do something, to which immediately before he had no appetite nor will, the *cause* of his *will,* is not the *will* itself, but *something* else not in his own disposing. So that whereas it is out of controversy, that of *voluntary* actions the *will* is the *necessary cause,* and by this which is said, the *will* is also *caused* by other things whereof it disposeth not, if followeth, that *voluntary* actions have all of them *necessary* causes, and therefore are *necessitated.*

When we desire to do something, the cause of our desire is not the desire or will itself, but something else. So free acts have necessary causes.

Seventhly, I hold that to be a *sufficient cause,* to which nothing is wanting that is needful to the producing of the *effect.* The same also is a *necessary* cause. For if it be possible that a *sufficient* cause shall not bring forth the *effect,* then there wanteth somewhat which was needful to the producing of it, and so the *cause* was not *sufficient;* but if it be impossible that a *sufficient* cause should not produce the *effect,* then is a *sufficient* cause a *necessary* cause, for that is said to produce an effect *necessarily* that cannot but produce it. Hence it is manifest, that whatever is produced, is produced *necessarily;* for whatsoever is produced hath had a *sufficient* cause to produce it, or else it had not been; and therefore also *voluntary* actions are *necessitated.*

Whatever exists has a sufficient cause to produce it, and so is necessary. Thus, all voluntary acts are necessitated.

Lastly, that ordinary *definition* of a *free agent,* namely, *that a* free agent *is that, which, when all things are present which are needful to produce the* effect, *can nevertheless not produce it,* implies a contradiction, and is nonsense; being as much as to say, the cause may be *sufficient,* that is to say, *necessary,* and yet the *effect* shall not follow. . . .

The last thing, in which also consisteth the whole controversy, namely that there is no such thing as an agent, *which when all things requisite to action are present, can nevertheless forbear to produce it;* or, which is all one, that there is no such thing as *freedom from necessity,* it is easily inferred from that which hath been before alleged.

That there is no freedom from necessity has thus been proved.

Some still feel if determinism is true, then holding people morally responsible is like holding robots morally responsible.

After hearing the arguments for soft determinism, libertarians in particular still find it wrong to hold people responsible for their actions if those actions are caused by natural laws over which human beings have no control. Nor is it any comfort to them to hear that people *choose* to do most of what they do, or that their choices stem from their desires or motives, if these desires, motives, and thus choices all are determined by natural laws. Holding people accountable in such circumstances seems to them like holding robots responsible for their actions.

Are human beings like robots? Soft determinists say we feel differently about people, and that's the only justification for treating them differently.

And perhaps that's the heart of the matter. Is there any reason to deal differently with human beings than with tables, chairs, television sets, or IBM computers? Is there something about human relationships or our social nature that is reason for regarding human beings as responsible for what they do, but not television sets or IBM machines? It seems appropriate to blame friends when they let you down, but not an IBM machine (you just get it fixed). The way we feel about people is essentially different from the way we feel about inanimate machines, and that different feeling is the justification—if there is any—for holding people but not machines responsible for their (uncompelled) actions.

Disagreements continue in part because of a lack of attention to the other side, but also because of other philosophic commitments.

Why, then, do disagreements on this topic continue? Partly, perhaps, from a lack of attention to the arguments on the other sides of the issue. But partly, they must be due to differences concerning other, related, philosophical questions, perhaps even to differences over the nature of the philosophical enterprise itself. For instance, someone whose religious convictions require that people be held responsible for certain of their actions cannot consistently hold the hard determinist position on the free will question. Although it isn't practical to deal with every related issue all at once, what we eventually say about them helps determine what answers we can accept to the question of free will versus determinism.

Summary of Chapter 2

1. The problem discussed in this chapter arises from an apparent contradiction between the almost universal idea that human beings have *free wills* and several other plausible-sounding ideas; namely, that (a) everything that happens, including every human action and choice, is determined or caused

by prior events or circumstances; (b) that if our actions and choices are determined, they aren't free; and (c) that we aren't morally responsible for actions or choices that are not free.

2. *Hard determinists* solve the problem by denying that we have free wills, concluding that in fact we aren't morally responsible for our actions or choices. They argue this way because they're convinced that determinism is true and free will, therefore, is an illusion. They tend to defend their view primarily by defending the determinist theory that everything is caused. Thus, they point to everyday experiences and beliefs that seem to imply things behave in a regular way (sugar doesn't make things taste sweet one day and sour the next), to everyday human behavior (even race car drivers can't choose to drive well while drunk), and also to the tremendous success of modern science in discovering causal connections (we can't choose to just flap our arms and fly to the moon).

Although many argue against hard determinism by arguing that determinism in general is wrong, the evidence favoring determinism is very strong, so that if we are to reject hard determinism it must be on the grounds that freedom of action and choice do not contradict determinism, so that we are indeed justified in holding people morally responsible even though their actions and choices are caused or determined.

3. *Libertarians* argue that free will is possible only if determinism is false, and that in fact at least in typical moral situations we do have free will. So we are justified in holding people morally responsible for what they choose and do.

Libertarians argue for their view on the grounds that, first, only their view makes it sensible to hold people morally responsible for their actions (they're completely unwilling to believe it doesn't make sense to do so), and second, we *feel* free when we make moral choices.

Opponents tend to object to libertarianism for three reasons. First, they believe determinism is true and we don't have uncaused or self-caused wills. Second, they argue that we don't feel free from *causal forces* (because causes aren't the sort of thing that can be felt), but rather from compulsion or coercion. And third, they argue that if we really did have uncaused will, then it would make no sense to hold us responsible for our actions, because they wouldn't stem from our characters, and thus would not be an indication of who we really are.

4. *Soft determinists* argue that hard determinists and libertarians go wrong in part because they use the wrong conception of freedom of the will. The relevant conception is that we are free when we choose and do what we want to do and aren't forced or compelled against our wills. They often distinguish

between two types of compulsion—*internal* and *external*—depending on whether the compelling force is inside or outside of our bodies.

Soft determinists defend their position by appealing to all the evidence favoring determinism in general, and also by pointing out that their view conforms to everyday practice. In everyday life when deciding whether people are to be held accountable for what they do, we don't ask whether actions are caused but rather whether or not they were compelled or forced. When people do what they want to do, we feel (with a few exceptions for definite reasons) that they are morally responsible for what they do.

Some people reject soft determinism because they reject determinism in general. Others reject it because they believe that so far soft determinists have not been able to handle certain kinds of cases and because they haven't adequately spelled out their criterion of compulsion. Furthermore, after having heard the soft determinist theory, libertarians in particular still find it totally implausible to hold people responsible for their actions if those actions are determined by past events or circumstances. If determinism is true, they argue, then human beings are just like robots, or complicated computers, and no one feels justified in blaming or punishing a computer when it malfunctions.

Finally, it was suggested that perhaps this is where the heart of the matter rests. We treat human beings, whether they are machines or not, differently from robots or computers because we somehow *feel* differently about them.

Questions for Further Thought

1. Would it make a difference to you in your daily life if you changed your mind on the free will question, for example, if you accepted hard determinism instead of soft, or vice versa?

2. What do you think of the argument in the last paragraph of the Spinoza reading in this chapter?

3. In everyday life, we often speak of this person as being strong willed and that one as weak willed. Does this have anything to do with the free will problem? More precisely, do strong-willed people have more freedom than weak-willed ones?

4. The judge in the famous 1920s Loeb-Leopold murder case was persuaded by Clarence Darrow's hard determinist arguments to spare Loeb and Leopold the death penalty. Suppose instead he'd argued that just as Loeb and Leopold were caused by their heredity and upbringing to murder in cold blood, so he (the judge) is caused by his heredity and upbringing to sentence Loeb and

Leopold to death, and he then did so? Would that make better sense than what he in fact did (take Darrow's advice and sentence the two to life imprisonment)?

5. What do you think of the following statement by the physicist Arthur H. Compton?

> One's ability to move his hand at will is more directly and certainly known than are Newton's laws. If these laws deny one's ability to move his hand at will, the preferable conclusion is that Newton's laws require modification.

6. How about this argument by sociologist Peter Berger?

> We see the puppets dancing on their miniature stage, moving up and down as the strings pull them around, following the prescribed course of their various little parts. We learn to understand the logic of this theater and we find ourselves in its motions. We locate ourselves in society and thus recognize our own position as we hang from its subtle strings. For a moment we see ourselves as puppets indeed. But then we grasp a decisive difference between the puppet theater and our own drama. Unlike the puppets, we have the possibility of stopping in our movements, looking up and perceiving the machinery by which we have been moved. In this act lies the first step towards freedom.

7. And how about this one by contemporary philosopher John Hospers?

> We talk about free will, and we say, for example, the person is free to do so-and-so . . . *if* he wants to—and we forget that his wanting to is itself caught up in the stream of determinism, that unconscious forces drive him into the wanting or not wanting to do the thing in question. The analogy of the puppet whose motions are manipulated . . . by springs inside is a telling one at almost every point. . . . It is no wonder that the protestations of philosophers that "the act which is the result of a volition, a deliberation, a conscious decision, is free" leaves . . . [psychiatrists] somewhat cold.

8. Theologians have argued for centuries over whether our having free will is compatible or not with God's knowing ahead of time exactly what we're going to choose to do. What do you think of the following argument by St. Augustine that the two are compatible?

> If you knew in advance that such and such a man would sin, there would be no necessity for him to sin. . . . You would not directly compel the man to sin, though you knew beforehand that he was going to sin. Nor does your prescience in itself compel him to sin even though he was certainly going to sin, as we must assume if you have real prescience. So there is no contradiction here. Simply you know beforehand what another is going to do with his own will. Similarly God compels no man to sin, though he sees beforehand those who are going to sin by their own will.

9. What is your opinion of the following attempt by St. Thomas to reconcile belief in free will with the belief that God determines our fates ahead of time?

> The predestined must necessarily be saved, yet by a conditioned necessity, which does not do away with the liberty of choice. . . . Man's turning to God is by free choice; and thus man is bidden to turn himself to God. But free choice can be turned to God only when God turns to it. . . . It is the part of man to prepare his soul, since he does this by his free choice. And yet he does not do this without the help of God moving him. . . . And thus even the good movement of free choice, whereby anyone is prepared for receiving the gift of grace, is an act of free choice moved by God. . . . Man's preparation for grace is from God, as mover, and from free choice, as moved.

10. Now what about Thomas Hobbes on the same subject (taken from the paragraph following the Hobbes excerpt in this chapter)?

> . . . I could add, if I thought it good logic, the *inconvenience* of denying *necessity*, as that it destroyeth both the *decrees* and the *prescience* of God Almighty; for whatever God hath purposed to bring to pass by *man*, as an instrument, or forseeth shall come to pass; a man, if he have liberty . . . from *necessitation*, might frustrate, and make not to come to pass, and God should either not *foreknow* it, and not *decree* it, or he should *foreknow* such things shall be, as shall never be, and *decree* that which shall never *come to pass*.

11. According to the Heisenberg uncertainty principle, a cornerstone of quantum physics, it's impossible to precisely determine the position and velocity of any single one of the basic particles (electrons, protons, and so on) that make up the physical universe, so that according to some physicists the laws governing these basic particles are *statistical*, not what is called *categorical* (or 100 percent). Some philosophers have taken this as evidence of "loose play" in the determinism that rules the world, and argued that perhaps we have free will after all, because exactly what happens to the electrons in our brain (on which what we choose depends) is not strictly determined—the will therefore might influence electrons to flow this way rather than that, resulting in our making this decision rather than that. Does this strike you as a good libertarian-type solution to the free will problem?

12. It has been argued that we can't divide actions into those that are externally compelled and those that are not, because all actions are externally compelled. After all, every action has *consequences*, which we either desire or not. Thus, choosing to hand over the money rather than be shot is just an extreme case of what we always do—choose the least evil or greatest good—only in this case one of the evils is so bad that our choice is more obvious. But there is just as much external compulsion in our choice, say, not to commit adultery (the evil perhaps being the loss of one's spouse, or guilt), just as much as a weighing of the consequences. The difference is just that the desires on each side are more balanced in the adultery example, so our choice is harder. Can the soft determinist's idea of external compulsion as a criterion of lack of freedom be saved from this argument?

The fact of having been born is a bad augury for immortality.—GEORGE SANTAYANA

Never take anything for granted.—OLD SAYING

Those who have compared our life to a dream were right. . . . We sleeping wake, and waking sleep.—MONTAIGNE

I cannot . . . believe that the individual survives the death of his body, although feeble souls harbor such thoughts through fear or ridiculous egotisms.—ALBERT EINSTEIN

Most of the greatest evils that man has inflicted on man have come through people feeling quite certain about something which, in fact, was false.—BERTRAND RUSSELL

For God created man to be immortal, and made him to be an image of his own eternity. Nevertheless, through envy of the devil came death into the world.
—THE WISDOM OF SOLOMON
(FROM THE APOCRYPHA)

The origin of the idea of immortal life is easy to discover; it is kept alive by hope and fear, by childish faith, and by cowardice.
—CLARENCE DARROW

Ultimate Skepticism—But what after all are man's truths?—They are his irrefutable errors.—NIETZSCHE

That life is worth living is the most necessary of assumptions, and were it not assumed, the most impossible of conclusions.
—GEORGE SANTAYANA

The blazing evidence of immortality is our dissatisfaction with any other solution.
—RALPH WALDO EMERSON

Death, the only immortal, who treats us all alike . . .—SAMUEL CLEMENS

What is past I know, but what is for to come I know not.
—2 ESDRAS 4:46 (FROM THE APOCRYPHA)

Skepticism is the chastity of the intellect.
—GEORGE SANTAYANA

3

Skepticism and Knowledge

A SKEPTIC IS A DOUBTER. **Skepticism,** as a philosophical attitude, systematically questions or doubts all claims to knowledge about the nature of the universe or humanity's place in it. The point of this wholesale doubting is to find out whether there are some things that cannot be doubted, and, if so, what they are and how they can be known, or whether nothing can be known for certain. But the main virtue for most of us in adopting this philosophical program of systematic doubt is that questioning our beliefs forces us to examine the workings of our own minds, to separate our beliefs into the founded and unfounded, certain and probable, profound and foolish, questioned and shielded from question, and to notice where beliefs conflict with each other, where (if anywhere) they seem acceptable without justification or reason and where not, which forms of reasoning seem good to us and which not so good, and so on. It thus gives us some of the tools needed to do a good job of evaluating the mind's vast stock of beliefs—the job that constitutes the philosophical enterprise.

Skeptics question all claims to knowledge and accept only what can be known for sure. But for us skepticism is a program for examining our beliefs more carefully, to see which can be justified.

1. Do We Have Knowledge of the Future?

Although a great deal of uncertainty attaches to the future, we still seem to know a lot about it. We know, for instance, that bread will nourish, the sun will rise every morning, sugar will sweeten coffee, and (if we know a bit of science) that every object in the universe will attract every other with a force depending on the masses of the objects and the distance between them (Newton's law of gravitation).

We seem to know a lot about the future.

The ordinary person knows thousands of such facts about the future, and the scientist thousands more.

But skeptics challenge this "knowledge."

They do, that is, unless dyed-in-the-wool skeptics are right. For the "compleat skeptic's" wholesale doubting of all knowledge includes, of course, doubt about whether the sun will rise tomorrow, sugar will sweeten coffee, and the gravitation law will still hold.

The Principle of Induction

Philosophers have held that knowledge of the future is based on induction.

Before examining the skeptic's argument for such an apparently outrageous position, let's briefly look at the way in which we acquire the knowledge we usually feel quite certain we have about the future. In particular, let's look at what many philosophers have held is the basic principle used in discovering knowledge about the future, the **principle of induction.**

The key to induction is finding patterns or resemblances in experience and inferring they'll continue.

The basic idea behind valid induction is that of *pattern*, or *resemblance.* We want our conceptions of the future, our ideas about what this or that will be like, to fit a pattern we glean from what this or that was like in the past. (The problem, of course, is to find patterns that fit *all* of what we've experienced in the past.) In its simplest form, the principle of induction tells us to expect that kinds of things linked in the past will be similarly linked in the future.

Examples of everyday uses of induction.

Take our knowledge that sugar sweetens coffee. Putting sugar into coffee is linked in our experience with its tasting sweet. No one has ever put sugar into coffee, or any other food for that matter, and found that it tasted sour, bitter, or salty, or anything except sweet. The principle of induction simply says that we should expect this observed constant conjunction between placing sugar in food and its tasting sweet to continue in the future. It tells us (using the vocabulary of statistics) to extrapolate from the "sample" (observed cases in which sugar was placed in food) to the "population" (all cases in which sugar is placed in food).

The Skeptic Challenges Induction

Skeptics demand a justification for the use of induction.

Suppose a skeptic challenges our belief, say, that bread eaten tomorrow will nourish us as it has in the past. The normal way to defend this belief would be to appeal to observed facts about the past (that bread has so far always nourished) and to the principle of induction (that past connections of this kind will hold in the future). But complete skeptics accept nothing without justification. They thus demand a justification for our appeal to the principle of induction.

Induction Works

An obvious thought is that we're justified in using induction because it "works." All science is based on inductive inferences of some sort or other, and everyone knows how successful science is. Everyone knows that scientific method, using induction, *works.*

Using induction is justified because it works.

However, it simply isn't true that we know induction works. At best we know just that up to now it *has worked.* Will it work in the future? It sometimes is claimed that in fact we have a very good reason for thinking that induction will work in the future; namely, that it has worked in the past. But this defense of induction is clearly not adequate. To argue that induction *will* work because it *has* worked is to argue inductively—it's to use induction to justify the use of induction. (The premise of such an argument is "Induction has been relatively successful up to now," and its conclusion is "Induction always will be relatively successful.") So when we argue this way, we use induction to justify itself, which means we argue circularly, and hence fallaciously.

Reply: All we know is that induction has worked. To infer it will work in the future because it did in the past is to use induction to justify induction and is circular reasoning.

Nature Is Uniform

Another popular solution to the problem of induction appeals to some sort of principle of the **uniformity of nature,** such as the principle that every event has a cause. For instance, if we assume that nature is uniform, we can reason from (1) the fact that, say, all examined pieces of copper are uniform with respect to electrical conductivity to (2) the conclusion that all pieces of copper whatsoever (examined or not) are uniform in conductivity.

If nature is uniform, we're justified in using induction.

But solutions of this kind don't work. First, even if nature is uniform, there is no guarantee that any uniformity observed up to now will turn out to be a true uniformity of nature holding in the future. The true ones may have escaped our notice, perhaps because they're extremely complicated or subtle. Second, the assumption that nature is uniform may itself be challenged. *Why* assume that nature is uniform? It's very hard to find an even plausible answer. (Remember, we can't argue that the principle of uniformity has been fruitful in the past and so will continue to be in the future. That argument would

*Reply:
(1) Nature may be uniform and any given induction still may fail.
(2) There is no reason, other than induction, to assume nature is uniform.*

71

be an inductive argument and, therefore, would use the very principle of reasoning we're trying to justify.)

Justifying Induction Is a Pseudoproblem

Using induction is justified because induction is one of the principles of good reasoning.

There are also the so-called *dissolutions* of the problem of induction, according to which the very problem is itself a pseudoproblem—something that looks like a problem but isn't. Several different "dissolutions" have been proposed. According to one, it isn't rational to doubt the principles of inductive reasoning because these principles themselves *determine** what it means to be rational. So if we doubt the rationality of using induction, we simply don't know what it means to be rational.

Reply: If using induction is part of being rational, skeptics ask why should we be rational?

Unfortunately, the problem won't dissolve that easily. Imagine visiting a culture where it's considered rational to believe everything said by the village idiot, because in the language of that society being rational *means* believing everything said by that idiot. In such a situation, it would make perfectly good sense to ask *why* we should be rational, if being rational means believing the village idiot. Similarly, says the skeptic, it makes perfectly good sense to ask why we should be rational, if being rational means accepting conclusions obtained by induction. So we can't solve the problem merely by claiming that part of what is ordinarily meant by being rational is to accept the conclusions of valid inductive arguments.

We Can't Justify Everything

It's not so bad if we can't justify induction, because we can't justify everything.

Finally, some people attempt to solve the problem by removing its sting. They argue that some principles of reasoning must be accepted without justification, simply because it isn't possible to justify every such principle. So it isn't all that terrible if we can't justify induction.

It's very important to understand the claim that some principles of reasoning or other must forever remain unjustified. Take any principle—say, Principle A—for which a justification is demanded. Such

---

*Along with what are called "deductive" principles. See pp. 249–51 of the author's *Logic and Philosophy*, 4th ed. (Belmont, Calif.: Wadsworth, 1982), for more on the difference between the two. Roughly, reasoning is deductively valid when its premises, if true, guarantee the truth of its conclusion (unlike inductive reasoning). Why deduction provides this guarantee is in dispute. One answer is the "spelling out" theory of deduction, which says the guarantee results from the fact that in valid deductive reasoning the claim made by the conclusion is already made as part of what is asserted by the premises.

a justification can't contain a use of that very same principle (we can't use A to justify itself), because that would be circular. (A circular justification must be fallacious because it depends on something exactly as doubtful as what it is supposed to prove.)

So the justification of A must contain a use of at least one principle other than A. Call this other principle B. If B is to be used in justifying A, B also must be justified. But again, B can't be used to justify itself. And we can't use A to justify B, because we want to justify B in order to justify A (so such a justification would be circular). Thus, some other principle, C, must be appealed to. And so on, to infinity. Thus, to avoid a circular justification, we would have to provide an infinite series of justifications, and that is impossible. It follows that some principle of reasoning or other must remain unjustified.

We can't justify a principle by itself, and an infinite series of justifications is impossible, so some principle must remain unjustified.

The Moral

The result seems to be this: We have to either accept some principles without justification or else give in to the skeptic and agree that everything is doubtful. Because we're incapable of doubting everything, going through the skeptic's arguments can be thought of as an interesting way to come to see that some principles of reasoning must be accepted without justification—except, of course, for the "justification" that it just seems right to us. All or most of our beliefs about the future obtained by using induction may in fact turn out to be false. But it runs counter to one of our most fundamental intuitions to believe that will happen.

The moral is that some principle or other must be accepted without justification, because the alternative, skepticism, is not possible for us.

Belief in Induction Compared to Belief in God

In Chapter 1, we talked about those who accept God as a matter of faith, and in this chapter about those who accept induction on the basis of intuition. But aren't faith and intuition pretty much the same thing? They certainly are very much alike. In particular, religious faith and intuitive belief in induction both are beliefs for which we seem unable to provide convincing reasons or justifications—other than that we just believe.

Faith in God and intuition favoring induction are very much alike.

Still, there are differences between the typical belief in God based on faith (or intuition, if you will) and the typical belief in induction based on intuition (or faith, if you will). In the first place, induction plays a part in just about every rational decision we ever make in our

Differences: (1) Induction is used every minute.

73

daily lives (for one thing, because we have to know the likely consequences of our actions before rational decisions can be reached), while faith in God does not.

(2) Induction alone tells us nothing about the world. Faith is intuition to a supposed fact.

Second, induction is a *principle of reasoning*. By itself, it tells us nothing about life or the nature of the universe. We need to apply it to *experience* to reach conclusions about the nature of things.

By way of contrast, belief in God is belief in a particular feature of reality, not in a principle of reasoning for finding out such features of reality. It involves a direct intuiting of the truth of the matter.

(3) Faith in God is less constant.

Third, people commonly gain, or lose, their faith in God, or change from faith in one God to faith in another. Faith in induction is much more constant.

(4) Everyone has faith in induction, not everyone in God.

Fourth, otherwise perfectly intelligent human beings often have no faith whatever in God. But just about everyone has faith in induction. (Skeptics may pretend, but they *use* induction every minute of their waking lives.)

(5) Inductive beliefs are alike; in gods very different.

Fifth, people believe in all sorts of quite different gods. Beliefs about induction are much more alike.

(6) Faith in God leads to more faith.

Sixth, faith in God is almost always connected with additional "leaps of faith" that reveal the tenets of some particular religion. Belief in induction yields its benefits without additional leaps of faith.

(7) Faith in God but not induction is comforting.

Seventh, religious faith typically holds out to us at least a chance to satisfy some of our deepest desires; for example, to have life after death and to be forgiven for our sins on earth. So it seems to many nonbelievers that religious faith has a tinge of wishful thinking about it. On the other hand, faith in induction is not comforting in itself, because the use of induction often forces us to believe what we would much rather deny (for instance, that illness, suffering, aging, and death are inevitable).

For some, religious faith contradicts results of induction.

Finally, it should be noted that religious faith (although not faith in God alone!) sometimes leads to the rejection of what all of our other beliefs and experiences confirm, and to the acceptance of what the rest of experience tells us to reject. A serious example these days is the rejection on religious grounds of the scientific theory of evolution. Of course, religious belief, even Christian belief, does not require rejection of evolution, witness the many Christian biologists who accept it. But many who are religious do reject it on the grounds that it conflicts with their religious beliefs (for instance, their belief that the universe was created and stocked with the basic plants and animals all in one week).

In Section II of his Enquiry Concerning Human Understanding, *the Scottish philosopher David Hume (1711–1776) argued that all knowledge of matters of fact (beyond immediate sense experience) is founded on the relation of cause and effect, and can't be justified by appeal to any valid principle of reasoning.*

David Hume: SCEPTICAL DOUBTS CONCERNING THE OPERATIONS OF THE UNDERSTANDING

All the objects of human reason or enquiry may naturally be divided into two kinds, to wit, *Relations of Ideas,* and *Matters of Fact.* Of the first kind are the sciences of Geometry, Algebra, and Arithmetic; and in short, every affirmation which is either intuitively or demonstratively certain. *That the square of the hypothenuse is equal to the square of the two sides,* is a proposition which expresses a relation between these figures. *That three times five is equal to the half of thirty,* expresses a relation between these numbers. Propositions of this kind are discoverable by the mere operation of thought, without dependence on what is anywhere existent in the universe. Though there never were a circle or triangle in nature, the truths demonstrated by Euclid would for ever retain their certainty and evidence.

Knowledge divides into relations of ideas and matters of fact. Truths like $3 \times 5 = 15$, known just by thinking about them, are relations of ideas.

Matters of fact, which are the second objects of human reason, are not ascertained in the same manner; nor is our evidence of their truth, however great, of a like nature with the foregoing. The contrary of every matter of fact is still possible; because it can never imply a contradiction, and is conceived by the mind with the same facility and distinctness, as if ever so conformable to reality. *That the sun will not rise tomorrow* is no less intelligible a proposition, and implies no more contradiction than the affirmation, *that it will rise.* We should in vain, therefore, attempt to demonstrate its falsehood. Were it demonstratively false, it would imply a contradiction and could never be distinctly conceived by the mind.

The contrary of a matter of fact is possible (unlike the contrary of a relation of ideas), and can't be known just by thinking about it.

It may, therefore, be a subject worthy of curiosity, to enquire what is the nature of that evidence which assures us of any real existence and matter of fact, beyond the present testimony of our senses, or the records of our memory. . . .

Then how do we learn matters of fact?

All reasonings concerning matter of fact seem to be founded on the relation of *Cause and Effect.* By means of that relation alone we can go beyond the evidence of our memory and senses. If you were to ask a man, why he believes any matter of fact, which is absent; for instance, that his friend is in the country, or in France; he would give you a reason; and this reason would be some other fact; as a letter received from him, or the knowledge of his former resolutions and promises. A man finding a watch or any other machine in

Reasoning about matters of fact is based on the relation of cause and effect, which allows us to go beyond sensory evidence.

a desert island, would conclude that there had once been men on that island. All our reasonings concerning fact are of the same nature. And here it is constantly supposed that there is a connexion between the present fact and that which is inferred from it. Were there nothing to bind them together, the inference would be entirely precarious. The hearing of an articulate voice and rational discourse in the dark assures us of the presence of some person: Why? because these are the effects of the human make and fabric, and closely connected with it. If we anatomize all the other reasonings of this nature, we shall find that they are founded on the relation of cause and effect. . . .

Knowledge of the relation of cause and effect isn't obtained a priori—just by reasoning—but by experiencing two different sorts of things constantly conjoined, e.g., the constant conjunction between fire and being burned.

I shall venture to affirm, as a general proposition, which admits of no exception, that the knowledge of this relation is not, in any instance, attained by reasonings *a priori*; but arises entirely from experience, when we find that any particular objects are constantly conjoined with each other. Let an object be presented to a man of ever so strong natural reason and abilities; if that object be entirely new to him, he will not be able, by the most accurate examination of its sensible qualities, to discover any of its causes or effects. Adam, though his rational faculties be supposed, at the very first, entirely perfect, could not have inferred from the fluidity and transparency of water that it would suffocate him, or from the light and warmth of fire that it would consume him. . . . When it is asked, What is the nature of all our reasonings concerning matter of fact? the proper answer seems to be, that they are founded on the relation of cause and effect. When again it is asked, What is the foundation of all our reasonings and conclusions concerning that relation? it may be replied in one word, Experience. But if we still carry on our sifting humor, and ask, What is the foundation of all conclusions from experience? this implies a new question, which may be of more difficult solution and explication. . . . I say that, even after we have experience of the operations of cause and effect, our conclusions from that experience are not founded on reasoning or any process of the understanding. . . . The bread, which I formerly ate, nourished me; that is, a body of such sensible qualities was, at that time, endued with such secret powers; but does it follow, that other bread must also nourish me at another time, and that like sensible qualities must always be attended with like secret powers? The consequence seems nowise necessary. At least, it must be acknowledged that there is here a consequence drawn by the mind; that there is a certain step taken; a process of thought, and an inference, which wants to be explained. . . .

Trying to prove the future will resemble the past involves circular reasoning.

We have said that all arguments concerning existence are founded on the relation of cause and effect; that our knowledge of that relation is derived entirely from experience; and that all our experimental conclusions proceed upon the supposition that the future will be conformable to the past. To endeavour, therefore, the proof of this last supposition by probable arguments, or arguments regarding existence, must be evidently going in a circle, and taking that for granted, which is the very point in question.

In reality, all arguments from experience are founded on the similarity which we discover among natural objects, and by which we are induced to expect effects similar to those which we have found to follow from such objects. . . . From causes which appear similar we expect similar effects. This is the sum of all our experimental conclusions. Now it seems evident that, if this conclusion were formed by reason, it would be as perfect at first, and upon one instance, as after ever so long a course of experience. But the case is far otherwise. Nothing so like as eggs; yet no one, on account of this appearing similarity, expects the same taste and relish in all of them. It is only after a long course of uniform experiments in any kind, that we attain a firm reliance and security with regard to a particular event. Now where is that process of reasoning which, from one instance, draws a conclusion, so different from that which it infers from a hundred instances that are nowise different from that single one? . . .

From cases that appear similar, we expect similar effects. If we reasoned to this similarity, one case would be as good as many, but it isn't, so we can't reason to it.

Should it be said that, from a number of uniform experiments, we *infer* a connexion between the sensible qualities and the secret powers; this, I must confess, seems the same difficulty, couched in different terms. The question still recurs, on what process of argument this *inference* is founded? . . . When a man says, I have found, in all past instances, such sensible qualities conjoined with such secret powers: And when he says, Similar sensible qualities will always be conjoined with similar secret powers, he is not guilty of a tautology, nor are these propositions in any respect the same. You say that the one proposition is an inference from the other. But you must confess that the inference is not intuitive; neither is it demonstrative: Of what nature is it, then? To say it is experimental, is begging the question. For all inferences from experience suppose, as their foundation, that the future will resemble the past, and that similar powers will be conjoined with similar sensible qualities. If there be any suspicion that the course of nature may change, and that the past may be no rule for the future, all experience becomes useless, and can give rise to no inference or conclusion. It is impossible, therefore, that any arguments from experience can prove this resemblance of the past to the future; since all these arguments are founded on the supposition of that resemblance. Let the course of things be allowed hitherto ever so regular; that alone; without some new argument or inference, proves not that, for the future, it will continue so. . . .

We don't infer a connection between cause and effect, for on what rule of argument is this inference founded? That similar qualities will always be conjoined with similar effects is not a factually empty statement or an obvious or necessary truth. Past regularities prove nothing about the future without proof that regularities will hold in future.

2. Does a World Exist External to Our Senses?

The world seems to divide between waking experiences of real objects and dream experiences of imagined objects.

Common sense divides experiences into those of real objects that exist outside of our minds, such as tables and chairs, other people, buildings, the earth, our own bodies, and those of imagined objects experienced in dreams, hallucinations, and imaginations. An imagined, dreamed, or hallucinated object—say, an imagined table—exists only in our minds, while a real table exists "out there," in the world outside our minds. Or, more precisely, real tables exist "out there," but imagined tables don't exist at all, although "tablelike" *experiences* do exist in our "streams of consciousness."

Well, then, how do we know that material objects like tables and buildings exist "out there" in the world? The answer is, of course, by experiencing them through the senses. Or so we all believe before our heads are turned by philosophy. For it is a fact that we can indeed doubt the existence of an external material world. Let's examine some of the arguments skeptics have presented for doubting that a world of material objects exists external to our minds or streams of consciousness.

Sensory Knowledge

Skeptics doubt our experiences are of things existing apart from our experiences.

Common sense takes experiences of such things as trees, animals, tables, the moon, other people, our own bodies, as *evidence* that a physical or material world exists outside of our minds, outside of our streams of consciousness, a world having roughly the qualities (colors, shapes, sounds) we experience it to have. Skeptics don't doubt that we have such experiences; they doubt rather that our experiences are *of* something external to our minds.

The essential difference between dream and waking experiences is not in content but continuity or regularity.

To understand the skeptic's view, think of the differences between the everyday, "real-life" experiences we have when awake and the experiences we have when, asleep, we dream. The two kinds of experiences usually differ in content, clarity, mood, or vividness. But not always. The way we find out for sure that something was a dream is to wake up, when whatever *continuity*** or *regularity* the dream possessed is broken and the everyday continuity and regularity of waking

---

*We learn what to expect in waking (but not dream) experiences by means of inductive reasoning; when our expectations are grossly violated—as when the scene changes suddenly— we can say that *continuity* is broken.

experiences take their place. The point is that *any* experiences might occur in any order, in a dream. The way we know that the monster chasing us last night was fiction is that it suddenly turned into Uncle George, and then we woke up, and both were replaced by the familiar patterns of everyday waking life. (The old idea that you can tell whether you're dreaming by pinching yourself has nothing to it. Some people, in fact, are plagued by dreams in which they pass the pinch test only to find out later that the pinch experience was part of a dream. They find out later because they wake up and continuity breaks down, not because the pinch test works.)

Now look carefully at the content of a typical vivid and lifelike dream, say, the dream of meeting that old friend. There can't be any doubt that you don't really see the old friend when you dream of him. What you do experience are *sensations*—visual sensations (images), auditory sensations (sounds), and so on. But if dream and waking experiences can be alike except for continuity or logic, and if what is experienced in dreams are sensations (auditory, visual, and so on), then what is experienced in real life must be sensations also. In particular, we have no reason to suppose that in dreams we just experience the sensations, while in real life we also experience something else, namely, material objects, because if we did we would be able to tell that we're dreaming while we're dreaming by noticing the absence of material objects.

In dreams, we experience sensations. So if waking experiences have the same content, they too are sensations.

The fact that it is sensations we experience when awake is one reason why the skeptic doubts the existence of a world of material substances apart from our experiences. If there is such a world, says the skeptic, we can't have knowledge of its existence, because we can only know about our experiences, and our experiences are of sounds, smells, tastes, shapes, colors, and the like. We can't experience material objects (or anything else) that might exist apart from our world of experiences.

Skeptics argue that if there is a physical world existing over and above our experiences, we can't know it.

Phenomenalism and Realism

The belief that we can only experience sensations (sounds, smells, shapes, colors, feelings, tastes), coupled with the belief that we are justified in believing only in those things it is possible to experience, leads to the view called **phenomenalism.** (This view also is called *idealism.* But that label has also been applied to complicated "meta-

Phenomenalism is the view that only experiences (and perhaps minds) exist, but not physical objects.

physical" systems [G. W. Hegel's is an example], which claim that mind and spiritual values are fundamental in the universe, systems most phenomenalists reject. Unfortunately, the term *phenomenalism* also is a bit ambiguous.) Phenomenalists believe that a material world separate from our experiences does not exist. *

Realism is the view that physical objects exist in addition to our experiences of them.

Other philosophers, called **realists,** believe that a physical or material world exists apart from experience and, indeed, believe that our waking experiences are "of" that material world. For instance, when we see a wooden box, we experience its shape, size, and so on. Realists thus accept the commonsense idea that the shape and size we experience *are* the shape and size of the box, and that the box exists "out there" in the world, outside of our minds, independent of our experiencing it.

Phenomenalists don't deny existence of boxes; they deny they are anything separate from our experiences of them. Boxes exist only as experiences.

Phenomenalists, on the other hand, claim that the box *is* the collection of touchings, seeings, hearings, and feelings we experience when we have "boxlike" experiences. They don't deny the existence of the box; they simply deny that the box exists apart from our experiences of it—or, in other words, that there is a material box separate from the experiences we have of it. Because experiences of sights, sounds, touches, and so on, exist only in our minds, and the box is just a collection of these experiences, it follows, they say, that the box also exists only in our minds.

A Thought Experiment

The realist's view of things is so ingrained in us that some find it difficult to understand the phenomenalist's theory. So let's try a "thought experiment" to help make phenomenalism easier to understand.

Thought experiment: Suppose God exists and removes all physical objects but makes sure our experiences are as they would have been.

Let's suppose, for a moment, that God does indeed exist, and has the power to create or destroy whatever he cares to. Now imagine that at exactly 12:01 A.M., January 1, 2001, God destroys all material objects in the universe, so that books, buildings, all of our bodies, and even the earth and stars cease to exist. But imagine that God doesn't destroy our *experiences* of these things. In other words, imagine God passes a continuous miracle so that all of us have exactly the same experiences we would have had if he hadn't destroyed the material universe.

---

* Some phenomenalists say that only experiences exist; others, that only experiences and the minds that have them exist. We'll deal later with the question of the existence of minds.

Would we know that God had done this? Would we notice anything different? The answer clearly is no, because we're assuming that God makes sure our experiences remain exactly the same as they would have been had he allowed the material world to continue to exist.

We wouldn't know he'd done so.

Now suppose that one year later, God recreates the material world exactly as it would have been had he not destroyed it a year earlier. Would we notice this second change? Again, the answer is no, because there would be no mark of this change in our experiences.

If he later put them back, we again wouldn't know.

Well, then, why assume God bothered to create a physical world in the first place? Why not stick to the facts we can observe and conclude that all that ever was created was a "world of experiences"? That's exactly the conclusion phenomenalists come to when they declare that books, buildings, and all the other objects we're familiar with are just collections of our experiences. (Of course, atheistic and agnostic phenomenalists don't postulate a creator.)

Phenomenalists claim we've no reason to believe he created physical objects in the first place.

Another Thought Experiment

Now let's try another thought experiment. We said before that *continuity*, not content, is the difference between dream experiences (which certainly are not experiences of material objects) and waking experiences (which realists claim *are* experiences of material objects). So let's imagine that some person, Smith, leads the following extremely peculiar sort of life. Every morning, he wakes up, gets dressed, has bacon and eggs, goes to work at the factory, works all day, goes home, eats supper, watches television, and at midnight goes to sleep. He then dreams that he wakes up, gets dressed, eats Wheaties, goes to college, comes home in the evening, eats dinner, watches television, and goes to sleep at midnight. At that point he (really) wakes up, gets dressed, has bacon and eggs, goes to work in the factory, and so on, until at midnight he goes to sleep and dreams that he wakes up, gets dressed, eats Wheaties, . . .

Second thought experiment: Imagine Smith leads a double life, the first a normal waking life, the second an unusual dream life having the same kind of continuity and pattern as his waking life.

In other words, imagine that Smith has two separate streams of experience, one his "real" waking life, the other his "illusory" dream life. But imagine that both lives have continuity, so that, in particular, the experiences of each "dream day" have continuity with those of all the other "dream days"—unlike the case for ordinary dreams.

Would Smith be able to tell which stream of experiences is real and which just dreams? The answer is quite clearly no; each stream

Would Smith know dream from waking experiences? No. He'd notice no difference.

81

The following excerpt is from A Treatise Concerning the Principles of Knowledge *by the Irish philosopher and cleric George Berkeley (1685–1753), in which he gives classic exposition of the view that "to be is to be perceived."*

George Berkeley: TO BE IS TO BE PERCEIVED

Knowledge is of experiences, emotions, intro-spections, or ideas formed by help of memory and imagination.

It is evident to any one who takes a survey of the objects of *human knowledge,* that they are either *ideas* actually imprinted on the senses; or else such as are perceived by attending to the passions and operations of the mind; or lastly, *ideas* formed by help of memory and imagination—either compounding, dividing, or barely representing those originally perceived in the aforesaid ways. By sight I have the ideas of light and colours, with their several degrees and variations. By touch I perceive hard and soft, heat and cold, motion and resistance; and of all these more and less either as to quantity or degree. Smelling furnishes me with odours; the palate with tastes; and hearing conveys sounds to the mind in all their variety of tone and composition.

When several ideas often accompany each other, we call them one thing.

And as several of these are observed to accompany each other, they come to be marked by one name, and so to be reputed as one *thing.* Thus, for example, a certain colour, taste, smell, figure and consistence having been observed to go together, are accounted one distinct thing, signified by the name apple; other collections of ideas constitute a stone, a tree, a book, . . .

In addition to experiences, there are the minds that have them.

But besides all that endless variety of ideas or objects of knowledge, there is likewise Something which knows or perceives them; and exercises divers operations, as willing, imagining, remembering, about them. This perceiving, active being is what I call *mind, spirit, soul,* or *myself.* By which words I do not denote any one of my ideas, but a thing entirely distinct from them, wherein they exist, or, of which is the same thing, whereby they are perceived; for the existence of an idea consists in being perceived.

Our experiences can't exist without our minds perceiving them. To say the table exists means that I see it and feel it.

That neither our thoughts, nor passions, nor ideas formed by the imagination, exist without the mind is what everybody will allow. And to me it seems no less evident that the various sensations or ideas imprinted on the Sense, however blended or combined together (that is, whatever objects they compose), cannot exist otherwise than in a mind perceiving them. I think an intuitive knowledge may be obtained of this, by any one that shall attend to what is meant by the term *exist* when applied to sensible things. The table I write on I say exists; that is, I see and feel it; and if I were out of my study I should say it existed; meaning thereby that if I was in my study I might perceive it, or that some other spirit actually does perceive it. There was an

To be is to be perceived. That things exist apart

odour, that is, it was smelt; there was a sound, that is, it was heard; a colour or figure, and it was perceived by sight or touch. This is all that I can understand by these and the like expressions. For as to what is said of the *absolute* existence of unthinking things, without any relation to their being perceived, that is to me perfectly unintelligible. Their *esse* is *percipi*; nor is it possible they should have any existence out of the minds or thinking things which perceive them.

It is indeed an opinion strangely prevailing amongst men, that houses, mountains, rivers, and in a word all sensible objects, have an existence, natural or real, distinct from their being perceived by the understanding. But, with how great an assurance and acquiescence soever this Principle may be entertained in the world, yet whoever shall find in his heart to call it in question may, if I mistake not, perceive it to involve a manifest contradiction. For, what are the forementioned objects but the things we perceive by sense? and what do we perceive besides our own ideas or sensations?

But, say you, though the ideas themselves do not exist without the mind, yet there may be things like them, whereof they are copies or resemblances; which things exist without the mind, in an unthinking substance. I answer, an idea can be like nothing but an idea; a colour or figure can be like nothing but another colour or figure. If we look but never so little into our thoughts, we shall find it impossible for us to conceive a likeness except only between our ideas. Again, I ask whether those supposed *originals*, or external things, of which our ideas are the pictures or representations, be themselves perceivable or no? If they are, then *they* are ideas, and we have gained our point: but if you say they are not, I appeal to any one whether it be sense to assert a colour is like something which is invisible; hard or soft, like something which is intangible; and so of the rest.

Some there are who make a distinction betwixt *primary* and *secondary* qualities. By the former they mean extension, figure, motion, rest, solidity or impenetrability, and number; by the latter they denote all other sensible qualities, as colours, sounds, tastes, and so forth. The ideas we have of these last they acknowledge not to be the resemblances of anything existing without the mind, or unperceived; but they will have our ideas of the *primary qualities* to be patterns or images of things which exist without the mind, in an unthinking substance which they call Matter. By Matter, therefore, we are to understand an inert, senseless substance, in which extension, figure, and motion do actually subsist. But it is evident from what we have already shown that extension, figure, and motion are only ideas existing in the mind, and that an idea can be like nothing but another idea; and that consequently neither they nor their archetypes can exist in an unperceiving substance. Hence, it is plain that the very notion of what is called *Matter*, or *corporeal substance* involves a contradiction in it. . . .

from perception is unintelligible.

That things exist outside the mind is unintelligible. That objects exist apart from the mind is contradictory.

They are just perceived things, and we perceive only sensations.

It can't be that although ideas of objects are in the mind, material objects resembling them exist outside the mind, because ideas can't be like anything but ideas.

Primary qualities *are said to exist as* matter *apart from our experiences, but not* secondary qualities. *But since ideas can be like nothing but ideas, the notion that matter is an inert, senseless, separate substance, is contradictory.*

But though it were possible that solid, figured, moveable substances may exist without the mind, corresponding to the ideas we have of bodies, yet how is it possible for us to know this? Either we must know it by Sense or by Reason. As for our senses, by them we have the knowledge only of our sensations, ideas, or those things that are immediately perceived by sense, call them what you will: but they do not inform us that things exist without the mind, or unperceived, like to those which are perceived. This the materialists themselves acknowledge. It remains therefore that if we have any knowledge at all of external things, it must be by reason inferring their existence from what is immediately perceived by sense. But . . . what reason can induce us to believe the existence of bodies without the mind, from what we perceive, since the very patrons of Matter themselves do not pretend there is any necessary connection betwixt them and our ideas? I say it is granted on all hands (and what happens in dreams, frensies, and the like, puts it beyond dispute) that it is possible we might be affected with all the ideas we have now, though no bodies existed without resembling them. Hence it is evident the supposition of external bodies is not necessary for the producing our ideas; since it is granted they are produced sometimes, and might possibly be produced always, in the same order we see them in at present, without their concurrence. . . .

Even if material objects do exist, we'll never know it. Ideas tell us only of ideas, and we can't reason or infer to physical objects because there is no necessary connection between our ideas and the existence of physical objects.

In short, if there were external bodies, it is impossible we should ever come to know it; and if there were not, we might have the very same reasons to think there were that we have now. Suppose—what no one can deny possible—an intelligence, without the help of external bodies, to be affected with the same train of sensations or ideas that you are, imprinted in the same order and with like vividness in his mind. I ask whether that intelligence hath not all the reason to believe the existence of Corporeal Substances, represented by his ideas, and exciting them in his mind, that you can possibly have for believing the same thing? Of this there can be no question. Which one consideration were enough to make any reasonable person suspect the strength of whatever arguments he may think himself to have, for the existence of bodies without the mind. . . .

Suppose a mind has experiences with no material objects causing them; that person would have the same reason to believe material objects exist as we do— namely none.

I do not argue against the existence of any one thing that we can apprehend, either by sense, or reflection. That the things I see with my eyes and touch with my hands do exist, really exist, I make not the least question. The only thing whose existence we deny is that which *philosophers* call Matter or corporeal substance. And in doing of this there is no damage done to the rest of mankind, who, I dare say, will never miss it.

That tables and chairs exist, we can't doubt. I only deny the existence of the philosopher's invention: matter.

of experience would be just as real to him as the other. We described one of them as his dream life—but in fact, says the skeptic, we have no right to do so unless we can show some distinguishing mark either of his alleged dream life or of his real life. And the example is designed to make sure that no such mark exists.

The first point of this thought experiment is that continuity or regularity is the essential difference between dream and waking experiences. It shows that if dreams did have the same sort of continuity as waking experiences, then there would be no way to tell one from the other.

The point: If dreams had normal continuity, they'd be the same as waking experiences.

The second point is that waking and dream experiences must be "of" the same sort of things (shapes, colors, sounds, smells, and so on). And the third point is that we therefore have no more reason to suppose we see, hear, smell, or touch material objects that exist apart from our experiences when we're awake than we do to suppose we see these objects when we're dreaming. Lacking such reason, skeptics deny the existence of a material world. They stick to the facts as they know them; namely, to the facts of the experiences of colors, shapes, sounds, and the like, and they take things such as tables and chairs, buildings and trees, to be just collections of these experiences. (More modest, or agnostic, skeptics simply deny that we have any reason to believe that there are material objects in addition to our experiences of them, without denying that such material objects actually exist.)

So, the two must be "of" the same sorts of things (experiences), so we have no reason to think objects exist apart from experiences of them. Tables, autos, etc., are just the total of our experiences of them.

3. Are There Other Minds?

People differ in many ways from objects such as tables and chairs, or phonograph records and IBM machines, but they differ in particular in having mental lives, in having experiences or streams of consciousness. A person, unlike a computer, is more than just a body. We can be quite certain of this in our own cases, because we can experience our own mental lives as well as our own bodies. (Remember that the dispute between realists and phenomenalists is not over whether we have bodies, but rather whether bodies are collections of experiences or exist apart from our experiences.)

We can also experience the bodies of other people, but we can't experience someone else's mental life—we can't have his or her ex-

Since we can't experience the

85

experiences of
others, why
believe that
others have
mental lives?

Are solipsists
correct that we
can't know other
minds exist?

Their saying so
is no proof others
experience pain.

periences (although in daily life we all suppose each other's experiences are basically alike). Why, then, believe that other people have mental lives? Why assume there is any other stream of consciousness in the universe than your own? There isn't any reason to believe this, says the skeptic, who therefore denies the existence of "other minds."

Those who deny that there is a mental life or stream of consciousness associated with any body other than their own are said to be **solipsists.** Are solipsists right at least in their claim that we can't know of the existence of other minds because we can't experience them?

Take the belief that someone else is in pain. One reason we might think so is that the person himself says so. But this alone is not sufficient. We could easily make a phonograph record that plays the words "I am in pain," but that wouldn't convince us that phonograph records experience pain. Similarly, we could easily construct IBM machines that light up with the words "I'm in pain," but that wouldn't convince us that computers experience pain or anything else.

The Argument from Analogy

We infer to the
existence of other
minds by anal-
ogy, noticing
how similar we
are in construc-
tion and actions:
the argument
from analogy.

Well, then, what grounds do we have, other than a person's saying so, for believing someone else is in pain, or has any sort of conscious-ness whatever? The answer most often given is that we reason to the existence of other streams of consciousness, other minds, by *analogy,* which is a kind of inductive reasoning. We notice, for instance, that we behave in certain characteristic ways when we're in pain, and assume by analogy that when others (who seem to be constructed pretty much as we are) respond in similar ways they too are in pain. For example, if we stick a pin in our finger, we respond in more or less the same way as other people do. We may say "ouch," pull our finger away, and so on. Because *we* feel pain when we exhibit such behavior, we assume by analogy that others do also.

Deception Is Not the Issue

Skeptics aren't
talking about
occasional decep-
tion. They claim
we never know
of other minds.

There is, of course, the problem of deception, familiar to all of us from knowledge of our own deceptive responses, and also from having been deceived by others. But skeptics aren't talking about occasional mis-takes due to deception. Their point is that we *never* know what some-one else is experiencing, we *never* have any good reason to believe

86

anyone else is experiencing anything whatever. Deception implies that there is something to conceal, such as our true intentions, because the point of deception is usually to get others to believe that we intend what in fact we don't. (A deceiver has to have something to conceal.) Solipsists simply deny there ever is reason to believe that anyone else has any mental life to hide, on the grounds that it's impossible for us to be directly aware of anyone else's inner experiences.

What about Cleverly Constructed Robots?

If we infer by analogy that other people are conscious because we are, why not assume also that cleverly constructed robots—programmed perhaps to say things like "ouch" when stuck with pins or "I need a doctor" when they malfunction—also are conscious? The usual answer is that robots aren't made of flesh and blood, and so aren't like us in relevant ways. But as more and more is learned about how the brain functions, some biologists have begun to believe that what makes one mental experience differ from another is not a mere difference in the arrangement of flesh and blood, but rather a difference in the patterns of brain nerve firings. (The point is that a particular pattern of electrical impulses can be produced in several different ways; there need not be a one-to-one correspondence between any particular arrangement of flesh and blood and some particular conscious experience.) What if this, or a similar theory, turns out to be true? Then the question arises as to whether computers programmed to mirror brain firing patterns should be thought of as having conscious experiences that mirror human conscious experiences. If we discover, for example, that a particular nerve firing pattern is always associated with a certain kind of pain experience, and program a computer so that its electrical circuits fire in that pattern, should we say that the computer feels pain and is conscious?

Why not assume robots think also? Usual reply: Robots aren't flesh and blood.

But suppose science finds that it's neural firing patterns that count. Would robots programmed to fire such patterns think?

What about Other Animals?

Of course, animals other than just human beings are made of flesh and blood. And all mammals seem to have the kind of neural circuitry required to have experiences such as pain and pleasure, emotions, and the like. Mice squeal in pain and terror when torn apart by a predator. Dogs moan out the loss of their masters. We thus seem to have both

Other animals have flesh and blood and similar brain firing patterns. When a dog moans, is it feeling pain?

87

physiological and behavioral evidence supporting an extension of the argument from analogy to cover at least some other animals (in particular those closest to us on the evolutionary ladder, such as gorillas and chimpanzees).

Some people think other animals are sentient beings.

All this has led some philosophers and lots of scientists to conclude (along with generations of dog and cat lovers) that at least the "higher" animals are conscious beings. This is a genuine belief for them, not just a rhetorical or theoretical posture (as solipsism surely must be for any otherwise sane person who espouses it). This is proved by the fact that some of them have stopped eating certain other animals, while others talk of "animal liberation," by which they mean that we human beings have moral obligations to other sentient animals.

Is the Argument from Analogy Defective?

Skeptics reject the argument from analogy, even supposing induction in general were o.k.

Skeptics, of course, are untouched by such arguments. They deny the validity of the argument from analogy, whether it is applied to humans or to animals, because all analogical arguments have conclusions that outrun their premises, just as do any other sorts of inductive arguments. But let's suppose we've already accepted induction in general and analogical reasoning in particular. There still is an additional reason to doubt the validity of analogical reasoning to the existence of other conscious beings.

Suppose you buy several General Motors cars, and each one has high maintenance costs and wears out after only sixty or seventy thousand miles. You can then reason by analogy that if you buy another GM car, it too will need lots of repairs and wear out quickly. This is a use of analogical reasoning, which practically everyone accepts as valid.

They do so because the analogy to other minds can't be tested, the way other inductions can.

The trouble is that analogical reasoning to other minds differs from these other legitimate uses of analogy in one serious way: we can test other—legitimate—uses of analogy (for instance, we can test the preceding analogy by buying another GM car and keeping track of its performance), but we can't test analogical reasoning by pointing to the existence of other minds (we can't test the truth of our conclusion that Jones is conscious, because we can't experience his experiences). Nor is this just a technological difficulty that can be remedied by greater knowledge. Someone's conscious experiences just aren't the sort of thing that anyone else can experience. So this particular use of analogy seems to be challengeable on special grounds, over and above the usual ones that lead skeptics to doubt induction in general.

Well, then, why accept the argument from analogy? Why believe in the existence of other minds? Because we do, and can't stop doing so. In particular, we accept the argument from analogy even after hearing the skeptical arguments against it (just as some believers accept the existence of God even after hearing all the proofs knocked down). We believe in other minds because even the most skeptical objections fail to generate a living doubt in us on the matter, or in the words of earlier chapters, we believe on the basis of intuition or faith.

The only answer to skeptics is that we have faith in the argument from analogy and can't doubt the existence of other minds.

4. Is There Life after Death?

Induction tells us to believe the sun will rise tomorrow—that there will *be* a tomorrow, and a day after tomorrow. But it also tells us to believe that the number of tomorrows any one of us can expect to experience in this life is limited—we all die sooner or later, and never very much later. The fact of death is perhaps the hardest fact we have to face—this "final swindle of human existence." Most of us defend ourselves from this fact most of the time simply by not thinking about it, thinking about it as little as possible, or by joking about it. But some of us, lots of us, handle death by assuming that the end of life here on earth is, at least for some, the beginning of a new life, perhaps in heaven. Are there good reasons for believing that the end of our life here on earth is not the end of our life?

Induction tells us our life here on earth will end.

But is there life after death?

Religious Faith

Most of those who believe in life after death do so on religious grounds. For them, belief in an afterlife is just part of the package of beliefs that make up their religious faith. Since we've already discussed religious faith, let's just add here that faith in an afterlife is an act of faith separate from simple faith in God, because the conception of God has nothing in it one way or the other about an afterlife. (There is no contradiction in believing in God and also believing that there is no life after death. Several religious groups, in fact, accept both these doctrines.)

Those who believe in life after death on religious grounds make a separate leap of faith.

89

René Descartes (1596–1650), mathematician and philosopher, used the skeptical program to doubt everything—until he arrived at something that he couldn't doubt; namely, that he existed. (He then used this truth to very unskeptically prove all sorts of other things.)

René Descartes: I THINK, THEREFORE I AM*
Meditation I: Of the Things Which May Be Brought within the Sphere of the Doubtful

Since so many of my beliefs have been wrong, I'll examine all of them.

It is now some years since I detected how many were the false beliefs that I had from my earliest youth admitted as true, and how doubtful was everything I had since constructed on this basis; and from that time I was convinced that I must once for all seriously undertake to rid myself of all the opinions which I had formerly accepted, and commence to build anew from the foundation, if I wanted to establish any firm . . . structure in the sciences. . . .

I can't be sure of sensory knowledge, because the senses sometimes deceive. But can I deny, say, that I am here, seated by the fire?

All that up to the present time I have accepted as most true and certain I have learned either from the senses or through the senses; but it sometimes proved to me that these senses are deceptive, and it is wiser not to trust entirely to any thing by which we have once been deceived.

But it may be that although the senses sometimes deceive us concerning things which are hardly perceptible, or very far away, there are yet many others to be met with as to which we cannot reasonably have any doubt, although we recognize them by their means. For example, there is the fact that I am here, seated by the fire, attired in a dressing gown, having this paper in my hands and other similar matters. And how could I deny that these hands and this body are mine. . . .

Yes, because I may be dreaming.

At the same time I must remember that I am a man, and that consequently I am in the habit of sleeping, and in my dreams representing to myself the same things or sometimes even less probable things, than do those who are insane in their waking moments. How often has it happened to me that in the night I dreamt that I found myself in this particular place, that I was dressed and seated near the fire, whilst in reality I was lying in bed! . . .

Furthermore, I may be deceived by some all-powerful God.

I have long had fixed in my mind the belief that an all-powerful God existed by whom I have been created such as I am. But how do I know that He has not brought it to pass that there is no earth, no heaven, no extended body, no magnitude, no place, and that nevertheless . . . they seem to me to exist just exactly as I now see them? And, besides, as I sometimes imagine

---

*René Descartes, *Meditations on First Philosophy*, trans. E. S. Haldane and G. R. T. Ross. Copyright 1912 by Cambridge University Press. Reprinted by permission.

that others deceive themselves in the things which they think they know best, how do I know that I am not deceived every time that I add two and three, or count the sides of a square, or judge of things yet simpler, if anything simpler can be imagined? But possibly God has not desired that I should be thus deceived, for He is said to be supremely good. If, however, it is contrary to His goodness to have made me such that I constantly deceive myself, it would also appear to be contrary to his goodness to permit me to be sometimes deceived, and nevertheless I cannot doubt that He does permit this. . . .

And I may be self-deceived, even when I add 2 plus 3, because I know people often are self-deceived.

I then suppose . . . some evil genius not less powerful than deceitful, has employed his whole energies in deceiving me; I shall consider that the heavens, the earth, colours, figures, sound, and all other external things are nought but the illusions and dreams of which this genius has availed himself in order to lay traps for my credulity. . . .

Suppose an evil genius is trying to deceive me.

Meditation II: Of the Nature of the Human Mind; and That It Is More Easily Known Than the Body

. . . I suppose, then, that all the things that I see are false; I persuade myself that nothing has ever existed of all that my fallacious memory represents to me. I consider that I possess no senses; I imagine that body, figure, extension, movement and place are but the fictions of my mind. What, then, can be esteemed as true? . . .

Doubting everything doubtable, do I arrive at something I can't doubt?

But how can I know there is not something different from those things that I have just considered, of which one cannot have the slightest doubt? Is there not some God, or some other being by whatever name we call it, who puts these reflections into my mind? That is not necessary, for is it not possible that I am capable of producing them myself? I myself, am I not at least something? But I have already denied that I had senses and body. Yet I hesitate, for what follows from that? Am I so dependent on body and senses that I cannot exist without these? But I was persuaded that there was nothing in all the world, that there was no heaven, no earth, that there were no minds, nor any bodies: was I not then likewise persuaded that I did not exist? Not at all; of a surety I myself did exist since I persuaded myself of something [or merely because I thought of something]. But there is some deceiver or other, very powerful and very cunning, who ever employs his ingenuity in deceiving me. Then without doubt I exist also if he deceives me, and let him deceive me as much as he will, he can never cause me to be nothing so long as I think that I am something. So that after having reflected well and carefully examined all things, we must come to the definite conclusion that this proposition: I am, I exist, is necessarily true each time that I pronounce it, or that I mentally conceive it.

No. I can't persuade myself that I don't exist. For I can't doubt or persuade myself if I don't exist.

An evil deceiver can't persuade me to think I'm nothing, as long as I think I'm something. "I am, I exist" is necessarily true whenever I think or speak it.

Séances and Mystical Experiences

Troubles with appeals to séance, and so forth: (1) Lots of con artists around; (2) why would the departed bother to give us such trivial information?

Some believe in life after death on the basis of mystical experiences, some from witnessing séances. They believe that departed souls sometimes appear in mystical visions, or that long-dead relatives speak to us at séances, and thus believe that an afterlife does indeed exist. The question, of course, is the reliability of afterlife revelations, a question just like the one about miracles discussed in Chapter 1. Let's add two small notes here. First, we know that there are con artists who sometimes even fool magicians. And second, the content of séances is usually so uninspired and useless as to make us wonder why those in the afterlife would bother.

Last-Minute Reprieves

Don't "near-death" experiences prove there is life after death?

There also is the evidence of those saved from death at the last minute. Typical are those who come close to death on the operating table, have their hearts stop beating, and then are "brought back to life." Some people who've gone through this experience report that they left their bodies and traveled through a dark tunnel toward an intense white light. They also report that their lives flashed in front of them and other similar experiences.

The people who report these experiences are in other respects just ordinary people, with no unusual axes to grind; their reports therefore should be as believable as any others concerning extreme circumstances. But believing these experiences occur and believing that we survive the deaths of our bodies are two different things. The crucial question is whether those who report these experiences were or were not dead—in the sense that their bodies had ceased to function. So far, there is no good evidence that these people were dead in this sense.* On the contrary, there is reason to think they were alive, because many people who have certain kinds of near-death experiences (for example, falling from an airplane onto a soft surface and surviving) during which they remain alive, and indeed even conscious, report having similar experiences.

No, because they're "alive" experiences. There is no evidence of return-to-life experiences.

_____

*However, such evidence is possible. A report later by a patient of an operating room event that occurred when instruments showed neither heart *nor* brain activity would be interesting evidence that human experiences might possibly continue after our bodies have ceased to function.

Evidence from This Life against an Afterlife

Those who doubt the existence of an afterlife generally do so for two reasons. First, there is the lack of positive evidence, just discussed. And second, evidence from this life indicates that conscious life is causally connected to body physiology. Because our bodies certainly do stop functioning at death, it's argued that our conscious lives must stop at death also.

On life after death: (1) no evidence for it; (2) evidence in this life is against it.

The idea that our mental lives are causally connected to the lives of our bodies is a familiar one. We know that those who drink a lot of alcohol get drunk, whether they want to or not. Similarly, breaking a leg causes pain—we have no choice in the matter. Insufficient iron in someone's diet makes that person feel tired. Reduced production of certain hormones reduces sexual potency and desire. Marijuana, cocaine, alcohol, mescaline, LSD, and other drugs alter mental states, sometimes producing hallucinations. The list of mind-body connections of this kind is very long and quite familiar to us from daily experience.

There are lots of examples of the connection between bodily states and mental states . . .

In addition, we know that destruction or malfunction of certain parts of the brain or nervous system results in destruction of parts of our mental life. Chloroform stops certain nerves from firing and thus renders us unconscious. Nerves cut in the wrist cause loss of sensation in the hand. Auto accident victims who've had various parts of their brains destroyed suffer all sorts of peculiar mental losses (some, for instance, find that they can't remember the beginnings of sentences long enough to finish them). When the optic nerve is cut, the inevitable result is blindness. And so on.

. . . and the destruction of parts of the brain leads to partial destruction of the mind . . .

It seems, then, that by destroying someone's nerves one by one we could slowly destroy the various aspects of consciousness, one by one, until, when the whole brain and nervous system have been destroyed, the person's whole mental life will have been destroyed. Thus it seems plausible to suppose that when we die, when the whole brain and nervous system stops functioning, our entire conscious life also stops. *

. . . so when at death, the whole brain is destroyed, it seems that our mental life must also be destroyed.

So if we count evidence from this life, we must admit that so far it is negative. Belief in an afterlife, at least at this stage in our knowledge, therefore must be based solely on faith.

---

*Some say that the soul survives death. But if the soul is not a conscious entity, its survival—whatever a soul may consist in—isn't what most people have in mind when they believe in life after death.

The ancient Greek philosopher Plato (427?–347 B.C.) and his pupil Aristotle (384–322 B.C.) have been perhaps the two most influential Western philosophers. In the following passages, Plato argues for the immortality of the soul while Aristotle argues in a way consistent with belief that the soul is mortal and perishes with the body at death. First, Plato (from the Phaedo, *translated by Benjamin Jowett):*

Plato: PHAEDO

*The soul is what brings the body life.
And the soul which brings life won't receive the opposite of what it brings.
The immortal is that which doesn't admit of death, and the soul doesn't admit of death.*

When the body dies, the soul must live on forever.

Tell me, [said Socrates,] what is that of which the inheritance will render the body alive? The soul, [replied Cebes]. . . . Then whatever the soul possesses, to that she comes bearing life? Yes certainly. And is there any opposite to life? There is, he said. And what is that? Death. Then the soul . . . will never receive the opposite of what she brings. . . .

And . . . what did we just now call that principle which repels the even? The odd. And that principle which repels the musical or the just? The unmusical, he said, and the unjust. And what do we call that principle which does not admit of death? The immortal, he said. And does the soul admit of death? No. Then the soul is immortal? Yes, he said. . . .

Seeing then that the immortal is indestructible, must not the soul, if she is immortal, be also imperishable? Most certainly. Then when death attacks a man, the mortal portion of him may be supposed to die, but the immortal retires at the approach of death and is preserved safe and sound? True.

Then, Cebes, beyond question the soul is immortal and imperishable, and our souls will truly exist in another world!

Now listen to Aristotle on the same subject:

Aristotle: DE ANIMA

Real substance may be viewed as matter, form, or the combination of the two. Matter is potential, form is its realization.

Real substance conforms to bodies, living or dead.

Real substance is the name which we assign one class of existing things; and this real substance may be viewed from several aspects, either, *firstly,* as matter, meaning by matter that which in itself is not any individual thing; or *secondly,* as form and specific characteristic in virtue of which an object comes to be described as such and such an individual; or *thirdly,* as the result produced by a combination of this matter and this form. Further, while matter is merely potential existence, the form is perfect realization. . . .

These real substances again are thought to correspond for the most part with . . . natural bodies. Now among such natural bodies, some have, others do not have life, meaning here by life the process of nutrition, increase and decay from an internal principle. Thus every natural body possessed of life would be a real substance, and which we may describe as composite.

Since then the body, as possessed of life, is of this compound character, the body itself would not constitute the soul: for body is not something attributed to a subject; it rather acts as the underlying subject and the material basis. Thus then the soul must necessarily be a real substance, as the form which determines a natural body possessed potentially of life. The reality however of an object is contained in its perfect realization. Soul therefore will be a perfect realization of a body such as has been described. . . .

The body of a living thing can't be its soul. Soul must be the form of a body, its perfect realization.

The definition we have just given should make it evident that we must no more ask whether the soul and the body are one, than ask whether the wax and the figure impressed upon it are one, or generally inquire whether the material and that of which it is the material are one; for though unity and being are used in a variety of senses, their most distinctive sense is that of perfect realization.

Soul and body can't be one and the same.

A general account has thus been given of the nature of the soul: it is, we have seen, a real substance which expresses an idea. Such a substance is the manifestation of the inner meaning of such and such a body. Suppose, for example, that an instrument such as an axe were a natural body: then its axehood or its being an axe would constitute its essential nature or reality, and thus, so to speak, its soul; because were this axehood taken away from it, it would be no longer an axe, except in so far as it might still be called by this same name. The object in question, however, is as matter of fact only an axe; soul being not the idea and the manifestation of the meaning of a body of this kind, but of a natural body possessing within itself a cause of movement and of rest. . . .

Soul is the manifestation of the inner meaning of a body.

The part of our definition which speaks of something as "potentially possessed of life" must be taken to mean not that which is thrown off its soul, but rather that which has it: the seed and the fruit is such and such a body potentially. In the same way then as cutting is the full realization of an axe, or actual seeing the realization of the eye, so also waking may be said to be the full realization of the body: but it is in the sense in which vision is not only the exercise but also the implicit capacity of the eye that soul is the true realization of the body. The body on the other hand is merely the material to which soul gives reality: and just as the eye is both the pupil and its vision, so also the living animal is at once the soul and body in connection.

Waking is the full realization of the body, and the living animal the soul and body in connection.

It is not then difficult to see that soul or certain parts of it (if it naturally admit of partition) cannot be separated from the body: for in some cases the soul is the realization of the parts of body themselves. It is however perfectly conceivable that there may be some parts of it which are separable and this

Parts of the soul can't be separated from body, but some parts may be, since they don't

because they are not the expression or realization of any particular body. And indeed it is further matter of doubt whether soul as the perfect realization of the body may not stand to it in the same separable relation as a sailor to his boat.

express any particular body.

The animate is distinguished from the inanimate or soulless by the fact of life. There are a number of ways in which a thing is said to live . . . as for example, reason, sense-perception, local movement and rest. Respecting these various powers, there are some animals which possess them all, others which have merely some of them, and others again which have but one only. . . . Soul then is the original and fundamental ground of all our life, of our sensation and of our reasoning. It follows therefore that the soul must be regarded as a sort of form and idea, rather than as matter and as underlying subject. For the term real substance is, as we have before remarked, employed in three senses: it may denote either the specific form, or the material substratum, or thirdly the combination of the two: and of these different aspects of reality the matter or substratum is but the potential ground, whereas the form is the perfect realization. Since then it is the product of the two that is animate, it cannot be that the body is the full realization or expression of the soul; rather on the contrary it is the soul which is the full realization of some body.

Soul is the basic ground of all our life, and is thus form and idea rather than underlying matter or subject; since it is a combination of form and matter that is animate, the body can't be the full realization of the soul, but must be vice versa.

This fact fully supports the view of those who hold that the soul is not independent of some sort of body and yet not to be identified with a body of any sort whatever. The truth is that soul is not body but it is something which belongs to body. And hence further it exists in a body and in a body of such and such a nature, not left undetermined in the way that earlier thinkers introduced it into the body without determining besides what and what sort of body it was, although it does not even look as though any casual thing admitted any other casual thing.

So soul is neither independent of body nor body itself.

This same conclusion may be reached also on *a priori* grounds. The full realization of each object is naturally reached only within that which is potentially existent and within that material substratum which is appropriate to it. It is clear then from these considerations that soul is a kind of full realization or expression of the idea of that which has potentially the power to be of such a character.

This is proved a priori also.

Summary of Chapter 3

Skepticism, as a philosophical attitude, questions or doubts all claims to knowledge, accepting only that which can be rationally justified. Athough none of us can be true skeptics, still it is useful to go through the skeptic's arguments.

1. The skeptic challenges the *principle of induction* (the principle that we should expect patterns or connections observed in the past to hold in the future), and thus challenges our belief that we have any knowledge about the future.

There are several common replies to the skeptic, several common attempts to justify induction.

    a. We're entitled to use induction because it works, both in everyday life and in science. The trouble with this defense of induction is that we only know induction has worked so far, not that it will work from now on.

    b. Because nature is uniform, we're entitled to use induction since the point of induction is to discover such uniformities. The problem with this solution is that, first, nature could be uniform, although the patterns we notice up to a given point are not the ones that persist. And, second, the principle that nature is uniform itself needs a justification, yet the only plausible "proof" uses the principle of induction and so is circular.

    c. The problem is a pseudoproblem, because it must be rational to use induction: using induction is part of what it means to be rational. The trouble this time is that if we define rationality so as to include the use of induction, then it's sensible to ask why we should be rational.

    d. Finally, we should note that it is impossible to justify every principle without either circular reasoning or an infinity of justifications, neither of which are satisfactory. So it isn't so terrible that we accept induction without justification. Whether this does or doesn't remove the "sting" from the problem, it is true that we can't justify everything without either circularity or infinite regress. (Note that belief in induction is like faith in God in that it is an unjustified belief, but is different from faith in God in several ways, in particular in being in itself neutral as to whether its use will be comforting or terrifying.)

2. *Skeptics* challenge the belief we all have in the existence of a material world that exists apart from our experiences of it. They do so on the grounds

that when we experience objects normally thought to be physical objects, all that we experience are sounds, sights, smells, tastes, and so on, all of which can exist in our minds independently of any physical object. The fact that we have such experiences in dreams, hallucinations, and the like, when no physical objects cause them is proof of the possibility that none of our experiences are related to material objects.

Phenomenalists, in effect, agree with skeptics in denying at least that we have any reason to believe a physical world exists apart from our experiences. *Realists*, on the other hand, believe in the existence of a material world apart from our experiences, which in fact our experiences are "of."

Because all of us in everyday life think along the lines of the realist, it is useful to consider thought experiments in order to understand the phenomenalist's position. Imagine that God removed all material substances from the universe but passed a continuous miracle, so that we all had exactly the experiences we would have had if he hadn't destroyed the physical world. Clearly, we wouldn't know he had done so, because our experiences would be the same as if he hadn't. What reason, therefore, do we have for assuming a material world existed in the first place?

Another thought experiment takes advantage of the fact that continuity and regularity enable us to tell dream experiences from waking ones, and asks us to imagine a person whose dream life does have continuity—one night's dreams taking up where the previous night's ended. Clearly, the person in question would not be able to tell dream from reality, which suggests that we have no more reason to assume our real-life experiences are of, or caused by, physical substances existing apart from our experiences than are our dream experiences.

3. Skeptics also challenge the commonsense belief that other people have streams of consciousness just like our own. They do so on the grounds that we never experience the content of another person's mind, never have their experiences, and have to infer by *analogy* to the existence of other streams of experience. The trouble with this, they point out (over and above their objections to induction, in general, analogy being a kind of induction) is that there is no way to check up on analogical reasoning of this kind—say, reasoning to the conclusion that Smith feels pain—unlike the usual case for analogical reasoning.

4. Skeptics are unwilling to believe in life after death, on the grounds of a lack of evidence. The religious person may believe in life after death on faith, but of course skeptics won't believe anything unsupported by reasons. There is, of course, much evidence in séances and near-death experiences, but this evidence, claims the skeptic, is very poor, to say the least. Séances are notoriously open to chicanery—to fraud—and anyway all such experi-

ences are part of *this* life, and thus far the skeptic can't tell us anything about some alleged other life. Furthermore, if we allow evidence from this life to count, skeptics would be the first to point to all the evidence linking our mental lives to functioning brains and nervous systems. Because our bodies surely are destroyed at death, the best inference, if any is valid, must be that our minds cease to exist at death.

Questions for Further Thought

1. Bishop Butler is said to have "refuted" Berkeley's idealism by kicking a stone as he said, "I refute it thus." *Did* he refute it thus?

2. It has seemed to some commentators that Berkeley's arguments (in the reading in this chapter) are on safer ground when he argues that if there are physical objects existing apart from our experiences we couldn't know it than when he claims there aren't any physical objects to know about. Their point is that Berkeley's second claim outruns his argument (isn't defended by his argument). Do you think it fair to say that *at best* phenomenalists can only argue with any plausibility that we can't know whether there is a material world or what it's like, not that no material world exists?

3. Or does the whole idea of phenomenalism seem outrageous to you? If so, how would you propose we refute it?

4. What do you think of Plato's argument for immortality (given by Socrates in the Plato reading in this chapter)?

5. Do you think that séances and that sort of thing give us any good evidence favoring life after death?

6. Does Descartes really prove he exists (in the reading in this chapter)?

7. Suppose scientists prove that how our body moves depends ultimately on the *patterns* of nerve firings in the body, similar patterns producing similar bodily motions (so that different sets of nerve firings might have the same pattern and thus produce the same actions). If we then construct a robot programmed to have the same sort of electrical firing patterns as do human beings, should we assume these electronic marvels are alive and have mental experiences?

8. Hans Reichenbach argued that we can in fact justify induction. His argument, roughly, was that potential users of induction are like hungry fishermen who come upon a lake. They can't prove there are any fish in the lake, but they can prove that, if they're going to catch any fish, they have

to cast their nets. Similarly (almost), we can't prove induction will work in the future, but we can prove that, if any method will work, induction will, so if we want to catch future truths, we're justified in casting our inductive nets.

To see his point, suppose (outlandishly) that we find some crystal ball gazer whose success rate in prediction is much better than ours when we use induction. Will her success rate be far higher in the future? Using induction to test that theory, we at first would have to conclude that it won't (because higher-level inductions make it more likely that her success is an accident rather than evidence of predictive powers). But soon her continued success would overrule our initial skepticism and make it more and more likely that she does have predictive power. Thus, using induction, we would predict whatever she predicted and so be as successful as she is.

Obviously, Reichenbach's theory is much more technical than that. But how does his main idea strike you? Can it solve the problem of induction?

9. There also is the theory that induction is justified because it is "self-correcting" and thus gets us nearer and nearer to the truth. In science, for instance, theories are tested and often refuted by the evidence; new inductive inferences are then drawn and tested, and sooner or later some will prove correct, while the failures are weeded out. So when we use induction we keep getting closer and closer to the truth and therefore are justified in using it. Does this argument work?

10. How would you reply to the following?

> Every belief is either accepted on its own merits or because of other beliefs. But these other beliefs also rest either on themselves or on some other belief. Now a belief that rests on no other belief is called *faith*. Therefore, at rock bottom every belief rests on faith. So why have atheists singled out faith in God for doubt?

11. Shouldn't skeptics doubt their own rule to doubt everything that can't be proved? After all, they can't prove their own rule, can they?

12. Bertrand Russell once used the example of turkeys who learn to associate the arrival of the farmer every morning with food, until one November morning when the farmer comes and wrings their necks. Does this support the skeptic's views on induction? (Are we turkeys waiting, perhaps, to have our necks wrung?)

13. (Question for those who know a bit of formal logic.) Many twentieth-century philosophers in the analytic camp (see Chapter 6 for more on the analytic turn in philosophy) have argued that induction is a pseudoproblem because it can't be solved. Genuine problems, they say, have to have solutions. Their point is that any valid proof has to be either inductive or deductive. An inductive proof would use the very thing to be proved, namely,

induction, and so would be circular and thus fallacious. And no deductive argument could possibly justify using induction either, because (in their view) the conclusion of a valid deductive argument merely spells out explicitly what is already contained (perhaps implicitly) in its premises, and it's quite clear that we have no such premises. The reason is that these premises themselves would have to be warranted either by an inductive argument, or a deductive one, or by mere observation. Observation can't do the job, because obviously we don't literally see laws of nature or see induction justified. And we've already seen that induction won't, either. So the premises of our deductive justification of induction themselves will have to be obtained deductively. Yet only what are sometimes called *tautologies* or *logical truths*—empty statements such as "Yellow is yellow," "Bachelors are unmarried," or "Nothing both is and isn't"—can be proved by deductions that either start from scratch (the null set of premises) or from premises that are logical truths. Therefore, there is no possible way to justify induction, so it isn't a real problem; the alleged problem is thus (as they would say) *dissolved*. Does this justification work?

The duties of universal obligation are five, and the moral qualities by which they are carried out are three. The duties are those between ruler and subject, between father and son, between husband and wife, between elder brother and younger, and those in the intercourse of friends. These are the five duties of universal obligation. Wisdom, compassion and courage,—these are the three universally recognized moral qualities of man.—CONFUCIUS

Nothing can possibly be conceived in the world, or even out of it, which can be called good without qualification, except a good will.—IMMANUEL KANT

Morality is the herd instinct in the individual.—NIETZSCHE

The exclusive worship of the bitch-goddess Success is our national disease.—WILLIAM JAMES

Sin is a queer thing. It isn't the breaking of divine commandments. It is the breaking of one's own integrity.—D. H. LAWRENCE

There is no sin except stupidity.
—OSCAR WILDE

Ugliness is a sin.—FRANK LLOYD WRIGHT

The maxim "Honesty is the best policy" is incomplete as it stands. Completed, it would read as follows: "Honesty is the best policy with those who are honest and the worst and stupidest policy with those who are dishonest."—THOMAS SZASZ

"Sins" are indispensable to every society organized on an ecclesiastical basis; they are the only reliable weapons of power; the priest lives upon sins; it is necessary to him that there be "sinning."—NIETZSCHE

Philosophers should diligently inquire into the powers and energy of custom, exercise, habit, education, example, imitation, emulation, company, friendship, praise, reproof, exhortation, reputation, laws, books, studies, etc.; for these are the things that reign in men's morals; by these agents the mind is formed and subdued.—FRANCIS BACON

The devil can cite Scripture for his purpose.
—SHAKESPEARE

Always do right. This will gratify some people, and astonish the rest.—SAMUEL CLEMENS

Unable to make what is just strong, we have made what is strong just.—BLAISE PASCAL

I have to live for others and not for myself; that's middle class morality.
—GEORGE BERNARD SHAW

All sin is a kind of lying.—ST. AUGUSTINE

There slowly grew up in me an unshakable conviction that we have no right to inflict suffering and death on another living creature unless there is some unavoidable necessity for it, and that we ought all of us to feel what a horrible thing it is to cause suffering and death out of mere thoughtlessness.
—ALBERT SCHWEITZER

Don't be silly, Ninety-nine. We have to shoot, kill, and destroy. We represent everything that's wholesome and good in the world.
—MAXWELL SMART (on the television program "Get Smart")

What we call "morals" is simply blind obedience to words of command.—HAVELOCK ELLIS

Morality and religion are but words to him who fishes in gutters for the means of sustaining life, and crouches behind barrels in the street for shelter from the cutting blasts of a winter night.—HORACE GREELEY

Morality is not properly the doctrine of how we may make ourselves happy, but how we may make ourselves worthy of happiness.
—IMMANUEL KANT

There is but one morality, as there is but one geometry.—VOLTAIRE

What is moral is what you feel good after and what is immoral is what you feel bad after.
—ERNEST HEMINGWAY

It must not be forgotten that although a high standard of morality gives a slight or no advantage to each individual man and his children over other men of the same tribe, yet an advancement in the standard of morality will certainly give an immense advantage to one tribe over another.—CHARLES DARWIN

4

Morality

PHILOSOPHERS COMMONLY DIVIDE statements into those about *facts* and those about *values*. The statement "The earth is roughly a sphere" is an example of a factual statement; "Suicide is wrong" an example of a statement of value.

In the case of factual statements, something outside of the speaker's mind—"the way the world is"—makes them either true or false. Thus, the statement "Snow is white" is true, because snow *is* white, while the statement "The earth is flat" is false, because the earth isn't flat.

But moral judgments seem to be different. If I argue that the Bible is mistaken in saying that the hare chews its cud and you claim that the Bible is correct, we can examine hares and settle the issue (it turns out that hares aren't cud chewers). However, if I argue that abortion is immoral and you that it's often perfectly all right, no appeal to ordinary facts (say, about the nature of the fetus, or how abortions are performed) can settle the issue. We might agree on all the facts of this kind and still disagree about whether abortion is immoral.

In other words, moral statements or judgments seem to be different from factual ones, and their truth or falsity, if they are true or false, judged in some other way than by examining some part of the universe, as we judge factual statements like "Snow is white." Well, then, how are moral claims to be judged? Are there peculiarly *moral* facts that make moral statements true just as other kinds of facts validate statements such as "Sugar tastes sweet" or "John is tall"? If not, what does make a true moral statement true?

There are statements of fact and of value.

The truth or falsity of factual statements depends on what the world is like. But what makes moral (value) statements true or false?

1. Religious Authoritarianism

Some say God's commands determine moral right and wrong.

Perhaps the most popular answer to the question "What makes true moral statements true?" is that *God's commands* (not to lie, not to kill) make statements such as "Lying is wrong" and "Killing is wrong" true. On this view, God's commanding us to do something *makes* that thing right and his commanding us not to do a thing makes that thing wrong. But there are serious difficulties with this idea.

How Can We Find Out What God Commands?

But how can we find out what he commands?

First of all, there is the problem of finding out what God commands us to do. (Let's assume here that we somehow know there is a God.) There are three standard answers to this problem (aside from an appeal to faith), none satisfactory.

Consult One's Conscience

We can consult our consciences. But they differ one from another.

Some say that our conscience tells us what God commands. So we should "let our conscience be our guide." But it is notorious that what conscience tells one person radically differs from what it tells another. (This is true in particular when moving from one culture to another, but it's also true to a lesser extent when going from person to person within a culture.) Eating human flesh is a serious violation of conscience for most of us in Western industrial societies, but gives New Guinea cannibals not the slightest twinge. Similarly, eating the flesh of cattle goes against the consciences of most Hindus, but Christians eat beef daily without serious qualms.

And that's not a mark of Divine origin.

We have here a reason for thinking that God does not speak to us through our consciences. Surely he wouldn't tell one of us that killing and eating human beings is a terrible sin while telling others it's an act of merit.

Of course, it doesn't follow that we shouldn't appeal to our consciences in deciding what we ought to do. How we feel about something is surely an important bit of information, and appealing to conscience is just a way of finding that out. (Another way to put it is that appeals to conscience are appeals to moral intuitions.) The point here is that in appealing to conscience, we can't be appealing to God's will, because consciences differ so radically from person to person and place to place. (Another problem with consulting our consciences is that we often fail to get an answer, or get a contradictory answer. Thus, many people today find their consciences confused on the issues of birth control, abortion, and many others.)

Consult Religious Authorities

A second way to find out what God commands is to consult religious authorities or experts. The trouble this time is that religious authorities have no magical way of discovering God's will that isn't available to the rest of us. Think of the immense variety of religions in the world, each with its own creed. Hindu priests, New Guinea shamans, Zen masters, Jewish rabbis, Muslim priests, and Christian ministers all give very different answers to questions about God's will. And even among Christians, Baptist ministers, Catholic priests, and Mormon elders certainly disagree on these questions.

We can consult religious authorities. But which ones? They all disagree with each other.

So the problem in consulting religious experts has always been to find a reason for listening to one rather than to the others. Unless the very choice of a religious authority is a matter of faith, religious authorities have to be chosen on the basis of evidence of reliability, as are any other authorities. Yet there seems to be no good evidence favoring one authority over another.

Consult the Bible

Finally, religious people appeal to miracles, mystical experiences, and the Bible to find out what God commands us to do. We've already discussed such appeals in Chapter 1, when we discussed reasons for believing God exists, but let's look at a few things the Bible says about moral right and wrong, to see if it sounds like a divinely inspired document.

We can consult the Bible.

The Bible's Moral Teachings Need Human Interpretation

First of all, what the Bible says about morality and God's commands tends to be *vague* (imprecise, unclear, fuzzy around the edges) and thus requires human interpretation before we can carry out those teachings. This is a serious problem, especially for those who read the Bible in a straightforward or literal way. For example, does the com-

But the Bible's moral teachings are vague and need interpreting.

105

mandment to honor our parents mean that we should *obey* them? Because the concept of honor is vague, we have no sure way of knowing.

The Bible's Moral Teachings Are
Inconsistent, Incomplete, and Counterintuitive

Taken literally, the Bible is contradictory, e.g., Christ contradicts the Old Testament.

Furthermore, it's hard to find any reasonably straightforward or literal interpretation of the biblical moral teachings that is not *inconsistent* or *contradictory.* In Exodus, we're told that "Thou shalt not suffer a witch to live" and "Whosoever lieth with a beast shall surely be put to death," both of which seem to contradict the commandment not to kill. * We're also told that "if any mischief follow, then thou shalt give life for life, eye for eye, tooth for tooth." Yet this too contradicts the commandment not to kill. Further, in the New Testament Christ says, "Ye have heard that it hath been said, An eye for an eye, and a tooth for a tooth: But I say unto you, that ye shall resist not evil: but whosoever shall smite thee on thy right cheek, turn to him the other also." Thus, Christ deliberately contradicts the Old Testament.

Biblical moral teachings don't cover all cases, and run counter to intuition.

In addition to being contradictory, the biblical moral teachings are *incomplete* (they don't cover every possible situation) and *counterintuitive.* They say next to nothing about the morality of abortion (because they don't say whether a fetus is a human being), fair wages or taxes, war, or even whether it's all right to cheat on exams. And where the Bible does pronounce, it sometimes says things contrary to strongly held intuitions and thus is counterintuitive. For example, the Bible condones slavery, and forbids all lending of money at interest, and insists on a second-class status for women.

But how do we interpret the Bible so as to be God's word?

Of course, those who believe the Bible is an allegorical or mythical document that has to be interpreted or analyzed deny it gives us contradictory or counterintuitive commandments when interpreted correctly. The trouble is that there isn't any particular reason for accepting one interpretation rather than another *as the word of God.*

---

* Because most of us don't know Hebrew and Greek, we have to read the Bible in translation, which means we have to depend on human interpretations. According to many experts, the commandment not to kill is better translated as saying not to *murder.* If it is, it doesn't contradict the quoted passages from Exodus, but then it becomes next to useless, because it doesn't tell us which killings are murder and which aren't.

The Bible Sometimes Requires the Impossible

Finally, it should be noted that when interpreted literally, the Bible sometimes requires us to do things we aren't able to do. Love, for instance, is beyond our power of choice (although we can influence our *chances* of loving). In particular, the command to love God obligates some of us to do something beyond our ability, something that for us is impossible.

The Bible requires the impossible of some, e.g., to love God.

Knowing What God Commands, Why Obey?

Another common objection to religious authoritarianism is that, even if we knew what God commands, there would still be the question of whether what he commands is right, and thus the question of whether we ought to obey out of duty or prudence. (In its standard form, the argument asks whether something is morally right because God commands it or whether he commands it because it's morally right.)

Should we obey God out of duty or prudence?

For those who believe in a morally perfect God who wouldn't command us to do evil, this problem is just a striking way of illustrating the first problem—how to find out what God commands. It should make us pay attention to the fact that in part we have to judge whether specific commands *are* the commands of God by seeing whether they agree with our intuitions about moral right and wrong. Our tendency to accept the Ten Commandments as the word of God stems in part from the fact that the commandments conform somewhat to our rough intuitions concerning adultery, bearing false witness, and so on.

We judge whether X is God's command in part by our intuition of its rightness.

But what if the Bible told us to lie, steal, and kill whenever it suits our purposes, no matter how much harm that may cause others? In that case, we'd be much less inclined to think of the Bible and its commandments as the word of God. What this seems to mean is that we have to evaluate given interpretations in terms of our own moral sentiments. But if we do that, we'll find out how we ourselves feel about moral right and wrong, not what God commands. (The issue is not academic, because many find the God described in the Old Testament in particular to be somewhat less than perfect, in fact saying things many find morally repugnant. One example is the statement "For I the Lord thy God am a jealous God, visiting the inequities of

If the Bible told us to lie, steal, etc., could it be God's word?

the fathers upon the children unto the third and fourth generation of them that hate me.")

2. Egoism

Egoism: We ought to benefit ourselves the most possible.

Many of us grow up being taught some form of religious authoritarianism. But as we see more of life, see the incredible amount of suffering and immorality around us, notice that the immoral often seem to do better than the moral, and notice the great differences between the moral codes of the various groups and religions, some of us become cynical and begin to see our duty as that of "looking out for Number One." This sort of cynicism is consistent with the moral theory called **egoism,** roughly the theory that everyone ought to do whatever is likely to benefit themselves the most, however it affects others. (Sometimes this cynicism is expressed in the belief that there is no such thing as morality, no moral facts—nothing that would make a moral statement right or wrong. Morality, according to the cynical, is a sham or delusion, or even a trap set by the clever to manipulate the gullible.)

Is benefit pleasure? Self-fulfillment?

Although the main thrust of egoism is clear, care is needed in spelling out details. There is first the question of what sort of benefit egoists are supposed to try to maximize for themselves. Some say pleasure and the reduction of pain, the hedonistic version, others self-fulfillment or the best possible satisfaction of our overall desires and goals. Second, there is the question of altruistic acts (acts intended to benefit someone else at the expense of the doer). Does a sensible egoism permit altruistic acts, or perhaps even require them? There are two sorts of cases where egoism would seem to require us to be altruistic. The first is where we expect our altruism to be reciprocated, so that our altruism is required by *prudence*, by the long-term expectation of overall personal gain. (An example is someone who does favors for a business acquaintance, expecting favors in return.)

Does egoism allow prudent altruism?

Does egoism allow imprudent altruism?

The other sort of case is simply where a person *desires* to benefit someone else, say, a close relative, friend, or lover. According to what is perhaps the most sensible version of egoism, our duty is to maximize pleasure for ourselves, doing good for others when we feel that it is just a way to maximize our own pleasure (assuming we're normal and get satisfaction from helping those we care about).

The German philosopher Immanuel Kant (1724–1804) believed that a moral imperative could not be merely hypothetical or "iffy" (as is the imperative "If you want to win an election, flatter the voters") but must hold categorically, with no if's about it, and thus be in his terms a categorical imperative. In the following excerpt from The Fundamental Principles of the Metaphysic of Morals *(translated by T. K. Abbott), Kant attempts to discover the content of the categorical imperative by means of pure reason alone, without regard for anything peculiar to human nature.*

Immanuel Kant: THE CATEGORICAL IMPERATIVE

. . . We will first inquire whether the mere conception of a categorical imperative may not perhaps supply us also with the formula of it, containing the proposition which alone can be a categorical imperative. . . .

The mere conception of a categorical imperative tells us its content: the necessity that maxims conform to the law itself.

When I conceive a hypothetical imperative, in general I do not know beforehand what it will contain until I am given the condition. But when I conceive a categorical imperative, I know at once what it contains. For as the imperative contains besides the law only the necessity that the maxims shall conform to this law, while the law contains no conditions restricting it, there remains nothing but the general statement that the maxim of the action should conform to a universal law, and it is this conformity alone that the imperative properly represents as necessary.

There is therefore but one categorical imperative, namely, this: *Act only on that maxim whereby thou canst at the same time will that it should become a universal law.* . . .

The categorical imperative: Act only on universalizable maxims.

We will now enumerate a few duties, adopting the usual division of them into duties to ourselves and to others, and into perfect and imperfect duties.

1. A man reduced to despair by a series of misfortunes feels wearied of life, but is still so far in possession of his reason that he can ask himself whether it would not be contrary to his duty to himself to take his own life. Now he inquires whether the maxim of his action could become a universal law of nature. His maxim is: From self-love I adopt it as a principle to shorten my life when its longer duration is likely to bring more evil than satisfaction. It is asked then simply whether this principle founded on self-love can become a universal law of nature. Now we see at once that a system of nature of which it should be a law to destroy life by means of the very feeling whose special nature it is to impel to the improvement of life would contradict itself, and therefore could not exist as a system of nature; hence that maxim cannot possibly exist as a universal law of nature, and consequently would be wholly inconsistent with the supreme principle of all duty.

Is suicide moral? The maxim would be: Take my life if self-love is benefited. But this can't be universalized because then the feeling (self-love) intended to further life would destroy it, which is contradictory.

Is it moral to borrow money not intending to repay? No, because the maxim would be: I'll borrow and promise to repay not intending to. And this can't be universalized without contradiction, because then promising would become impossible.

2. Another finds himself forced by necessity to borrow money. He knows that he will not be able to repay it, but sees also that nothing will be lent to him, unless he promises stoutly to repay it in a definite time. He desires to make this promise, but he has still so much conscience as to ask himself: Is it not unlawful and inconsistent with duty to get out of a difficulty in this way? Suppose, however, that he resolves to do so, then the maxim of his action would be expressed thus: When I think myself in want of money, I will borrow money and promise to repay it, although I know that I never can do so. Now this principle of self-love or of one's own advantage may perhaps be consistent with my whole future welfare; but the question now is, Is it right: I change then the suggestion of self-love into a universal law, and state the question thus: How would it be if my maxim were a universal law? Then I see at once that it could never hold as a universal law of nature, but would necessarily contradict itself. For supposing it to be a universal law that everyone when he thinks himself in a difficulty should be able to promise whatever he pleases, with the purpose of not keeping his promise, the promise itself would become impossible, as well as the end that one might have in view in it, since no one would consider that anything was promised to him but would ridicule all such statements as vain pretences. . . .

Is it moral not to help the poor? No, because the will would contradict itself in universalizing the maxim of this act, since we may need help ourselves some-time.

4. A fourth, who is in prosperity, while he sees that others have to contend with great wretchedness and that he could help them, thinks: What concern is it of mine? Let everyone be as happy as Heaven pleases, or as he can make himself; I will take nothing from him nor even envy him, only I do not wish to contribute anything to his welfare or to his assistance in distress! . . . But although it is possible that a universal law of nature might exist in accordance with that maxim, it is impossible to *will* that such a principle should have the universal validity of a law of nature. For a will which resolved this would contradict itself, inasmuch as many cases might occur in which one would have need of the love and sympathy of others, and in which, by such a law of nature, sprung from his own will, he would deprive himself of all hope of the aid he desires.

The maxims of some actions can't even be conceived without contradiction, while others can't be willed without contradiction.

These are a few of the many actual duties, or at least what we regard as such, which obviously fall into two classes on the one principle that we have laid down. We must be *able to will* that a maxim of our action should be a universal law. This is the canon of the moral appreciation of the action generally. Some actions are of such a character that their maxim cannot without contradiction be even *conceived* as a universal law of nature, far from it being possible that we should *will* that it *should* be so. In others this intrinsic impossibility is not found, but still it is impossible to *will* that their maxim should be raised to the universality of a law of nature, since such a will would contradict itself. It is easily seen that the former violate strict or rigorous (inflexible) duty; the latter only laxer (meritorious) duty. Thus it has been completely shown by these examples how all duties depend as regards the nature of the obligation (not the object of the action) on the same principle. . . .

[It] is extremely important that we must not allow ourselves to think of deducing the reality of this principle [the categorical imperative] from the *particular attributes of human nature*. For duty is to be a practical, unconditional necessity of action; it must therefore hold for all rational beings (to whom an imperative can apply at all), and *for this reason only* be also a law for all human wills. On the contrary, whatever is deduced from the particular natural characteristics of humanity, from certain feelings and propensions, nay, even, if possible, from any particular tendency proper to human reason, and which need not necessarily hold for the will of every rational being; this may indeed supply us with a maxim, but not with a law; with a subjective principle on which we may have a propension and inclination to act, but not with an objective principle on which we should be *enjoined* to act, even though all our propensions, inclinations, and natural dispositions were opposed to it. . . .

The categorical imperative doesn't follow from human nature, but must hold for all rational beings.

Supposing, however, that there were something *whose existence* has *in itself* an absolute worth, something which, being *an end in itself*, could be a source of definite laws, then in this and this alone would lie the source of a possible categorical imperative, i.e., a practical law. . . .

If then there is a supreme practical principle or, in respect of the human will, a categorical imperative, it must be one which, being drawn from the conception of that which is necessarily an end for everyone because it is *an end in itself*, constitutes an *objective* principle of will, and can therefore serve as a universal practical law. The foundation of this principle is: *rational nature exists as an end in itself*. Man necessarily conceives his own existence as being so: so far then this is a *subjective* principle of human actions. But every other rational being regards its existence similarly, just on the same rational principle that holds for me: so that it is at the same time an objective principle, from which as a supreme practical law all laws of the will must be capable of being deduced. Accordingly the practical imperative will be as follows: *So act as to treat humanity, whether in thine own person or in that of any other, in every case as an end withal, never as means only*. . . .

Rational nature exists as an end in itself. We think of our own existence this way (subjective principle), but others do also making it an objective principle to treat people as ends, never just means.

Egoists believe we have no moral duty to others.

However, what egoists have to agree on, to be egoists, concerns the moral concepts of *fairness* and *justice* (as well as other moral concepts, such as retribution). For the basic idea behind egoism is that there is no *moral duty* requiring us to do what we otherwise wouldn't want to do; it isn't that we should never act altruistically. It's as though egoists want to tell us that if we happen to have any feelings of *duty* or *obligation* toward others (as opposed to just nice feelings or the desire to help them), we ought to lie down and wait till they go away. In short, egoism tells us that we have no moral duties toward others; our moral duty, if we have one, is to always look out for Number One.

Critical Evaluation of Egoism

Egoism is consistent, complete, and precise, but not intuitive. It doesn't take account of our sense of fairness or justice.

Egoism has the virtue of being a more or less consistent, complete, and precise moral theory. The main reason for rejecting it is just that it violates the desire almost all of us have to be *fair*, or *just*, a desire that is often much stronger than competing selfish desires.* If we are to best look out for our own overall strongest interests, we thus have to consider our feelings in favor of fairness and justice in addition to our occasional desires to benefit others. (For example, fairness often seems to require us to keep promises, to fulfill contracts, even when doing so harms us personally.)

Therefore, egoism fails as a moral theory, at least for most of us, even if we accept the idea that we should try to maximize our own interests, because it fails to take account of our sometimes very strong interest in being fair or just to others (at least if they're fair to us).

Psychological Egoism

Psychological egoism: As a matter of fact, we must behave selfishly.

There is an interesting variety of egoism, sometimes called **psychological egoism.** This is the theory that *as a matter of fact* human beings are constructed so that they must behave selfishly. Psychological egoists claim that all actions are in fact selfishly motivated and that unselfish actions are therefore impossible. So they claim that it can't ever be our duty to act unselfishly (because it can't ever be our duty to do the impossible).

---

*For the moment, we beg the objectivity-subjectivity issue discussed later in the chapter. Rejecting egoism for the reason just given is consistent with subjective theories of morality, but perhaps not with objective theories.

In defending psychological egoism, egoists often appeal to cases of apparent altruism that on closer inspection or deeper insight turn out to be selfish, such as the apparently unselfish parents whose real motives for sending their children to college turn out to be status, avoidance of guilt, and financial security in later life.

Much apparent altruism is really selfish.

Psychological Egoism Refuted

There can be no doubt that much of what passes for altruism is really cleverly selfish, as a great deal of modern psychology attests (in particular, regarding recent ideas about self-deception and unconscious motivation). But many apparently altruistic actions cannot be explained in this way. Some parental "sacrifice" surely is selfish, but much more is not, the extreme cases being the legendary mothers who rush into burning buildings to save their children at extreme risk to their own lives. Other classic examples of actions that seem hard to classify as selfish include soldiers who fall on hand grenades to save the lives of buddies; lovers who sacrifice for those they love; and heroic firemen and policemen who save others at great risks to their own necks. It seems then that psychological egoism must be incorrect.

But some altruism seems to be genuine, e.g., mothers sacrificing for children. So psychological egoism fails.

Philosophical Egoism

When confronted with examples like mothers rushing into burning buildings or soldiers falling on hand grenades, some egoists try to save the day by *defining themselves into victory* (although they obviously would not put it that way). That is, having failed to support their theory by appeal to facts about human nature, they support it by subtle manipulation of the meanings of key words or of the content of key concepts.

For example, philosophical egoists argue that even acts motivated by a mother's desire to benefit her children are selfishly motivated because they're done to satisfy the *mother's* desire for her children's benefit, not, say, to satisfy the desires of her children to benefit themselves. The distinctive claim that makes an egoist a **philosophical egoist** is this: Since all actions are done because of the desires or motives of those who do them, all actions are by their nature selfish, so that it cannot ever be our moral duty to act unselfishly.

Philosophical egoism: All acts are done to satisfy our own desires and motives. Hence, they're selfish.

113

Philosophical Egoism Refuted

Philosophical egoism is a very slippery sort of theory, because it trades on confusion resulting from changes it makes in the meanings of the key expressions "selfish action" and "unselfish action." As defined by a philosophical egoist, *selfish actions* are actions people do to satisfy their own motives or desires; *unselfish actions* (were such actions possible) would be actions entirely divorced from the doers' desires, done rather to satisfy the desires or motives of others.

But the true meanings of these two expressions are crucially different. It isn't that one but not the other is intended to satisfy the desires or motives of the person who does the action—philosophical egoists are right that all actions flow from the desires or motives of the doer. The difference is rather that an *unselfish action* is commonly thought of as one motivated by a desire to help *someone else,* while a selfish action is taken to be one motivated by a desire to help oneself. It is, after all, precisely those motivated by desires to benefit themselves who are generally thought to be selfish, while those frequently motivated by desires to benefit others are thought to be unselfish.

As soon as we bring the usual criteria of selfish and unselfish actions to bear, philosophical egoism falls to pieces. There clearly are many cases of unselfish actions (that is, actions done from a desire of the doer to benefit others), so that we aren't forced to conclude that egoism is correct. Room is thus left for other sorts of moral theories. But the trick that makes philosophical egoism initially plausible (changing the content of key ideas or the meanings of key terms) is worth bearing in mind so that we don't fall prey to it when thinking about other philosophical topics.

3. Utilitarianism

Religious authoritarianism determines moral right and wrong by appeal to God, or religious documents, or experts. Egoism does so by appeal to a person's (primarily) selfish desires and goals. The position called **utilitarianism** (from the word *utility*) classifies actions as either morally right or morally wrong in terms of the degree to which they're either useful or harmful. The utilitarian's basic principle is that the morally right action in a given circumstance is the one that has the greatest usefulness of any action possible in that circumstance.

114

Right Actions Produce the Greatest Benefit for All Concerned

But this statement needs to be explained. There is, first, the question of whose utility is to count in calculating right actions. The answer is that utilitarians intend right actions to be those most useful to *all concerned*, not just to the doers of the actions.* The right action in any situation is the one that will produce the greatest overall utility for human beings without regard for who benefits from it or by how much.

But most useful for all concerned, no matter how the utility is distributed.

There is also the more technical question whether right actions are those which it is *rational to believe* will have the greatest overall utility or those that *in fact* will have. Most utilitarians say right actions are those that in fact will have the greatest utility. But some say it is those that it is rational to believe will have the greatest utility.

It doesn't make much difference which of these meanings we choose, provided we're clear which one has been chosen. If we say it is actions that are in fact most useful, it will follow that sometimes those who do immoral acts won't be blamable—for instance, when they try to do the right thing but fail because of ignorance. And sometimes those who do morally right acts will nevertheless be blamable—for instance, when they intend to bring about less than the most possible utility but by mistake accidentally bring about the most possible.

Act Utilitarianism

There is also the question whether it is particular actions that are to count or types of actions. If we say it is particular actions that count, we get the position called **act utilitarianism,** which requires us to find the particular action in each situation that will have greater utility than any other action we could do in that situation. If we say it is types of actions that count, we get the moral theory called **rule utilitarianism,** which requires us to find the set of moral rules (each rule selects out a type of action) that has greater utility than any other set of moral rules (not necessarily in any particular situation, but in the

Act utilitarianism: Consider the utility of the particular act in question. Rule utilitarianism: Act according to the set of rules that yields more utility than any other set.

---

*There is an older use of the word *utilitarianism,* according to which egoism also is a utilitarian theory, called *egoistic utilitarianism,* as opposed to *universalistic utilitarianism,* today just called *utilitarianism.*

long run). The difference between act and rule utilitarianism will be made clearer when rule utilitarianism is discussed.

(Another technical question concerns whether we should opt for the set of moral rules that, *if followed,* would have the greatest utility, or rather for the set that, in fact, given how people are going to behave, will have the greatest utility. The two are very different because of the large gap between what people ought to do and what they in fact are going to do.)

Hedonistic Theories

Some say utility is self-fulfillment, or more knowledge. But most say it's pleasure and the absence of pain.

Finally, there is the question as to what utility ultimately consists in. Some say it consists in producing self-fulfillment, some an increase in knowledge, beauty, or the like. But most utilitarians have in mind *pleasure* and the absence or reduction of *pain.* For them, utilitarianism requires that our actions be designed to maximize pleasure (or minimize pain). A theory that takes pleasure as the ultimate human good and pain as the ultimate human evil is said to be a **hedonistic** theory. Because most utilitarians intend to be hedonists in this sense, let's concentrate on hedonistic utilitarianism, starting with act utilitarianism.

The Hedonic Calculus

Hedonistic utilitarianism: Choose the act that yields the greatest overall balance of pleasure over pain.

Suppose for a moment that pleasures and pains can be measured and given numerical values, so that we could speak, say, of Mary Smith (a classical music lover) getting 100 units of pleasure from listening to a Mozart piano concerto and John Jones (who is bored by such music) getting − 50 units of pleasure (that is, 50 units of pain). Then before choosing to do some Action A, rather than B, C, or D, act utilitarianism would require that we calculate the total amount of pleasure (pain) likely to result for all those affected by Action A, and then do the same for B, C, and then D. Our duty would be to do whichever of these actions has the highest numerical value and thus will produce the greatest overall pleasure.

Take a trivial case. Suppose Smith is going to treat Jones to a night out, and is about to buy tickets for that evening, the choice being between a football game, a Mozart concert, and the latest movie blockbuster. Smith calculates that she'll get 100 units of pleasure from going to the concert, 50 from seeing the movie, and 75 from the football game. And she calculates that Jones will get 75 units of pleasure from the football game, 125 from the movie, and −50 from the concert. Adding up the figures, she finds the following:

	Concert	Movie	Football
Smith	100	50	75
Jones	−50	125	75
Total	50	175	150

According to act utilitarianism, Smith should buy two tickets to the movie, because that will yield the greatest pleasure for all concerned of any action she can do. Notice that going to the football game is not expected to yield as much pleasure for Smith, the doer of the action, as going to the concert, or as much pleasure for Jones as going to the movie. A completely egoistic theory would require Smith to consider just her own pleasure and thus buy tickets to the concert. A completely altruistic theory would require that she consider just Jones's pleasure and thus buy tickets to the movie. Act utilitarianism requires her to maximize not some particular person's pleasure but rather the *total amount* of pleasure that she can bring about in that situation. She is required to choose the action expected to yield the greatest overall pleasure even if it doesn't maximize her own pleasure.

We shouldn't maximize our own pleasure, but total human pleasure, however distributed.

In the preceding example, only two people are involved. But the procedure is the same for any number. Suppose a third person, John Green, is going to go along with Smith and Jones, and that Smith calculates Green will get 75 units of pleasure from the concert, 50 from the movie, and 100 from the football game. The figures then would look like this:

	Concert	Movie	Football
Smith	100	50	75
Jones	−50	125	75
Green	75	50	100
Total	125	225	250

According to act utilitarianism, in this case Smith should buy tickets to the football game, because that will yield the greatest pleasure for all concerned.

We can't predict pleasures precisely, but still should try to.

Of course, no utilitarian would claim that it's actually possible to give precise numerical values to pleasures or pains expected to result from particular actions. For now at least, and perhaps forever, that is a theoretical limit to reach for. But even now we often can make reasonable estimates. For instance, husbands and wives often can be pretty sure that committing adultery in certain cases will cause much more pain for all concerned (in particular for their spouses) than refraining from that act, perhaps one reason adultery isn't more common than it is.

Pleasures Differ in Intensity, Duration, Fecundity, and Likelihood

More intense pleasures count more.

Correct judgments of pleasures and pains require that several factors be taken into account. First, pleasures and pains differ in *intensity* (sexual intercourse, for instance, generally yields more intense pleasure than does eating Wheaties). More intense pleasures count more than less intense ones.

Longer-lasting pleasures count more.

Second, pleasures differ in *duration*. The pleasure of a good meal is fleeting compared to the satisfaction that results from having created a great work of art. Longer-lasting pleasures obviously count more than shorter ones.

More likely pleasures count more.

Furthermore, some pleasures are *more likely* to result than others. This point is especially important in considering cases where an immediate pleasure competes with a distant one. We're often confronted with a choice between spending money now—say, for an expensive meal we're pretty sure will give us pleasure—and saving it for later, say, to help pay for a world cruise expected to give us much greater pleasure. The future, unfortunately, is uncertain, so that the *likelihood* of actually getting pleasure from a meal eaten today is greater than it is from a world cruise a few years from now. Sometimes, a bird in the hand *is* worth two in the bush. The greater the likelihood that pleasure or pain will result, the greater the weight that should be attached to it. If pleasure A is twice as likely as pleasure B, it should count twice as much in our calculations (other things being equal).

Finally, it's notorious that some pleasures lead to other pleasures, while some lead to pain, and that some pains lead to more pain while some lead to great pleasure. In other words, some pleasures and pains have greater *fecundity*, or *fertility*, than others. In calculating pleasures and pains, we have to consider the long run. There may well be greater pleasure now in going out on the town rather than practicing to improve an income-producing skill, but practicing, itself perhaps a pain in the neck, may lead to much greater pleasure later. (This is one of those things about life we're taught as children that actually turns out to be true.) *More fertile pleasures count more.*

There are thus at least four pleasure factors to consider in deciding which actions will yield the greatest balance of pleasure over pain: intensity, duration, fecundity, and the likelihood of obtaining the pleasure.

Some claim that pleasures differ in quality as well. The nineteenth-century utilitarian John Stuart Mill, perhaps the most important of all utilitarians, believed (this should come as no surprise) that intellectual pleasures were of higher quality than those obtained from, say, eating, carousing, or sexual intercourse. Although few of us are likely to agree with Mill's ranking of pleasures, it is plausible to suppose that the various sorts of pleasure do differ in quality as well as intensity and duration. *Pleasures also differ in quality, some say.*

The Plausibility of Utilitarianism

Utilitarianism is attractive for two reasons. One is that it makes sense of moral obligation by tying it to human benefit. If we think of morality as consisting of a set of rules for right and wrong action, like the cultural rules of a given society, the question arises as to why we should follow such rules. Utilitarianism answers this question by tying morality to human purpose. It says in effect that right actions are those that best further human purposes (in its hedonistic form, this means increasing human pleasure), which seems to be a good reason for complying. *Utilitarianism is attractive because: (1) It ties morality to human benefit;*

In addition, utilitarianism takes account of the essentially social nature of the human predicament. It's part of our nature to have regard for the welfare of at least some other human beings as well as for our own. Indeed, our own welfare seems inextricably tied to that of others in our group (no one can be happy when everyone else is *and (2) it takes account of our social natures, our interest in the welfare of humanity.*

119

miserable). In choosing to do actions that maximize human pleasure, we thus seem to be furthering our interest both in the general welfare of humanity and in our own personal welfare.

Utilitarianism Is Counterintuitive

Utilitarianism seems counterintuitive; it violates our sense of fairness, e.g., it may require the conviction of an innocent suspect, or the breaking of promises.

Several serious objections have been raised against utilitarianism. One is that in certain unusual sorts of cases it violates our sense of fair play or justice, and thus is *counterintuitive.* * Suppose several terrifying sex murders occur, and all evidence points to a particular suspect who is apprehended by the police. What if the prosecuting attorney discovers at the last minute that the suspect is innocent? Should he placate the general public clamoring for the suspect's neck, thus taking the life of an innocent person? Or should he free the suspect and start a riot among the fearful and angry populace? Utilitarianism requires that he convict and punish the suspect if, as is sometimes the case, the resulting overall pleasure-pain ratio will be greater than if the suspect is set free. Yet it seems intuitively wrong to punish an innocent victim.

Or consider the case of a secret promise. Suppose you promise your dying grandmother that you'll deliver her secret fortune to a rich nephew likely to squander it in Las Vegas. Should you keep the promise or should you, perhaps, give the money to a needy family with six hungry children? It would appear that on utilitarian grounds you should break your promise and give the money to the needy family, because more overall pleasure is likely to result. Yet this seems intuitively unfair to your grandmother and her rich nephew, and thus seems to be the morally wrong thing to do.

It's Long-Run Pleasures That Count

Pro utilitarianism: No wrong results if we consider long-term

Some have defended utilitarianism by arguing that those who think it leads to such counterintuitive results fail to consider the long-term consequences of actions. Thus, it has been argued that convicting

---

*Another objection, very hard to evaluate, is that human life itself seems to have great value (witness the extent to which people struggle for even a few more moments of life); yet there seems no straightforward way to equate, say, one day of life with a certain amount of pleasure or satisfaction.

innocent victims weakens the respect for law essential to the satisfactory operation of government, and that breaking a promise weakens the practice of promise keeping essential for many day-to-day activities.

pleasures, e.g., lying weakens the practice of promising.

But this defense is not satisfactory. In the first place, practices such as promise keeping can withstand many breakings—they are made and kept every day even though it's well known that promises are often broken. And second, breaking a promise can't possibly harm the general practice of promising if no one knows that the promise has been broken, as in our example. Similar remarks apply to the prosecuting attorney case. Even the most naive learn sooner or later that justice, although not entirely blind, certainly does not have anything like 20-20 vision. Yet governments do manage to function. In the innocent suspect case, convicting an innocent person the general public firmly believes is guilty can't possibly harm the credibility of the institutions of law or government in the eyes of that public.

Con utilitarianism: (1) Practice of promising can withstand many breakings; and (2) a lie can't harm the practice if it isn't known.

The point of these examples is that morality seems to require something other than just the maximizing of pleasure. In most cases, it also requires the *fairness* of keeping promises, telling the truth, and not convicting innocent suspects. Suppose Actions A and B both yield a great deal of overall pleasure, but that A yields a bit more than B. If the two actions are otherwise pretty much the same except that A involves theft, adultery, and promise breaking, while B does not, then surely B is preferable to A. Yet utilitarianism would require that we do A, because it yields greater pleasure. Most of us would disagree, which shows that most of us find nonutilitarian factors such as fairness or justice relevant to moral deliberation.

So utilitarianism does seem to violate our sense of fairness or justice.

The lifeboat case, where someone must be thrown overboard to keep the boat from sinking, also illustrates this point. If Smith is a convicted mass murderer while Jones has led a saintly life, it seems right to toss the guilty Smith to the sharks, not the innocent Jones. Yet act utilitarianism requires us to throw Jones overboard in cases where doing so will result in greater human pleasure in the long run (perhaps because Smith has a cure for cancer, or knows vital enemy military secrets). The point of this example is that utilitarianism does not take account of our intuition that the *moral standing* of a person (based on his past performance) is relevant to decisions about how to treat that person.

Utilitarianism is wrong because it doesn't account for moral standing.

121

Rule Utilitarianism

Rule utilitarianism: *Choose the set of rules that maximizes pleasure.*

Some of the standard objections to act utilitarianism have led theorists to propose that the principle of utility be applied not to particular actions but to types or classes of actions. They thus adopt *rule utilitarianism*, the theory that an act is right or wrong depending on whether it follows from or violates a correct moral *rule*, where a set of rules becomes correct by having greater long-run utility than all alternative sets.

Arguments in Favor of Rule Utilitarianism

Pro rule utilitarianism: *It can handle counterexamples to act utilitarianism.*

The basic claim of those in favor of rule utilitarianism is that it can handle counterexamples to act utilitarianism. Take the innocent suspect case. Although it may be true that convicting and executing innocent suspects sometimes has greater utility than setting them free, the *rule* always to convict innocent suspects does not appear to have as great utility as the rule to convict only those who are guilty, because the practice of convicting the innocent leads to fear (who can say who the next innocent victim will be?) and disrespect for the law.

The rule to keep promises has greater utility than to break them.

Or take the promise-to-grandmother example. Although breaking one's promise will have greater utility than keeping it in this particular case, the general rule to keep promises has greater utility than the general rule to break them, because the practice of breaking promises tends to destroy the very practice of promising itself.

Objections to Rule Utilitarianism

Con rule utilitarianism: *It doesn't handle objections to act utilitarianism.*

The trouble is that rule utilitarianism doesn't seem to successfully handle the objections to act utilitarianism, and has serious difficulties of its own.

The rule to convict only the guilty has less utility than some complicated rules.

Consider the innocent suspect example. It's true that the general rule to convict only guilty parties has greater utility than the rule to always convict innocent ones as well. But it doesn't have greater utility than several more complicated rules. An example is the rule to convict innocent parties whenever they're believed by the general public to be guilty and failing to do so will create fear and hysteria or lead to a riot. A rule of this kind wouldn't foster disrespect for the law and wouldn't increase fear or hysteria.* Yet it violates strong intuitions many of us have against punishing an innocent suspect.

Or take the promise-to-grandmother example. While it is true that the general rule to keep promises has greater utility than the rule to always break them, it doesn't have greater utility than many other, more complicated, rules. An example is the rule to keep promises, except when breaking them in all likelihood will not be discovered, and (partly because it won't) will probably lead to greater happiness.

The rule to break promises when it won't be known has greater utility, but seems wrong.

Is Rule Utilitarianism Really Different from Act Utilitarianism?

In fact, because there always is a particular sort of rule to appeal to, we can show that rule utilitarianism handles counterexamples no better than does act utilitarianism, and in fact that rule and act utilitarianism are the very same theory under different names.

In fact, rule and act utilitarianism may be the same theory with different names.

In the promise-breaking example, the rule is just to break promises whenever breaking them has greater long-run utility than keeping them.** In the innocent suspect case, the rule is to convict innocent parties whenever doing so has greater long-run utility than setting them free. And so on for other cases.

The point is, the set of rules that truly maximizes utility will tell us in every case to do exactly the same actions required by act utilitarianism. Rule utilitarianism will thus be just as intuitive, or counterintuitive, as act utilitarianism, and in fact will really just be the same theory under a different description and name.

In reply to all this, some utilitarians argue that even if extremely complicated rules will yield greater utility than simpler ones, we may not be able to discover them, or know which particular actions satisfy

Pro rule utilitarianism: We should

---

*Notice that such disrespect would be justified only if it were morally wrong to convict the innocent. But if utility is the criterion of moral rightness, and if convicting innocent parties really does sometimes maximize pleasure, then no disrespect for the law is justified, because convicting an innocent person under those circumstances would be the morally right thing to do. The point is that those who lose respect for the law if it convicts innocent suspects when that will maximize pleasure cannot be utilitarian in their basic instincts.

**Those who object to the reference to utility in this rule should notice that it can be replaced by a description of the kinds of circumstances in which the person promised doesn't know the promise has not been kept, the beneficiary doesn't know of the promise, and so on. We have to know what those circumstances are, otherwise we wouldn't know that this is a case in which breaking the promise will have greater utility than keeping it.

consider only less complicated rules.

Con: If rule utilitarianism requires what act utilitarianism does, they're the same. If not, what reason is there for obeying rule utilitarianism?

Why obey a rule that doesn't maximize utility?

them. Therefore, we should be looking for simpler general rules that come close to maximizing utility. Others argue that there are no such complicated rules to be discovered in the first place.

But both these replies miss the mark. Either rule utilitarianism always tells us to do exactly what act utilitarianism requires, or else it doesn't. If it does, then rule and act utilitarianism are just the same theory described differently, and rule utilitarianism will have the same defects as act utilitarianism. If it doesn't, then rule utilitarianism will sometimes require us to do actions that have less than the most possible utility, and thus violate the very intuition that makes utilitarianism plausible to start with (namely, that morally right actions are those having the greatest possible social usefulness).*

Consider the promise-to-grandmother case. Rule utilitarians have to justify a rule to keep that kind of promise by arguing that it has greater utility than any other possible rule. But if maximum utility is the goal, why accept any rule that ever tells us to do an act likely to have less than the most possible utility? The only reason would be a greater affection for following rules than for maximizing utility, something a utilitarian can't have and remain a utilitarian.

A Hard "What If" Question for Utilitarianism

Whatever the true facts, what if convicting innocent suspects, etc., led to greatest utility? A true utilitarian has to say such acts are our duty, which seems wrong.

Much arguing between utilitarians and their opponents consists in disagreeing about just what utilitarianism tells us to do in certain situations (for instance, in the innocent suspect case). Utilitarians argue that their theory doesn't yield counterintuitive results in these cases when applied to the true facts about the consequences of the various choices open to us. And in truth, no one can be sure about such consequences. Even so, we can still ask "What if" questions. What if (whether or not it ever happens in reality) there are occasional cases in real life in which long-term human benefit is maximized by convicting innocent suspects, by having gladiators fight to the death in the Coliseum before huge, bloodthirsty crowds, or by subverting

---

*This does not mean that it isn't prudent to devise general rules of conduct. In real life, we can't always stop and investigate the long-run consequences of every possible action open to us. We thus need rough-and-ready rules to guide everyday decisions. But a utilitarian should break those rules whenever it's clear that they aren't likely to maximize utility. They thus aren't the kind of rules *rule* utilitarians have in mind.

promises made to dying relatives? A true utilitarian must say that in such cases it would be right to maximize overall human benefit. Anyone who can't swallow that thereby exhibits a taste for justice independent of any taste for increasing human satisfaction, and is therefore not a good candidate for utilitarianism. *

4. Equality

Utilitarians believe that justice is achieved by maximizing utility. Others point to different factors, such as *equality*. However, several different kinds of equality are often appealed to: in particular, equality of pleasure or satisfaction, of wealth or income, and of opportunity.

Ideas about equality in the distribution of pleasures or wealth run into the quick objection that slackers certainly deserve less than hard workers, and those guilty of serious crimes less than the more virtuous.

Equality of Opportunity

But equality of opportunity is another matter. People compete for all sorts of things, in particular for food, mates, and status. Justice, it is claimed, requires that everyone have an equal chance in this competition; in other words, it requires that the competition be *fair*. The "friend" who woos and wins your spouse behind your back doesn't play the mating game (competition) fairly, nor does the person who spreads lies that harm your reputation.

Some claim justice requires equality of opportunity, so that competition will be fair.

Similarly, it's often held that those who grow up in immensely wealthy or powerful families—Rockefellers or Mellons—have an unfair advantage over the rest of us, because their greater power gives them much better opportunities. Henry Ford II quickly rose through ranks of the Ford Motor Company to become its president at age thirty-eight; no one supposed he won that position in a fair competition. Those who cry for equal opportunity believe it is unjust that some get to run the 100-yard dash of life with a 50-yard head start.

Those who have great wealth have an unfair advantage over others.

---

*The same is true of the mass of people if in fact they respond with disrespect for law (as some utilitarians suggest they would) when they find out about such things as the conviction of innocent people.

In this excerpt from his book Utilitarianism, *English philosopher John Stuart Mill (1806–1873) explains and attempts to prove the principle of utility.*

John Stuart Mill: **WHAT UTILITARIANISM IS**

Right actions promote happiness; wrong ones just the opposite. Happiness equals pleasure and absence of pain.

. . . The creed which accepts as the foundation of morals "utility" or the "greatest happiness principle" holds that actions are right in proportion as they tend to promote happiness; wrong as they tend to produce the reverse of happiness. By happiness is intended pleasure and the absence of pain; by unhappiness, pain and privation of pleasure. . . . pleasure and freedom from pain are the only things desirable as ends; . . . all desirable things . . . are desirable either for pleasure inherent in themselves or as means to the promotion of pleasure and the prevention of pain. . . .

Some pleasures are of higher quality than others.

If I am asked what . . . makes one pleasure more valuable than another, merely as a pleasure . . . there is but one possible answer. Of two pleasures, if there be one to which all or almost all who have experience of both give a decided preference, irrespective of any feeling of moral obligation to prefer it, that is the more desirable pleasure. . .

Those who can enjoy both higher- and lower-quality pleasures prefer the higher. They'd rather be a human being dissatisfied than a pig satisfied. The pig has a different opinion because he knows only one side.

Now it is an unquestionable fact that those who are equally acquainted with and equally capable of appreciating and enjoying both do give a most marked preference to the manner of existence which employs their higher faculties. Few human creatures would consent to be changed into any of the lower animals for a promise of the fullest allowance of a beast's pleasures; no intelligent human being would consent to be a fool, no instructed person would be an ignoramus, no person of feeling and conscience would be selfish and base, even though they should be persuaded that the fool, the dunce, or the rascal is better satisfied with his lot than they are with theirs. . . It is better to be a human being dissatisfied than a pig satisfied; better to be Socrates dissatisfied than a fool satisfied. And if the fool, or the pig, are of a different opinion, it is because they only know their own side of the question. The other party to the comparison knows both sides. . . .

OF WHAT SORT OF PROOF THE PRINCIPLE OF UTILITY IS SUSCEPTIBLE

We can't prove ultimate ends by reason or by experience.

Questions of ultimate ends do not admit of proof. . . . To be incapable of proof by reasoning is common to all first principles, to the first premises of our knowledge, as well as to those of our conduct. But the former . . . may be the subject of a direct appeal to the faculties which judge of fact—namely, our senses and our internal consciousness. Can an appeal be made to the same faculties on questions of practical ends? . . . Questions about ends are, in other words, questions about what things are desirable. The utilitarian doctrine is that happiness is desirable, and the only things desirable, as an end; all other things being only desirable as means to that end. What ought to be required of this doctrine, what conditions is it requisite that the doctrine should fulfill—to make good its claim?

Utilitarianism says happiness is the only desirable end. Can this be proved?

The only proof capable of being given that an object is visible is that people actually see it. The only proof that a sound is audible is that people hear it; and so of the other sources of our experience. In like manner, I apprehend, the sole evidence it is possible to produce that anything is desirable is that people do actually desire it. If the end which the utilitarian doctrine proposes to itself were not, in theory and practice, acknowledged to be an end, nothing could ever convince any person that it was so. No reason can be given why the general happiness is desirable, except that each person, so far as he believes it to be attainable, desires his own happiness. This, however, being a fact, we have not only all the proof which the case admits of, but all which it is possible to require, that happiness is a good, that each person's happiness is a good to that person, and the general happiness, therefore, a good to the aggregate of all persons. Happiness has made out its title as *one* of the ends of conduct and, consequently, one of the criteria of morality.

The only proof a thing is desirable is that people desire it.

Each person desires his own happiness. So a given person's happiness is a good to that person and the general happiness a good to the collection of all persons.

But it has not, by this alone, proved itself to be the sole criterion. To do that, it would seem, by the same rule, necessary to show not only that people desire happiness, but that they never desire anything else. Now it is palpable that they do desire things which, in common language, are decidedly distinguished from happiness. They desire, for example, virtue and the absence of vice no less readily than pleasure and the absence of pain . . .

But people desire other things, like virtue.

But does the utilitarian doctrine deny that people desire virtue, or maintain that virtue is not a thing to be desired? The very reverse. It maintains not only that virtue is to be desired, but that it is to be desired disinterestedly, for itself. . . . This opinion is not, in the smallest degree, a departure from the happiness principle. The ingredients of happiness are very various, and each of them is desirable in itself, and not merely when considered as swelling an aggregate. The principle of utility does not mean that any given pleasure, as music, for instance, or any given exemption from pain, as for example health, is to be looked upon as means to a collective something termed happiness, and to be desired on that account. They are desired and desirable in and for themselves; besides being means, they are a part of the end. Virtue, according to the utilitarian doctrine, is not naturally and originally part of the end, but it is capable of becoming so; and is desired and cherished. . . .

This doesn't contradict the happiness principle. For virtue, health, etc., are part of the end of happiness.

Of course, spelling out what constitutes equality of opportunity in more complicated cases is much more difficult and has generated mountains of debate.

Equality May Conflict with Other Goods

But what happens when equality of opportunity conflicts with other goods?

Furthermore, equality of opportunity has to be weighed against other moral considerations with which it sometimes conflicts. One reason people work and save is to give their children greater opportunities for success. It seems fair that those who honestly put aside a nice nest egg be allowed to spend it on their children if that is their desire. Yet in doing so they give their children a great advantage in competition with poorer children. There is thus a conflict between the "right" of parents to use their money as they see fit, and the right of young people to a fair chance in their competition with others. The problem is how to resolve this and similar conflicts, a problem that as yet has not received a widely accepted answer.

5. Forward- versus Backward-Looking Theories

Utilitarianism is forward-looking and doesn't take account of moral standing, as do backward-looking theories.

Utilitarianism is a *forward-looking* or *consequentialist* moral theory. It tells us that our actions are right or wrong because of their future consequences. (It looks to the past only to learn what the consequences will be of doing a particular action now.) One objection raised against utilitarianism, as we saw, is that it fails to take account of how people have behaved toward each other in the past. That is, it fails to take account of the *moral standing* of those affected by our actions. Theories that do take moral standing into account can be said to be *backward-looking* theories.

The point of backward-looking theories is that justice or fairness requires us to treat people differently depending on how they've dealt with us and others in the past and on how we've dealt with them.

6. Retribution

Retribution: repaying an unfair harm by punishment.

A key notion in this backward-looking conception of justice or fairness is *retribution*. In the sense intended here, **retribution** is the "repayment" of immoral behavior by punishment (thinking of blame as a kind of punishment). (In a wider sense, retribution also includes re-payment of especially meritorious behavior by a reward—thinking of praise as a kind of reward.) Examples are the punishment of traitors by death, murderers by life imprisonment, thieves by several years in jail, drunk drivers by thirty days in the clink, and little kids caught lying by a week's lost allowance. In retribution, the punishment must fit the crime, because it involves a *paying back,* a *re*-tribution.

The punishment must fit the crime because it's a retribution, a paying back.

Retribution Differs from Deterrence

Retribution should not be confused with its cousin **deterrence,** which is the discouraging of undesired behavior by harming those caught doing it. An example is a parking ticket, which is given to discourage illegal parking, not to punish immoral drivers.

Of course, punishment usually does tend to discourage wrongdoing, which may well be the reason for the evolution of a strong sense of retribution. But a true retributivist argues for punishment on the grounds of its "rightness" or "fittingness," or because of a sense of moral outrage or betrayal.

Deterrence: harming wrongdoers to discourage wrongdoing.

Retributivists don't harm wrongdoers to deter, but because they deserve punishment.

Utilitarians Opt for Deterrence

It's quite clear that utilitarians believe in deterrence—in harming wrongdoers to discourage future wrongdoing—but not in punishment, at least not in the sense intended here. For punishment sometimes produces more overall harm than benefit (in particular, the satisfaction gained by the harmed parties is often less than the pain inflicted on the person punished). Even when it produces more benefit than harm it often fails to *maximize* benefit (because other actions would produce even more human satisfaction). And anyway, the purpose of a utilitarian system of penalties is to discourage wrongdoing, and thus to increase overall human benefit; the purpose of a strictly retributivist system of punishment is to repay wrongdoers for their having immorally harmed us.

Utilitarians deny the rightness of retribution, and opt for deterrence when it will maximize pleasure in the long run.

7. Reciprocity and Contracts

It is generally held that those who freely enter into agreements with others are morally obligated to keep them—other things being equal.

Examples are married couples who agree not to have sex with anyone else, and businesspeople who borrow money on a promise to pay it back with interest. It is also generally believed that lying and other kinds of deceptive behavior are morally wrong under most circumstances. But there is disagreement as to what it is about lying or breaking promises that makes them immoral. Some, for instance, claim that there is something intrinsically wrong with lying, or failing to keep promises; others argue that lying and cheating are wrong, when they are, because of the evil consequences they produce.

Are lying, etc., wrong intrinsically or because of their evil consequences?

Reciprocity

Moral obligations arise because of reciprocal agreements.

But according to another view, moral obligations arise in these and similar cases because of some prior agreements or bargains involving **reciprocity.** Thus, in a typical case, Smith may agree to lend Jones money now in the expectation that Jones will pay it back with interest later, so that both parties to the agreement benefit. (Cooperative ventures also usually involve some form of reciprocity.)

Agreements may be explicit or implicit.

In the case of borrowing money, the reciprocal obligations are generally *explicit* ("I loan you money now, you repay with interest later"). In the case of not lying, they're usually *implicit* ("I'll tell you the truth, you tell me the truth").

Reciprocity is backward-looking.

Reciprocity, like retribution, is a backward-looking idea. For example, in the absence of any prior agreement, explicit or implicit, there isn't any reason to give back money someone has given us, or to tell the truth when asked a question. (No one feels obligated to tell the truth to enemy soldiers in wartime or to business competitors who ask about trade secrets.)

Contract Theories

Contract theory: Moral obligations arise from reciprocal agreements, e.g., social contracts.

According to what are sometimes called **contract** theories of morality, all moral obligations arise from reciprocal arrangements of one kind or another. The best-known contract theories are *social contract* theories, which derive the legitimacy of governments and other social arrangements from explicit or implied agreements among the citizens. But some argue that all moral obligations arise from contracts explicit or implicit. One such contract theory is based on the idea that human beings are essentially social animals who must cooperate with others of their species, in particular others of their own group, in order to survive and have a chance for a decent life.* Yet it is precisely (most of) these other human beings who are our most serious competitors for the necessities as well as the goodies of life—in particular food, shelter, status, safety (especially from other human beings), and mates. Morality, on this view, is the oil needed to grease the cooperative machinery necessary for human social survival.

Morality oils the machinery of human cooperation.

In addition to the idea of reciprocity, a good contract theory should appeal to the notions of fairness and retribution, already mentioned. In the first place, a person is obligated only to live up to *fair* arrangements. It would be foolish of someone to live up to an arrangement that takes much more than it gives back. (It would be foolish, for example, to think slaves have *obligations*—as opposed to reasons of prudence—forcing obedience to their masters, given the patent unfairness of slave societies.) It's a different matter, of course, if a person freely agrees to an arrangement knowing it is unfair. And, second, it is precisely the failure of others to live up to fair reciprocal arrangements, with resulting harm to others, that generates the sense of outrage underlying the practice of retribution.

We're obligated only to live up to fair agreements. Our sense of retribution arises because of outrage at cheating on fair agreements.

Thus, the ideas of fair reciprocity and of retribution go together nicely to form a coherent moral theory. Our duty, according to this sort of contract theory, is to make only fair agreements, and to keep all fair arrangements we make or otherwise assent to (provided others do, or are likely to). Furthermore, we're justified in striking back to gain retribution against those who fail to keep fair bargains they've made with us. (It's exactly the temptation to cheat on such bargains by not reciprocating that constitutes the urge to sin—sinning, on this view, is the selfish violation of fair contracts.)

Basic moral principle: Make only fair agreements, and keep them provided others do.

We're justified in striking back at cheaters.

Because contract theories (and theories concerning equal opportunity) are usually discussed in the context of social or political philosophy (where they're referred to as *social* contract theories), let's put off further discussion on these theories until later, noting at this point that the particular contract theory just referred to, based on an evolutionary theory of human nature, provides a ready answer to the difficult question of what would cause anyone to be motivated to sacrifice selfish interests to satisfy moral obligations when they can get

The reason for keeping agreements with others is our sense of fairness, which makes possible the human ecological niche.

---

*See the author's "Making the World Safe for Reciprocity," in *Reason and Responsibility*, 6th ed., ed. Joel Feinberg (Belmont, Calif.: Wadsworth, 1981).

The nineteenth-century German philosopher Friedrich Nietzsche believed that the usual moral idea about not harming or exploiting others is "a Will to the denial of life," a "slave morality" almost the opposite of the "master morality" he advocated for a "select class of beings." This excerpt is from Beyond Good and Evil *(translated by Helen Zimmern).*

Friedrich Nietzsche: MASTER AND SLAVE MORALITY

Every higher civilization arose when barbarians—more complete men, or beasts—attacked and enslaved physically and psychically weaker peoples.

Every elevation of the type "man," has hitherto been the work of an aristocratic society—and so will it always be—a society believing in a long scale of gradations of rank and differences of worth among human beings, and requiring slavery in some form or other. . . . Let us acknowledge unprejudicedly how every higher civilisation hitherto has *originated!* Men with a still natural nature, barbarians in every terrible sense of the word, men of prey, still in possession of unbroken strength of will and desire for power, threw themselves upon weaker, more moral, more peaceful races. . . .

Master morality considers enslavement of the weak to be for the sake of the superior masters. It's sensible for those of equal worth and power to treat each other well. But as a basic social idea, this is a denial of life, which is a will to power. We exploit by nature.

The essential thing, however, in a good and healthy aristocracy is that it should *not* regard itself as a function either of the kingship or the commonwealth, but as the *significance* and highest justification thereof—that it should therefore accept with a good conscience the sacrifice of a legion of individuals, who, *for its sake,* must be suppressed and reduced to imperfect men, to slaves and instruments. . . .

To refrain mutually from injury, from violence, from exploitation, and put one's will on a par with that of others: this may result in a certain rough sense in good conduct among individuals when the necessary conditions are given (namely, the actual similarity of the individuals in amount of force and degree of worth, and their co-relation within one organisation). As soon, however, as one wished to take this principle more generally, and if possible even as *the fundamental principle of society*, it would immediately disclose what it really is—namely, a Will to the *denial* of life, a principle of dissolution and decay. Here one must think profoundly to the very basis and resist all sentimental weakness: life itself is *essentially* appropriation, injury, conquest of the strange and weak, suppression, severity, obtrusion of peculiar forms, incorporation, and at the least, putting it mildest, exploitation . . . life *is* precisely Will to Power.

Two types of morality: master morality and slave morality.

In a tour through the many finer and coarser moralities which have hitherto prevailed or still prevail on the earth, I found certain traits recurring regularly together, and connected with one another, until finally two primary types revealed themselves to me, and a radical distinction was brought to light.

There is *master-morality* and *slave-morality*;—I would at once add, however, that in all higher and mixed civilisations, there are also attempts at the reconciliation of the two moralities; but one finds still oftener the confusion and mutual misunderstanding of them, indeed, sometimes their close juxtaposition—even in the same man, within one soul. The distinctions of moral values have either originated in a ruling caste, pleasantly conscious of being different from the ruled—or among the ruled class, the slaves and dependents of all sorts. In the first case, when it is the rulers who determine the conception "good," it is the exalted, proud disposition which is regarded as the distinguishing feature, and that which determines the order of rank. The noble type of man separates from himself the beings in whom the opposite of this exalted, proud disposition displays itself: he despises them. Let it at once be noted that in this first kind of morality the antithesis "good" and "bad" means practically the same as "noble" and "despicable";—the antithesis "good" and *"evil"* is of a different origin. The cowardly, the timid, the insignificant, and those thinking merely of narrow utility are despised; moreover, also, the distrustful, with their constrained glances, the self-abasing, the dog-like kind of men who let themselves be abused, the mendicant flatterers, and above all the liars;—it is a fundamental belief of all aristocrats that the common people are untruthful. "We truthful ones"—the nobility in ancient Greece called themselves. . . . A morality of the ruling class, however, is more especially foreign and irritating to present-day taste in the sternness of its principle that one has duties only to one's equals; that one may act towards beings of a lower rank, towards all that is foreign, just as seems good to one, or "as the heart desires," and in any case "beyond good and evil": it is here that sympathy and similar sentiments can have a place. The ability and obligation to exercise prolonged gratitude and prolonged revenge—both only within the circle of equals—artfulness in retaliation, *raffinement* of the idea in friendship, a certain necessity to have enemies (as outlets for the emotions of envy, quarrelsomeness, arrogance—in fact, in order to be a good *friend*): all these are typical characteristics of the noble morality, which, as has been pointed out, is not the morality of "modern ideas," and is therefore at present difficult to realise, and also to unearth and disclose.—It is otherwise with the second type of morality, *slave-morality.* Supposing that the abused, the oppressed, the suffering, the unemancipated, the weary, and those uncertain of themselves, should moralise, what will be the common element in their moral estimates? Probably a pessimistic suspicion with regard to the entire situation of man will find expression, perhaps a condemnation of man, together with his situation. The

Master morality equates good with noble and bad with despicable; cowards are despised.

In its treatment of inferiors, master morality is "beyond good and evil."

Slave morality is pessimistic, condemning, distrustful of good.

slave has an unfavourable eye for the virtues of the powerful; he has a scepticism and distrust, a *refinement* of distrust of everything "good" that is there honoured—he would fain persuade himself that the very happiness there is not genuine. On the other hand, *those* qualities which serve to alleviate the existence of sufferers are brought into prominence and flooded with light; it is here that sympathy, the kind, helping hand, the warm heart, patience, diligence, humility, and friendliness attain to honour; for here these are the most useful qualities, and almost the only means of supporting the burden of existence. Slave-morality is essentially the morality of utility. Here is the seat of the origin of the famous antithesis "good" and *"evil"*:—power and dangerousness are assumed to reside in the evil, a certain dreadfulness, subtlety, and strength, which do not admit of being despised. According to slave-morality, therefore, the "evil" man arouses fear; according to master-morality, it is precisely the "good" man who arouses fear and seeks to arouse it, while the bad man is regarded as the despicable being. . . . A last fundamental difference: the desire for *freedom*, the instinct for happiness and the refinements of the feeling of liberty belong as necessarily to slave-morals and morality, as artifice and enthusiasm in reverence and devotion are the regular symptoms of an aristocratic mode of thinking and estimating.—Hence we can understand without further detail why love *as a passion* . . . must absolutely be of noble origin. . . .

At the risk of displeasing innocent ears, I submit that egoism belongs to the essence of a noble soul; I mean the unalterable belief that to a being such as "we," other beings must naturally be in subjection, and have to sacrifice themselves. The noble soul accepts the fact of his egoism without question, and also without consciousness of harshness, constraint, or arbitrariness therein, but rather as something that may have its basis in the primary law of things:—if he sought a designation for it he would say: "It is justice itself." He acknowledges under certain circumstances, which made him hesitate at first, that there are other equally privileged ones; as soon as he has settled this question of rank, he moves among those equals and equally privileged ones with the same assurance, as regards modesty and delicate respect, which he enjoys in intercourse with himself. . . . The noble soul gives as he takes. . . . The notion of "favour" has . . . neither significance nor good repute; there may be a sublime way of letting gifts as it were light upon one from above, and of drinking them thirstily like dewdrops; but for those arts and displays the noble soul has no aptitude. His egoism hinders him here: in general, he looks "aloft" unwillingly—he looks either *forward*, horizontally and deliberately, or downwards—*he knows that he is on a height.*

away with not doing so. According to this theory, the evolution of a sense of fairness concerning the reciprocal arrangements that allow society to function well, and of feelings of guilt when failing to keep such agreements, promoted the group cooperation required to obtain the necessities of life and to compete successfully with surrounding groups. The human ecological niche could not have evolved without the (nonkin) altruism made possible by the evolution of these moral sentiments.

8. Metaethical Theories

The moral theories we've discussed so far are said to be **prescriptive** or **normative** theories. They tell us which actions are morally right and which morally wrong. Utilitarianism, for example, tells us that actions maximizing benefit for all concerned are right, all others being wrong.

Prescriptive theories say which acts are right and which wrong.

But there is another sort of moral theory, called **metaethical** or **second-order** theory, that considers questions *about* normative theories or about the statements or judgments they prescribe. Typical metaethical questions concern the meanings of moral terms such as *right, wrong, good, bad,* and *ought,* how we can justify particular moral claims or theories; and whether moral truths, if there are any, are objective or merely subjective. Let's concentrate here on the question whether moral claims and theories are objective or subjective.

Metaethical theories tell us about prescriptive theories.

Metaethical question: Are there objective moral truths?

Objectivity versus Subjectivity

Perhaps the most popular tradition in Western philosophy takes moral values, moral right and wrong, to be objective, not merely subjective. According to this tradition, something about the very fabric or nature of the universe, or of rationality itself (as opposed to a given person's perhaps defective reasoning ability), *prescribes* moral right and wrong, so that we all are obligated to obey, whatever may be our peculiar individual makeup.

Some say moral values are objective, following from the nature of reality or of reasoning.

But there have always been those who have argued that moral values, moral right and wrong, are subjective, and thus might differ from person to person. (However, it is often held that basic human

135

Others say moral values are subjective.

moral values tend to be quite similar—every culture, for instance, has rules against adultery, theft, lying, and so on—so that a certain amount of intersubjective agreement concerning subjective values is possible.)

Factual type statements, like "the earth is a sphere" are objective because something in the world makes them true.

Although the concepts of objectivity and subjectivity are notoriously vague and ambiguous, what is at issue can perhaps be grasped through examples. Take the statement mentioned at the beginning of the chapter; namely, "The earth is roughly a sphere." Statements of this kind are almost universally regarded as **objective,** meaning that something about the way the world is, in this case its roughly spherical shape, makes them true (if they are true). We may believe the earth is flat, wish that it were flat, or pretend that it is flat, but the objective fact will remain that the earth is a sphere. No opinion to the contrary, no belief, no wish, can change that fact.

But statements of taste, like "steak tastes good" are subjective. We can differ over them and both be right.

But now consider the statement "Steak tastes better than roast beef." Statements of this kind are often held to be **subjective,** in that they merely express the taste or opinion of the speaker rather than an objective fact about the world (other than the fact that steak tastes better to that speaker). If you say steak tastes better than roast beef and I say the reverse, we both may be right in that steak tastes better to you while roast beef tastes better to me. (This claimed subjectivity of taste is the reason for the popularity of the saying that there's no disputing about taste.)

Moral subjectivists say moral values are like tastes. There is no objective right or wrong about them. They reflect our feelings or responses, not an independent reality.

Similarly, an ethical subjectivist might argue that if you say it's always wrong to lie, and I say lying is sometimes all right, we both may be right, in that you feel one way about lying and I another. We may fight about it, of course. You may want to hold me to your standard, and blame me if I fail to live up to it. And I may try to convince you that you "really" don't feel lying is always wrong, perhaps by citing cases where this feeling conflicts with some stronger feeling. The point is that, according to subjectivists, there is no objective right or wrong about the matter independent of our feelings about it. There isn't anything about the nature of reality, other than your feeling as you do and my feeling as I do, that can be appealed to, unlike the case where we might disagree about the shape of earth. (If I insist the earth is flat, you can take me down to the sea and show me how the tops of ships come into view before the rest, or send me on a round-the-world cruise, and settle the matter. There is no comparable way to settle moral disputes, according to subjectivists.)

Moral Subjectivism Is a Negative Thesis

From what we've said so far, it should be clear that moral subjectivists deny the existence of something rather than asserting the existence of something else. They deny the existence of objective moral values— values that exist independently of how we feel about them, as 2 plus 2 equals 4 no matter how we feel about it. Their task is thus to show that alleged objective moral values don't exist, or more specifically, that the evidence or reasons given in favor of their existence are not acceptable. Thus, to prove beyond a shadow of a doubt that subjectivism in ethics is true, subjectivists would have to knock down every attempt to establish an objectively based morality, which in practice is next to impossible. Instead, they have attempted to refute the most popular objective theories or tried to show that the various kinds of possibilities are unpromising.

The moral subjectivist's task is to show that objective values don't exist. They try to show particular attempts to prove objectivity fail.

In addition, they've given explanations for the uses of moral terms such as *right, good,* and *ought,* so as to explain why these terms might seem to be objective, or in fact (as some say) are used objectively, even though there is nothing objective for them to refer to. For example, some have pointed to the use of these terms in association with standards of judgment in various fields, as in judging gymnastic or diving competitions; the standards determine what makes one performance better than another but themselves are determined by subjective attraction to qualities such as gracefulness and quickness.

They also show how moral terms come to seem objective, but aren't.

Isn't Justice, or Fairness, Objective?

On first glance, it may appear that moral values can be and indeed surely are objective. Take justice, or fairness. We know very well, it may be claimed, that it's unjust to convict innocent parties—recall the objection to utilitarianism that it would unfairly require punishment of innocent parties. And fair wages, it might be argued, are determined by amount of effort required, or quality or amount of goods produced. So there must be objective criteria for justice, or fairness.

It seems as though justice, or fairness, are objective.

It certainly is true that objective standards of justice of this kind have often been proposed. But suppose two different standards of this kind are put forth. How are we to decide which one we ought to follow? Or, to put the point a different way, having defined justice in some objective way, what justification would there be for saying

137

*But if two
criteria of justice
are proposed,
why choose one
over the other?
Or if we do
define justice
objectively, why
be just rather
than unjust?*

that we ought to try to be just, rather than unjust? What moral principle, or principle of reasoning, could lead us to that conclusion? (This is like the case where rationality is defined in such a way that accepting whatever the village idiot says is considered to be rational; in that case it seemed relevant to ask why anyone would want to be rational.) In other words, although we can easily adopt objective standards of value for justice or fairness, doing so merely shifts the question to why anyone would be obligated to accept those standards.

Everyday Value Terms Are Thought of as Objective

*Even if everyday
moral value
terms are objec-
tive, this doesn't
prove an objec-
tive reality corre-
sponds to them.*

In addition, we can't prove the objectivity of moral values just by appeal to the terms used in everyday, or in philosophical, moral discourse. The fact that someone uses, say, the term *ought* so as to imply objectivity proves nothing about whether there are in fact objective oughts, just as inclusion of the concept of flatness in the conception of the earth proves nothing about the flatness of the earth. Objectivity doesn't arise just because it is claimed to exist. (Some analytic philosophers—to be discussed in Chapter 6—account for the mistaken idea that such statements are objective in terms of a common human tendency to "reify," or project onto the external world, our attitudes or responses to things, as when we say the steak is better tasting than the roast beef, or that the mold on the cheese is disgusting. When coupled with the social nature of moral discourse, this tendency to externalize our own values leads to objectification as a way of getting interpersonal moral agreement.)

What Are Objective Values?

*Attempts to
show values are
objective mask
the lack of con-
nection between
ordinary objec-
tive facts and al-
leged objective
moral values.*

According to subjectivists, attempts to justify claims to objectivity in morality mask the true problem, which is the lack of connection between ordinary objective facts and alleged objective moral facts. Just what is, or conceivably could be, the objective connection between the objective fact of someone beating and maiming a child and the alleged objective fact that such a thing is morally wrong? Or to put it another way, what mysterious faculty sees first the cruelty of such an action, second the wrongness of it, and third the connection between the two?

In Appendix 1 to his Enquiry Concerning the Principles of Morals, *David Hume argues (consistently with the main thrust of his empiricist philosophy as expounded for instance in the excerpt reprinted in Chapter 3 on matters of fact and relations of ideas) that "reason alone can never produce any action, or give rise to volition. . . . Reason is, and ought only to be, the slave of the passions, and can never pretend to any other office than to serve and obey them." Having dethroned reason as the origin of moral right and wrong, he then enthrones moral sentiment in its place, championing the position here called* subjectiv-ism. *(In the last paragraph quoted—from* A Treatise of Human Nature—*he more tightly draws the distinction between that which is and that which ought to be, claiming that no valid principle exists for reasoning from what is to what ought to be.)*

David Hume: REASON IS THE SLAVE OF THE PASSIONS

One principal foundation of moral praise being supposed to lie in the usefulness of any quality or action, it is evident that reason must enter for a considerable share in all decisions of this kind; since nothing but that faculty can instruct us in the tendency of qualities and actions, and point out their beneficial consequences to society and to their possessor. . . .

Since reason is needed to decide the utility of actions, it's needed in making moral decisions.

But though reason, when fully assisted and improved, be sufficient to instruct us in the pernicious or useful tendency of qualities and actions; it is not alone sufficient to produce any moral blame or approbation. Utility is only a tendency to a certain end; and were the end totally indifferent to us, we should feel the same indifference toward the means. It is requisite a *sentiment* should here display itself, in order to give a preference to the useful above the pernicious tendencies. This sentiment can be no other than a feeling for the happiness of mankind, and a resentment of their misery; since these are the different ends which virtue and vice have a tendency to promote. Here therefore *reason* instructs us in the several tendencies of actions, and *humanity* makes a distinction in favour of those which are useful and beneficial.

Reason tells us which acts are useful and which harmful. Sentiment tells us to choose the useful.

[To prove reason alone is not sufficient, consider the following:] It is easy for a false hypothesis to maintain some appearance of truth, while it keeps wholly in generals, makes use of undefined terms, and employs comparisons, instead of instances. This is particularly remarkable in that philosophy, which ascribes the discernment of all moral distinctions to reason alone, without the concurrence of sentiment. It is impossible that, in any particular instance, this hypothesis can so much as be rendered intelligible, whatever specious figure it may make in general declamations and discourses. Examine the crime

The theory that reason alone determines moral right makes no sense for particular cases, e.g., reason alone can never show the demerit in ingratitude.

of *ingratitude,* for instance; which has place, wherever we observe good-will, expressed and known, together with good-offices performed, on the one side, and a return of ill-will or indifference, with ill-offices or neglect on the other: anatomize all these circumstances, and examine, by your reason alone, in what consists the demerit or blame. You never will come to any issue or conclusion.

What is the matter of fact we call crime?

Enquire then, where is that matter of fact which we here call *crime;* point it out; determine the time of its existence; describe its essence or nature; explain the sense of faculty to which it discovers itself. It resides in the mind of the person who is ungrateful. He must, therefore, feel it, and be conscious of it. But nothing is there, except the passion of ill-will or absolute indifference. You cannot say that these, of themselves, always, and in all circumstances, are crimes. No, they are only crimes when directed towards persons who have before expressed and displayed good-will towards us. Consequently, we may infer, that the crime of ingratitude is not any particular individual *fact;* but arises from a complication of circumstances, which, being presented to the spectator, excites the *sentiment* of blame, by the particular structure and fabric of his mind. . . .

And what faculty discovers it? No, we must feel it. Crime is no fact but a sentiment in us aroused by facts.

Virtue then is what pleases us, vice the opposite.

The hypothesis which we embrace is plain. It maintains that morality is determined by sentiment. It defines virtue to be *whatever mental action or quality gives to a spectator the pleasing sentiment of approbation;* and vice the contrary. . . .

Reason can't justify ultimate ends.

It appears evident that the ultimate ends of human actions can never, in any case, be accounted for by *reason,* but recommend themselves entirely to the sentiments and affections of mankind, without any dependence on the intellectual faculties. Ask a man *why he uses exercise;* he will answer, *because he desires to keep his health.* If you then enquire, *why he desires health,* he will readily reply, *because sickness is painful.* If you push your enquiries farther, and desire a reason *why he hates pain,* it is impossible he can ever give any. This is an ultimate end, and is never referred to any other object.

We can't justify one thing by another indefinitely; some values must be accepted on their own.

Perhaps to your second question, *why he desires health,* he may also reply, that *it is necessary for the exercise of his calling.* If you ask, *why he is anxious on that head,* he will answer, *because he desires to get money.* If you demand *Why? It is the instrument of pleasure,* says he. And beyond this it is an absurdity to ask for a reason. It is impossible there can be a progress *in infinitum;* and that one thing can always be a reason why another is desired. Something must be desirable on its own account, and because of its immediate accord or agreement with human sentiment and affection.

Virtue is desirable as an end.

Now as virtue is an end, and is desirable on its own account, without fee and reward, merely for the immediate satisfaction which it conveys; it is requisite that there should be some sentiment which it touches, some internal taste of feeling, or whatever you may please to call it, which distinguishes moral good and evil, and which embraces the one and rejects the other.

Thus the distinct boundaries and offices of *reason* and of *taste* are easily ascertained. The former conveys the knowledge of truth and falsehood: the latter gives the sentiment of beauty and deformity, vice and virtue. The one discovers objects as they really stand in nature, without addition or diminution: the other has a productive faculty, and gilding or staining all natural objects with the colours, borrowed from internal sentiment, raises in a manner a new creation. Reason being cool and disengaged, is no motive to action, and directs only the impulse received from appetite or inclination, by showing us the means of attaining happiness or avoiding misery: Taste, as it gives pleasure or pain, and thereby constitutes happiness or misery, becomes a motive to action, and is the first spring or impulse to desire and volition. From circumstances and relations, known or supposed, the former leads us to the discovery of the concealed and unknown: after all circumstances and relations are laid before us, the latter makes us feel from the whole a new sentiment of blame or approbation. . . .

I cannot forbear adding to these reasonings an observation, which may, perhaps be found of some importance. In every system of morality which I have hitherto met with, I have always remarked that the author proceeds for some time in the ordinary way of reasoning, and establishes the being of God, or makes observations concerning human affairs; when of a sudden I am surprised to find, that instead of the usual copulations of propositions, *is*, and *is not*, I meet with no proposition that is not connected with an *ought*, or an *ought not*. This change is imperceptible; but is, however, of the last consequence. For as this *ought* or *ought not*, expresses some new relation or affirmation, it is necessary that it should be observed and explained; and at the same time that a reason should be given for what seems altogether inconceivable, how this new relation can be a deduction from others, which are entirely different from it. But as authors do not commonly use this precaution, I shall presume to recommend it to the readers; and am persuaded, that this small attention would subvert all the vulgar systems of morality, and let us see that the distinction of vice and virtue is not founded merely on the relations of objects, nor is perceived by reason.

Reason tells us of truth and falsehood, taste of the sentiments of vice and virtue. Taste, but not reason, gives us motives to act.

Authors of moral systems start by saying what is the case but then slide into what ought to be. But they never tell us how the one leads to the other. This failure alone defeats all objective moral theories.

Morality is not discovered. It has to be made. We decide what is morally right and wrong on the basis of subjective desires.

Subjectivists, finding no answers to these questions, conclude that morality is not discovered either by examining some part of the world or by spinning out rational principles (as Kant has done in the excerpt earlier in this chapter). Morality, a subjectivist has to claim, must be *made. We* have to *decide* on the rules, say of social cooperation, on the basis of our subjective desires and attitudes, or what may be called our "motivating interests." On the basis of these motivating interests, we must decide, by using our reason, what we should do and what we should try to require others to do. The language of morality is the language used in this social enterprise.

Summary of Chapter 4

Unlike factual disputes (say, over whether the earth is flat), moral ones (say, over the morality of suicide) cannot be settled just by appealing to facts. What then *is* relevant?

1. According to religious authoritarianism, God's commands determine right and wrong. In reply, opponents ask, first, how can we know what God commands? (1) We can't appeal to our consciences, because consciences differ, but presumably God's commands are consistent; and (2) we can't appeal to religious authorities, because they have no information not available to us. (Also, they differ in their opinions one from another, and we have no reason to prefer one over the others.)

Furthermore (3) we can't appeal to miracles or the Bible, as argued in Chapter 1, and in addition what the Bible says about morality hardly bears the mark of divinity, being *inconsistent* (if taken literally), *incomplete, imprecise,* and *counterintuitive.* (It also sometimes requires us to do the impossible.)

Even supposing we knew what God commands, there would still be the question whether what he commands is *right,* and thus whether we should obey out of duty or fear (prudence). But to figure out whether his commands are right, we would have to evaluate them in terms of our own moral sentiments, so that we would really just be discovering how *we* feel about the matter, not what God commands.

2. Egoism is the view that it is always our moral duty to do whatever is best for ourselves. In its most sensible form, this means that there is no special *moral* obligation to consider when acting; we should just do whatever is prudent, and maximizes our desires, whether selfish or altruistic, ignoring any inclinations toward such things as fairness or justice. Egoism may be the most rational moral theory for those who lack a moral sense, who have no

great regard for justice or fairness. But for most of us, it wouldn't be consistent with rationality, because most of us have a reasonably high regard for justice.

Confronted with this, some egoists move to the variation here called *psychological egoism,* which argues that it is a psychological fact that human beings can't act unselfishly, so that it can't be our moral duty to do so. Thus, egoism must be correct. But occasional cases seem to exist (such as mothers rushing into burning buildings to save their babies) that don't seem consistent with psychological egoism.

Therefore some take the tack that all of our actions must be selfish because all of our actions are done from *our own* motives, desires, and inclinations, not from someone else's, and thus always have to be selfish. This view is here called *philosophical egoism.*

Opponents of this form of egoism point out that it assumes *selfish actions* are those done to satisfy our own desires and *unselfish actions* those done to satisfy the desires of others. But in fact we mean by selfish actions those done from our own desires to benefit ourselves and by unselfish actions those done from our own desires to benefit someone else. And in this sense, unselfish actions are not at all impossible; in fact, they occur all the time.

3. The theory of *utilitarianism* says that morally right actions are those that maximize overall utility (in the hedonistic version, this means maximizing *pleasure*—taking account of quantity, intensity, duration, fecundity, and perhaps quality) without regard for its distribution. According to *act utilitarianism,* we should consider each act; according to *rule utilitarianism,* we should consider types of actions. Rule utilitarianism thus says to follow that set of rules that on the whole maximizes utility compared to all other sets of rules.

Utilitarianism seems plausible because of our strong social nature. But it also seems to be counterintuitive, at least for retributivists, as the innocent suspect and overcrowded lifeboat examples illustrate.

Although it may seem that rule utilitarianism is not open to these objections, many claim it is—rule and act utilitarianism come down to the same thing in practice, because the rule to *maximize utility* always has greater utility than any set of competing rules. Furthermore, if rule and act utilitarianism really were different, following rule utilitarianism would go against the very intuition—that justice requires the maximizing of social utility—that made utilitarianism attractive in the first place.

4. Some argue that justice requires *equality,* not of the distribution of pleasure or goods, but of *opportunity.* However, this requirement conflicts with our feelings that those who earn wealth should be able to spend it as they see fit, including buying their children a better than equal chance of success in life.

143

5. Utilitarianism is a *forward-looking* theory, telling us to decide what to do on the basis of future consequences. One objection to it is that it fails to take account of things such as *moral standing*, as *backward-looking* theories do.

6. Some point to *retribution* as the key to understanding moral justice, having in mind *punishment* for immorality (and perhaps reward for especially meritorious behavior). Although utilitarianism is very likely consistent with *deterrence*, it doesn't seem to jibe with the idea of retribution.

7. Other writers believe that *reciprocity* is the key to justice. On this view, entering into fair reciprocal arrangements obligates us to carry them out. This approach is consistent with the *contract* view of morality, which says that moral obligations arise out of fair contracts, implicit or explicit. A limited version of this approach is the popular *social contract* theory, which states that social arrangements are fair when they can be cast as fair contracts between all the parties in society.

8. *Metaethical Theories.* The moral theories discussed so far are *prescriptive* or *normative,* prescribing morally right and wrong actions. On the other hand, *metaethical* theories examine the language or concepts of morality and the proposed prescriptive theories themselves, asking, for instance, what terms such as *good, right,* and *ought* mean.

One important metaethical question is whether moral right and wrong are *objective* or *subjective.* The most popular idea in Western philosophy has always been that they are objective, and thus the same for all at every time and place. But some have always claimed they are subjective, and thus differ from person to person and time to time, much like taste.

Subjectivists argue as they do because they fail to see what the alleged objectivity of moral claims could consist in, or how we could discover their objective nature. In particular, they don't seem to be discoverable by observing any nonmoral features of the universe, and there are no special principles of reasoning available. So they must be obtained by intuition, or faith, and thus, like religious faith, differ from person to person and time to time, a mark of their subjective nature.

But aren't things such as justice, or fairness, objectively definable? Specifically, can't we give objective criteria for fair contracts? Suppose we could (although many believe we can't). Then what justification would we have for demanding that others be fair, except that we want them to be? (We can't appeal to the apparent objective nature of everyday moral terms, any more than we can prove Santa Claus exists just by giving the term *Santa Claus* objective criteria of application, because there would still be the question of whether anything satisfies those criteria.)

Questions for Further Thought

1. Do you think the retributive theory of justice is right, or do you think harming those who do wrong is justified only by the need to deter or rehabilitate? On what basis, other than an appeal to intuition, can such a question be settled?

2. Supposing that you believe in God and he hasn't made a personal visit to you in a vision, how do you think we can find out what God commands? Or do you think we don't have to worry about that, but should decide moral questions some other way? If so, how?

3. In an actual case (*Parade* magazine, March 4, 1979), a married man committed adultery as the key act in cracking an international drug ring. When his wife found out, she sued for divorce on grounds of adultery. Forgetting the legal question (which in this case would have been Greek to most Americans), did the wife act on solid moral grounds?

4. Many cultures around the world have practiced infanticide with no moral stigma attached. Ancient Greece and Rome are examples; so are the present-day Yanomamo Indians of South America. In Asia, Indians, Chinese, and Japanese would "thin the rows." The reason given in most cases is roughly the same—inability to care for the newborn, especially along with other children. How do you feel about this? Does your attitude reflect acceptance of some particular theory about moral right and wrong? Is your opinion influenced at all by the fact that millions of otherwise perfectly ordinary people in many places and at many times have felt infanticide was the best thing to do under their (adverse) circumstances, and didn't feel they were committing murder?

5. Philosophical egoism is perplexing to many because the logic of that view sounds at first blush to be quite good, yet its conclusion is unpalatable. Just what is the argument anyway, and how is it to be refuted? (Or do you think it's correct?)

6. The discussion of morality in this book, as in most, has to do with the obligations of one human being to another. But some writers have always felt that this is too narrow a view. What do you think of Albert Schweitzer's opinion as expressed in the following passage?

> The great fault of all ethics hitherto has been that they believed themselves to have to deal only with the relations of man to man. In reality, however, the question is what is his attitude to the world and all life that comes within his reach. A man is ethical only when life, as such, is sacred to him, that of plants and animals as that of his fellow men, and when he devotes himself helpfully to all that is in need of help.

7. Do you think the fact-value division used in introducing this chapter is a good one? If so, what consequences flow from the fact that there is such a division? If not, what experienceable facts ground the "value facts" you think exist?

8. What do you think of David Hume's argument (in the reading in this chapter) that reason is and ought to be the slave of the passions?

9. How about his argument that there is no valid principle of reasoning from facts (what *is* the case) to values (what *ought* to be the case)?

10. Feelings favoring moral objectivism are strong in most of us. We find it hard to think we aren't justified in our outrage at those who commit monstrous moral sins, or that our judgment of immorality is not more than just a personal attitude. But isn't that similar to the case of taste in art or food? Just about every musician of any talent would insist that Mozart definitely is better than Irving Berlin or Lawrence Welk. Similarly, gourmets are unanimous in rating McDonald's and other fast food as junk compared to first-class French or Chinese cuisine. Couldn't it be, perhaps, that this general agreement in taste, especially among those who train their palates, leads us to mistakenly believe that our values, including moral values, have an objective quality all their own?

11. When confronted with the question "*What if* the facts are such that convicting innocent suspects, lying, stealing, and breaking promises really do often maximize utility?" some utilitarians reply that the facts *aren't* that way so it doesn't matter what would be the case if they were. What is your view on this question?

12. What do you think of John Stuart Mill's argument (in the excerpt in this chapter)?

> The only proof capable of being given that an object is visible is that people actually see it. The only proof that a sound is audible is that people hear it. . . . In like manner . . . the sole evidence it is possible to produce that anything is desirable is that people do actually desire it.

13. What is your reaction to this quote from the same paragraph?

> No reason can be given why the general happiness is desirable, except that each person . . . desires his own happiness. This, however, being a fact, we have not only all the proof which the case admits of, but all which it is possible to require, that happiness is a good, that each person's happiness is a good to that person, and the general happiness, therefore, a good to the aggregate of all persons.

14. My personal opinion is that human beings evolved roughly as the theory of evolution says they did, and also that the moral sentiments favoring

fairness, retribution, and the like, as well (in part) as sentiments such as empathy, admiration, and contempt, evolved because they served a specific function in the overall human ecological niche, namely, to greatly increase *cooperation* among otherwise competing members of a society (especially in getting food and in defending against attacks by other societies). Does this view strike you as having something to it? In what ways do you think it is wrong? Does it support any of the theories discussed in this chapter?

No man is an island.—JOHN DONNE

I begin by taking. I shall find scholars afterwards to demonstrate my perfect right.
—FREDERICK THE GREAT

Give me the liberty to know, to utter, and to argue freely according to conscience, above all liberties.—JOHN MILTON

What can be the "personal freedom" of an unemployed person who goes hungry and finds no use for his toil?—JOSEPH STALIN

Power tends to corrupt, and absolute power corrupts absolutely.—LORD ACTON

As wealth is power, so all power must infallibly draw wealth to itself by some means or other.
—EDMUND BURKE

Democracy is the worst form of government, except for all the others.
—ATTRIBUTED TO WINSTON CHURCHILL

We cannot divide ourselves between right and expedience. Policy must bow the knee before morality.—IMMANUEL KANT

Liberty is the sure possession only of those who have the courage to defend it.—PERICLES

Politics is the conduct of public affairs for private advantage.—AMBROSE BIERCE

A politician will do anything to keep his job—even become a patriot.
—WILLIAM RANDOLPH HEARST

Government is a contrivance of human wisdom to provide for human wants.
—EDMUND BURKE

He mocks the people who proposes that the Government shall protect the rich and that they in turn will care for the laboring poor.
—GROVER CLEVELAND

Every actual state is corrupt. Good men must not obey the laws too well.
—RALPH WALDO EMERSON

Why was government instituted at all? Because the passions of men will not conform to the dictates of reason and justice without restraint.—ALEXANDER HAMILTON

A government is free in proportion to the rights it guarantees to the minority.
—ALFRED M. LANDON

The State is the Divine Idea as it exists on Earth.—HEGEL

All government, of course, is against liberty.—H. L. MENCKEN

I beg my friends the liberals to tell me if ever in all history there was a government which was based exclusively upon the consent of the people, and which was ready to dispense altogether with the use of force. There never has been and never will be such a government.—BENITO MUSSOLINI

It will be proper to take a review of the several sources from which governments have arisen, and which they have been founded. They may all be comprehended under three heads—1st, Superstition; 2d, Power; 3d, the common interests of society, and the common rights of man. The first was a government of priestcraft, the second of conquerors, and the third of reason.—THOMAS PAINE

If we will not be governed by God, we must be governed by tyrants.—WILLIAM PENN

The art of government is the organization of idolatry.—GEORGE BERNARD SHAW

Is it not possible that an individual may be right and a government wrong? Are laws to be enforced simply because they are made? Or declared by any number of men to be good, if they are *not* good?—HENRY DAVID THOREAU

If I wished to punish a province, I would have it governed by philosophers.
—FREDERICK THE GREAT

. . . A bill of rights is what the people are entitled to against every government on earth.—THOMAS JEFFERSON

A society is rich when material goods, including capital, are cheap, and human beings dear. . . . The interest of those who own the property used in industry . . . is that the capital should be dear and human beings cheap.
—RICHARD H. TAWNEY

5

Social and
Political Philosophy:
Ethics and Society

IN CHAPTER 4, we discussed ethical or moral questions primarily from the point of view of individual or personal morality. We asked, for instance, whether an *individual* should keep promises when there is greater utility in breaking them. Now let's look at ethical issues from the viewpoint of social or political morality, realizing, of course, that the two are not distinct (human beings are of necessity social animals, so that personal problems are bound to merge with social ones).

We'll look at ethical issues from the viewpoint of sociopolitical philosophy.

It is often said that *politics*, as engaged in every day by real-life politicians and elected officials, is completely divorced from morality. The constant striving of politicians for personal political power and the regular attempts by powerful factions in society to gain selfish ends supports such a view. But this clearly is just part of the story. Every politician and pressure group tries to justify its position by appealing to social values—to social justice and "the public interest."

The idea that politics is divorced from morality is only part of the story.

Even when appealing to the selfish interests of one group or another, politicians try to mask that selfish appeal in the rhetoric of the public good. The reason, of course, is that the vast majority of us do in fact have regard for the social welfare, even if that regard often conflicts with and may be overruled by purely selfish desires. *No* man is an island. (Anyway, we don't want to be too cynical. All but the very worst politicians have moral scruples that on occasion are stronger than their selfish motives.)

149

1. What Makes Social Institutions Legitimate?

The popular view is that governments are legitimate when they have the consent of the governed.

What makes some social institutions morally right, or legitimate, and some not? In particular, what makes a government legitimate? The most popular answer these days is that governments are legitimate to the extent they have the consent of the governed. (Most other theories seem dated. Hardly anyone, for example, believes monarchies are legitimate because kings rule by divine right, a view that once had many champions.)

We'll consider utilitarianism, natural rights theory, and social contract theory.

But there is disagreement as to how governments should be selected and what governments can legitimately *do*, in particular what they can *force* individuals to do. Before considering specific issues, let's look at three popular theories about the general nature of legitimate rule by governments: (1) the utilitarian theory (having in mind mainly *rule* utilitarianism); (2) the theory of natural rights; and (3) social contract theory. (The three, of course, are not mutually exclusive. John Locke, for example, argued both for a social contract theory and a theory of natural rights.)

The Utilitarian Social Theory

Utilitarianism: A society is just when its rules maximize utility for that society.

Historically, utilitarianism was developed in large part to defend a liberal democratic view of the nature of a just society. Roughly speaking, utilitarians believe that a society is *just* when its laws and customs are likely to produce more benefit (utility) for the whole of society than would any other laws and customs. And this definition certainly seems plausible. Shouldn't social institutions serve the people who live under them? And what better way to serve the people as a whole than by maximizing benefit for its members?

Utilitarianism fails to take account of retribution.

The trouble is that utilitarianism as a social theory suffers from most of the defects raised in Chapter 4 against utilitarianism as a general moral theory. In particular, it fails to take into account the various reasons we have for wanting benefits to human beings distributed in some special way, and not simply maximized. A good example of this is the claim of retributivists that benefits must at least in part be distributed according to just desserts, so that sinners and slackers get

150

less and the virtuous and hard working get more, even if that means reducing the whole pie of benefits. *

In fact, according to critics, utilitarianism is consistent with and will on occasion lead to the very evil some of its most ardent champions (for instance, John Stuart Mill) intended it to overcome, namely, the "tyranny of a majority over a minority" in society. For it does seem that sometimes those policies that maximize social utility do so at the expense of some small group in society treated as "scapegoats." Thus, given the realities in India as they have existed for centuries, it may be that having a caste of untouchables who do the nation's miserable tasks (such as collecting "night soil") has maximized social utility by giving the vast majority psychological benefit and cheap, docile labor. But justice, or fairness, most would claim, forbids benefiting the large majority at the terrible expense of a tiny minority. Similarly, had the government in Uganda evenly distributed the wealth taken from its Asian minority (when they were kicked out of the country) among the black majority, it probably would have increased overall benefit. But surely such theft is not morally right.

Utilitarianism permits scapegoats and other unfair practices.

Natural Rights Theory

Another popular theory about governments is that people have **natural rights** (discovered by reason alone, according to some writers) that limit and shape legitimate governments and other social institutions. The U.S. political system was and is based in part on this idea. (Recall these words from the Declaration of Independence: "We hold these truths to be self-evident, that all men are created equal, that they are endowed by their Creator with certain unalienable Rights, that among

Natural rights theory: People have rights (discovered by reason alone) to life, and so on.

---

*However, remember the reply by some defenders of utilitarianism—mentioned in Chapter 4—that in fact utilitarianism is consistent with our intuitions about the just distribution of benefits. To add one detail, it's sometimes argued that in a utilitarian system those who work harder would be given more in return because higher wages act as an incentive to greater productivity, thus increasing the whole pie of benefits. Furthermore, some argue that the immense differences in wealth, often claimed to be unjust, would be ruled out by utilitarianism because of the principle of diminishing returns (that as a person's wealth increases beyond a certain small amount the benefits that can be gained from it by that person become less and less), so that we maximize overall social benefit by spreading wealth more evenly.

these are Life, Liberty, and the pursuit of Happiness.—That to secure these rights, Governments are instituted among Men, deriving their just powers from the consent of the governed.")

Against natural rights theory: There is no way to decide which rights are natural. They can't be self-evident, because people disagree about them.

Different writers, of course, argue for different and conflicting natural rights. John Locke, for instance, argued for a natural right to property, a right some socialist-minded natural rights advocates deny, and a right that the writers of the Declaration of Independence deliberately omitted from that document, even though they were strongly influenced by Locke. But the main problem for natural rights theorists is to provide good reason or justification for believing in any particular natural right. Thus, to the claim that natural rights are "self-evident," as the Declaration of Independence states, a powerful reply is that it is hard to see such rights as self-evident when people disagree as to exactly which rights are in fact natural rights (anything self-evident ought to be agreed to at least by a large majority of rational beings).

There is no obvious connection between facts and moral "truths."

Furthermore, recall the discussion in Chapter 4 on the objectivity-subjectivity of moral obligation. Subjectivists claim that there could be no possible connection between ordinary everyday facts, such as the round shape of the earth, the heaviness of lead, or the human desire for happiness, and the alleged objectivity of, say, the natural right to own property. But if such rights are not self-evident, and we can't have evidence supporting them, how can such rights be established?

For example, what is the connection between the fact of farming land and owning it?

Take the claim that we can discover a natural right to own property by means of some reasoning process. Subjectivists want to know just what the objective connection is between, say, the objective fact that a family has lived on and farmed a particular piece of land (even for centuries) and the alleged objective moral fact that that family has a natural right to the land. What mysterious rational faculty, what so far overlooked but valid principle of reasoning, leads us from the fact of their living on the land to their alleged natural right to own it? Subjectivists find no answer to such questions, and so reject natural rights theory as pie in the sky.

Experience may show that our aims are furthered by having a right to property,

Of course, there still may be very good reasons for deciding we want a society in which people own property, have free speech, and so on. Experience may show that granting these rights is the best way to satisfy certain of our interests (as John Stuart Mill argued for certain liberties as the best way to maximize social utility). But that is a

152

completely different sort of argument, and isn't open to advocates of a theory of *natural* rights.

but that's not a natural right.

Social Contract Theory

Historically, social contract theories also were often proposed as a way to defend and explain the liberal democratic idea of a free society. John Locke's theory, so important to American history, is an example. (But some writers—Thomas Hobbes, for example—argue that the main provision of a social contract would [should?] give the power of government to an absolute monarch.)

The basic idea of a social contract theory is that the legitimacy of government must stem from the consent of the governed, as though everyone had gotten together and agreed to a contract spelling out the machinery of government and other social arrangements. Various contract theories differ in detail, depending on what other ideas they incorporate. According to one such theory which considers a just society to be one in which fair contracts are carried out and no unfair ones are made, a law or social custom is *fair* or *just* only when it considers the interests of everyone in society equally, laying down rules for fair competition and cooperation among its members.

Social contract theory says that governments should have consent of the governed, as though created by a fair contract.

Illustration of Social Contract Theory

To see what some social contract advocates have in mind by this, imagine a situation that simulates a "state of nature," in which people are thrown together but haven't agreed to any rules of cooperation. Let's say several families consisting of sixty people have been ship-wrecked on a tropical island in the middle of the Pacific with little hope of ever being rescued. They've got to cooperate to survive, and anyway are bound to associate with each other just because that's the way people are. So they need rules of cooperation and association, and at the very least a leader. (In actual cases where this has happened, the stranded people have generally adopted the rules and customs of their native lands. But let's suppose this can't be done for some reason, so that the people have to start from scratch.)

What sort of system would they choose if they were rational and were trying to be as fair as possible (and didn't want to use force to

What sort of system would

153

gain an advantage)? First of all, mere survival would require granting the "state," or its leaders, some power or other over individuals in the group, for one thing because they might have to require serious sacrifices on the part of a few for the good of the group as a whole. For instance, they might have to require that the few able-bodied young men train and stand ready to risk their lives in case of attack by natives from nearby islands. Everyone would benefit from this, even those risking their necks, because all of any given person's interests would be bound up with the survival of the group. Of course, some people would be likely to benefit more than others. A young man who died in battle wouldn't have done as well as those who didn't have to fight and thus survived.

Second, to be fair, any rule that might harm some people more than others (forgetting retribution, for the moment), but is nevertheless justified somehow or other (say, by group survival), would have to be *impartial*—the rule itself could not be designed to benefit one party more than any other, or to give any particular person an advantage. Thus, a rule requiring able-bodied young men from some families but not others to fight would be unfair—assuming, of course, there is no "tradeoff," with young men from other families being required, say, to risk their necks digging for coal.

Third, any *required* cooperative activity would have to apportion benefits in terms of relative share of the whole effort.* For example, if John and Fred are required to take part in a wild boar hunt, and John's part is twice as great as Fred's, justice would require that he be given twice as many pigs as Fred in return for his effort. If Harry made all of the spears used in the hunt, his share of the rewards would have to reflect the value of those spears (however that would be rightly judged) to the success of the hunt. Similarly, if Sarah provided information about where the most wild boars could be found, fair rules would require that she get her share of the swag, even though she may never go on the hunts themselves.

Finally, our little society would have to do something to reduce cheating on the rules to a tolerable level, cheating being inevitable given human nature. Thus, if rules against adultery were required, it

ra tional, fair-minded people adopt on a desert island?
(1) The state would have power over individuals.

(2) Rules would be impartial.

(3) Benefits of cooperative effort would be divided according to effort.

(4) We'd have to have rules against cheating.

---

*For the moment, let's assume that amount of effort is what counts. Later, we'll consider other likely candidates; for example the value of the resulting product, or the unpleasantness of the task.

might be right to punish those who continually chase after other people's husbands or wives.

Rules for Fair Cooperative Ventures

It is sometimes held that the guiding principle in determining the fairness of rules for (necessary?) cooperative ventures is whether everyone involved is better off with a particular rule and the cooperation it enhances than without it (or with some other rule). But there is another side to the matter that often is overlooked. Suppose pigs become the principal wealth in our hypothetical society. A rich person thus would be someone who owns lots of pigs. Assume further that customs evolve in which pigs are used as the "bride price," as cattle are used in some parts of Africa. To have a chance for a choice bride, a young man would need lots of pigs to pay for his bride. In this sort of situation, justice would require more than that each wild boar hunter ends up better off than he was before the hunt. What good is it to George if he gets two pigs for his effort if Harry gets ten for an equal effort? He now has less chance than before to get a decent bride. That's why merely being better off than before doesn't yield justice, and we need to add the idea of rewards in proportion to a person's share of a common venture.

A distributive rule isn't fair just because all are better off with it, because of in-group competition. Justice requires distribution reflecting share of work.

Still, cases sometimes arise where it's impossible to distribute goods according to an otherwise fair principle. Everyone gets the benefit of a successful defense of the society, or successful attack on another, yet a few bear most of the risk and effort. How could it be both rational and moral for the few to be burdened with such an arrangement? It could be, according to the theory in question, and is, *if*, first the few need the benefit badly enough (as everyone needs group survival) *and* if no fairer arrangement is possible (as, for example, it would be ridiculous to require everyone to fight, including ninety-year-olds and cripples). Life is like that. Human beings just *do* find themselves in situations where no completely fair arrangement is possible (or, to put it another way, where the burdens or benefits must fall unequally or inequitably). In such cases, reason and morality say that this is the best possible course.

In some cases, no fair distribution is possible.

Of course, a just society arranges things so that situations of this kind happen as infrequently as possible. It would be wrong, to use Richard Nixon's favorite phrase, to have some benefit *gratuitously* from

But a just society minimizes unfairness.

The American founding fathers were greatly influenced by European political philosophers of the seventeenth and eighteenth centuries, in particular John Locke (1632–1704) and Jean Jacques Rousseau (1712–1778). The following excerpts are from Locke's Treatise of Civil Government *(second treatise).*

John Locke: **THE SOCIAL CONTRACT**

OF THE STATE OF NATURE

People once were in a state of nature, free of other's constraints.

To understand political power aright, and derive it from its original, we must consider what state all men are naturally in, and that is a state of perfect freedom to order their actions and dispose of their possessions and persons as they think fit, within the bounds of the law of nature, without asking leave, or depending upon the will of any other man. . . .

The state of nature is a state of liberty, but not of licence, say, to kill others, nor to take one's own life, liberty, etc.

But though this be a state of liberty, yet it is not a state of licence; though man in [a state of nature] have an uncontrollable liberty to dispose of his person or possessions, yet he has not liberty to destroy himself, or so much as any creature in his possession, but where some nobler use than its bare preservation calls for it. The state of nature has a law of nature to govern it, which obliges every one; and reason, which is that law, teaches all mankind who will but consult it, that, being all equal and independent, no one ought to harm another in his life, health, liberty, or possessions. For men being all the workmanship of one omnipotent and infinitely wise Maker . . . they are His property, whose workmanship they are, made to last during His, not one another's pleasure. . . .

OF PROPERTY . . .

But everyone has a right to his own person, labor, etc.

Though the earth and all inferior creatures be common to all men, yet every man has a property in his own person; this nobody has any right to but himself. The labour of his body and the work of his hands we may say are properly his. Whatsoever, then, he removes out of the state that nature hath provided and left it in, he hath mixed his labour with, and joined to it something that is his own, and thereby makes it his property. It being by him removed from the common state nature placed it in, it hath by this labour something annexed to it that excludes the common right of other men. For this labour being the unquestionable property of the labourer, no man but he can have a right to what that is once joined to, at least where there is enough, and as good left in common for others. . . .

OF POLITICAL OR CIVIL SOCIETY . . .

Man being born, as has been proved, with a title to perfect freedom, and an uncontrolled enjoyment of all the rights and privileges of the law of nature equally with any other man or number of men in the world, hath by nature a power not only to preserve his property—that is, his life, liberty, and estate—against the injuries and attempts of other men, but to judge of and punish the breaches of that law in others as he is persuaded the offence deserves. . . . But because no political society can be nor subsist without having in itself the power to preserve the property, and, in order thereunto, punish the offences of all those of that society, there, and there only, is political society, where every one of the members hath quitted this natural power, resigned it up into the hands of the community . . . and thus all private judgment of every particular member being excluded, the community comes to be umpire; and by understanding indifferent rules and men authorized by the community for their execution, decides all the differences that may happen between any members of that society concerning any matter of right, and punishes those offences which any member hath committed against the society with such penalties as the law has established; whereby it is easy to discern who are and who are not in political society together. Those who are united into one body, and have a common established law and judicature to appeal to, with authority to decide controversies between them and punish offenders, are in civil society one with another; but those who have no such common appeal—I mean on earth—are still in the state of nature, . . .

Since no society can endure without power to preserve property and punish offenders, individuals come to give up their rights to be umpires. A civil society is one where a common law decides disputes.

OF THE ENDS OF POLITICAL SOCIETY AND GOVERNMENT

The great and chief end, therefore, of men's uniting into commonwealths, and putting themselves under government, is the preservation of their property; to which in the state of nature there are many things wanting.

First, There wants an established, settled, known law, received and allowed by common consent to be the standard of right and wrong, and the common measure to decide all controversies between them. For though the law of nature be plain and intelligible to all rational creatures; yet men, being biased by their interest, as well as ignorant for want to study of it, are not apt to allow of it as a law binding to them in the application of it to their particular cases.

Secondly, In the state of nature there wants a known and indifferent judge, with authority to determine all differences according to the established law. For every one in that state, being both judge and executioner of the law of

Governments are formed to preserve private property.

(1) We need a standard of right and wrong.

(2) We need an impartial judge to implement the law.

nature, men being partial to themselves, passion and revenge is very apt to carry them too far, and with too much heat in their own cases. . . .

Thirdly, In the state of nature there often wants power to back and support the sentence when right, and to give it due execution. They who by any injustice offend, will seldom fail, where they are able by force to make good their injustice; such resistance many times makes the punishment dangerous, and frequently destructive to those who attempt it. . . .

(3) We need power to uphold the law.

OF THE EXTENT OF THE LEGISLATIVE POWER

The great end of civil society is to establish legislative power to preserve society and the people in it.

The great end of men's entering into society being the enjoyment of their properties in peace and safety, and the great instrument and means of that being the laws established in that society: the first and fundamental positive law of all commonwealths, is the establishing of the legislative power; as the first and fundamental natural law, which is to govern even the legislative itself, is the preservation of the society, and (as far as will consist with the public good) of every person in it. . . .

(1) Legislatures can't be arbitrary in treating those in society.

First, It is not nor can possibly be absolutely arbitrary over the lives and fortunes of the people. For it being but the joint power of every member of the society given up to that person, or assembly, which is legislator; it can be no more than those persons had in a state of nature before they entered into society, and gave it up to the community. . . .

(2) Legislatures can't make arbitrary decrees.

Secondly, The legislative, or supreme authority, cannot assume to itself a power to rule by extemporary arbitrary decrees, but is bound to dispense justice, and decide the rights of the subject by promulgated standing laws, and known authorised judges. . . .

(3) They can't take away property without consent, because the point of societies is to preserve property.

Thirdly, The supreme power cannot take from any man any part of his property without his own consent. For the preservation of property being the end of government, and that for which men enter into society, it necessarily supposes and requires that the people should have property, without which they must be supposed to lose that by entering into society, which was the end for which they entered into it, too gross an absurdity for any man to own. . . .

Taxation without majority representation is tyranny.

'Tis true governments cannot be supported without great charge, and it is fit every one who enjoys a share of the protection should pay out of his estate his proportion for the maintenance of it. But still it must be with his own consent, *i.e.,* the consent of the majority giving it either by themselves or their representatives chosen by them. . . .

(4) Legislators can't give their power to others.

Fourthly. The legislative cannot transfer the power of making laws to any other hands; for it being but a delegated power from the people, they who have it cannot pass it over to others.

the patriotism of others. (In World War II, President Roosevelt suggested a ceiling of $25,000 on income in view of the tiny salaries given those fighting and dying overseas. He appealed to the immorality of some getting rich off the backs of those defending the nation, and he surely was right even though his proposal was hooted down.) In our hypothetical society, it would be wrong, say, to distribute the rewards of a hunt unfairly, given that there are simple ways to divide them fairly.

2. Social Justice and Liberty

Political differences in democratic societies tend to focus on the two related concepts of **social justice** and **liberty.** Just about everyone in a democracy believes in both of these, but different people interpret or stress them differently. So-called liberals and left-wingers tend to stress social justice, in particular equality before the law and the elimination of poverty, or at least the elimination of great differences between rich and poor (economic justice). Conservatives, libertarians, and right-wingers tend to stress individual liberty or freedom, in particular economic freedom and individual initiative. In recent times, liberals have tended to favor more government interference in private lives so as to increase social justice (for example, consider laws against racial, ethnic, or religious prejudice, and the original intent of the graduated income tax). Conservatives or libertarians have tried to reduce the role of government as an agent of social change or economic leveling (recall the conservative opposition to the use of government to speed racial equality, or their success over the years in watering down the economic leveling effect of the graduated income tax and the various inheritance taxes).

Liberals tend to stress social justice. Conservatives stress individual freedom, particularly economic freedom.

Of course, all such definitions are only roughly true. There is a strong historical connection between conservatives and government repression of certain kinds of private behavior (think of the recent right-wing attempts to make or keep abortion and homosexual behavior illegal). On the other hand, liberals (along with libertarians) have been in the forefront in defending freedom of religion, freedom of speech, and so on, in opposition to nonlibertarian right-wing elements in society (think of recent fights over publication of the

But conservatives sometimes favor political repression, while liberals defend free speech, etc.

159

Pentagon Papers, or the successful CIA attempts at prior censorship of books critical of intelligence operations).

3. Economic Justice: Free Enterprise versus Socialism

In the nineteenth century, Karl Marx argued for a kind of economic determinism, and predicted that the capitalistic "free enterprise" system of the emerging Western industrial world would soon give way to a socialistic economic system (leading sooner or later to communism). We now can see that he was wrong about the arrival of socialism (so far, at any rate), but he certainly was right to emphasize the crucial nature of economic factors in human societies, even if he went overboard on the matter.

Today the basic economic question concerns choosing capitalism or socialism.

Today, the issue (outside the Soviet sphere, where there is no freedom to genuinely discuss the matter) is whether (1) a **free enterprise, capitalistic** system, or (2) a **socialistic** system, or (3) some combination of the two, is most likely to produce social justice or yield the biggest pie of wealth to distribute. The chief difference between capitalism and socialism concerns the ownership and direction of the "means of production," in particular factories, and large distributive or service organizations (such as the telephone company or Safeway). (In the Soviet Union, of course, farms and even private homes are generally owned and always controlled by the state.)

This issue is economic, not strictly political.

It is important to see that the issue of free enterprise versus socialism concerns what sort of *economic* system we should have. It isn't about the best form of government. It has nothing to do with who has governmental power—except, of course, indirectly (Marxists and many other socialists argue that in a capitalistic system the immensely wealthy Rockefellers, Mellons, and Hunts will inevitably control whatever political machinery happens to exist). In particular, it is important to see that in a democratic society in which the people elect their governmental officials, they may choose either type of economic system or any combination of the two without giving up their democratic ideals.

In the United States in recent times, conservatives, libertarians, the right wing, and the Republican party have favored free enterprise. Liberals have been seriously divided on the issue.

It would be nice if there were some easy way to decide whether, say, utilitarianism or social contract theory favors one side or the other on this basic economic issue. But the truth of the matter is that there is a great distance between broad general theory and specific economic issues that is very hard to bridge. It's hard to know the actual consequences of any economic policy (no doubt one serious reason for the failure of recent governments to solve the problems of unemployment and inflation).

It's hard to know what ethical theories imply for specific questions.

Take social contract theory. Would a fair contract among all factions in the United States today consist in part in an agreement to have a socialistic economy? Debates on this are endless. No one can be sure. On the one side are those who point to the inefficiency of governments as compared with private enterprises. If we choose socialism, it is said, and governments own and manage large economic units, they are bound to manage them inefficiently, so that everyone has less and goods will be of inferior quality. (Countries under the control of the Soviet Union are cited as examples.) It is also often claimed that socialism gives too much power to governments, threatening freedom.

For example, would a fair social contract lead to socialism or capitalism? Does socialism lead to fewer goods?

On the other hand, socialists argue that free enterprise inevitably leads to immense and unfair differences in wealth, and to extreme poverty for some even in the richest countries. Furthermore, there is the great risk of relative economic slavery (what good is the freedom to choose one's own job at a time when the only jobs available pay near-starvation wages, they ask), and therefore of at least some measure of political inequality. Socialism, on the other hand, they see as increasing our chances of obtaining political equality while reducing the likelihood of vast differences in wealth, thus producing greater social justice and more true freedom. (In addition, they argue that the poor record of socialism in dictatorships like the Soviet Union is not relevant when considering *democratic* socialism.)

Does free enterprise lead to unfair differences in wealth?

In practice, however, the choice in America today is between various forms of capitalism involving different degrees of government control. Should governments regulate certain industries on which all depend (such as the airlines, broadcasting industries, and telephone companies)? Do governments have a duty to provide every citizen in one way or another with certain vital services (medical, educational) if private enterprise fails to provide them? Interestingly, certain "so-

The practical choice today concerns the precise blend of socialism and capitalism.

161

cialistic" services are believed in by almost everyone—Ayn Rand being perhaps the chief exception—public highways being the best example. And it should be noticed that almost every champion of both capitalism and socialism believes that governments must coin and regulate money and provide for the common defense, although *how* these are to be provided always makes for exciting debate. Only a very few extreme anarchists oppose such basic government services.

Should we have a "closed shop" system in which only union members can be hired by a unionized company? Or should we insist on the principle of an "open shop"? Is a genuinely graduated income tax that "socks the rich" best? Should governments provide things like food or medical care for those who otherwise would have to do without? What about being an employer of last resort?

Some of the more serious issues don't get sufficient attention; for instance, the question of seniority and who should be fired in hard times.

It's surprising how seldom the moral aspects of some of these questions are seriously raised, while others (abortion, birth control, etc.) hog the limelight. Take the question of worker layoffs in hard times, such as those experienced recently by the auto, steel, and construction industries. Unions in the United States have regularly fought for higher wages for their members and against firings that are arbitrary or political; but they rarely try to protect the jobs of union members laid off in hard times. The result is that economic recessions or depressions place a heavy burden on some workers while others are unhurt. The general rule is "Last hired, first fired." But what *moral* virtue is there in seniority that makes it the most important consideration? Would it be more just to defend the jobs of all workers—say, by sharing time off in recessions, or lowering everyone's pay—so that the burden is more equally distributed?

What Are Fair Wages?

Wages in the United States are based mainly on what someone is willing to pay, resulting in great differences in income and wealth.

The question of fair wages is vital to almost everyone these days, given that most of us are wage earners. The system in operation in the United States today is one in which the marketplace—what you can get someone to offer—is the main ingredient in deciding wages. (The strength of unions as compared to management at any given time also is important.) The result has been immense differences in wages and wealth among the various classes in this supposedly classless society.

Well, imagine we wanted to have a society in which all workers received fair wages. How would we decide what is fair? Several plausible principles come to mind.

Equal Pay for Equal Work

Whatever other principles turn out to be right, justice does seem to require that those who do exactly the same work should receive the same wages. Whatever an auto assembly-line worker ought to be paid, every worker who does the same job equally well ought to receive the same pay. This seems to follow from the general principle of reasoning that says we should treat equal cases equally, or what amounts to the same thing, that there must be a difference between two cases if it is rational to treat the two cases differently.

Those who do the same work should get the same wages.

In fact, the major objection to the idea of equal pay for equal work is that there may be relevant differences of *need* between workers who do the same job. If Smith has six kids and Jones only one, Smith has a greater need than Jones, and so, some argue, ought to receive more pay.

Should those who need more get more pay?

But even supposing justice somehow requires that we give Smith more money than Jones because of greater need, this inequality would be due to the *overall* balance of just desserts and not because Smith deserves more pay in return for his work. This point becomes clear when we realize that need is independent of employment—whatever reason we might have for giving people money according to need would exist whether they worked or not; for instance, if they were handicapped and couldn't work. (The case would be different, of course, if Smith were able to but refused to work.) However, raising the issue of need does show that questions of wages are part of the broader and more difficult problem of the total distribution of wealth.

Justice may require giving more to the needier, but that wouldn't be wages.

Does Utilitarianism Imply a Principle of Need?

It sometimes is argued that to be consistent utilitarians should support a principle of need as the best way to maximize overall social utility. The reason is that according to what is sometimes called the "principle of marginal utility," increases in income beyond a certain minimum will result in smaller and smaller increases in utility—the more you

Because of the principle of marginal utility, utilitarianism may imply distribution

163

according to need . . .

make, the less each dollar is worth to you (the reason why a thousand dollars is of little consequence to a multimillionaire). (A familiar example of a similar idea is that for each dollar spent on a high-fidelity phonograph, you get smaller and smaller increases in the quality of sound. A $1000 setup definitely does not sound twice as good as one that costs only $500.)

Is Social Contract Theory Inconsistent with a Principle of Need?

But social contract theory does not seem to imply a principle of need, because no fair contract would make a richer party give wealth to a needier, poorer one.

On the other hand, it may be that social contract champions have to stand against a principle of need (perhaps beyond a certain minimum—sometimes called the "subsistence" or "poverty" level) if they are to be consistent. Where is the justice, on their view, in reducing one person's pay in order to give it to someone else who does nothing extra to deserve it except for having more needs? In our example, why should Jones have to help pay the costs of Smith's kids just because Jones chose to have fewer children? Or to put it another way, even if Jones wants to do whatever duty requires, how can Smith's decision to have lots of children give Jones the burden of another moral duty? How could a *fair* contract exist between Smith and Jones requiring one to take care of the offspring of the other?*

Some claim this would make social contract theory inhumane. But the theory just spells out moral or legal obligation; it doesn't forbid charity or other altruism.

The usual reply to arguments of this kind is that it is heartless, even inhumane. But there are at least two good replies to this charge of heartlessness. First, we assumed in the Smith and Jones example that neither Smith nor Jones were poverty stricken. Even the most heartless social contract theorists might allow that any fair social contract must protect every member of society from certain things, destitution being one of them (personal safety being another).

Second, and of extreme importance, social contract theory attempts to spell out the boundaries of *legitimate legal obligation*—part of moral obligation. It wants to tell us what governments can *force* us to do without becoming tyrannical. It doesn't rule out charity. And it doesn't

---

*There are very odd situations where this would be possible. In our tropical island example, all the young adults might get together and agree on some cooperative plan for raising children. Not knowing ahead of time who would have many and who few children, they might agree to spread the *risk* evenly, as we do with insurance policies, so that a person who in fact had few offspring would still fairly be burdened with the care of many.

forbid the people in any society from agreeing by whatever fair pro-
cedures they establish to do whatever benevolent acts they wish to
do. The function of governments, according to social contract theory,
is not just to assure fair competition between the members of the
society, or to assure success for those things requiring cooperation
(such as defense). It also is intended to provide a fair way for getting
done whatever the members of society want done that isn't unfair to
any members who object to it. It is, in other words, a theory about
what we might *owe* to others in society, not what we might *choose* to
give them by means of the machinery of government.

More Pay for More or Higher-Quality Productivity

Hand in hand with the idea of equal pay for equal work is the idea
that those who produce more, or make things that are more valuable
to us, deserve higher wages. If Smith bakes twice as many pies as
Jones, it seems plausible that Smith ought to be paid twice as much
as Jones. Similarly, if Smith's pies are better, he or she ought to get
more per pie.

Those who produce more or better should get more pay.

Again, the main objection is humanitarian. People differ greatly
in ability. A physically weak person may be able to produce much less
than a strong one, even when working much harder. In addition,
when the principle is applied to the case of great geniuses, the plausibility of the principle declines considerably. For instance, all modern
life depends on science, and most scientific advances depend at least
in part on a few basic principles, theories, and inventions. The in-
ventors of the microscope, telescope, and eyeglasses, to mention three
obvious examples, benefited humanity thousands of times more than
most of us conceivably could. Do they deserve to be thousands of
times richer? Practically all modern science owes some debt to Isaac
Newton. Did he (or do his heirs) deserve to be multibillionaires?

Objections: (1) It's inhumane; (2) it would lead to great differences in wealth, because some can produce such valuable things.

But even in less extreme cases the principle of more pay for more
useful work seems to break down. It's hard, of course, to know the
real value of things. But there can't be any doubt that there is one
thing that no human society can exist without, namely food. (Our
own society could not exist without lots of other things as well, but
food is the one thing every society must have to survive.) Does this
mean that farmers should be the economic princes of any culture?

Would more pay for more important products yield a counterintuitive distribution of wealth?

More Pay for More Effort

Some say more pay for more effort.

One problem with the humanitarian idea that we should give everyone equal pay is that it fails to take account of our extreme distaste for slackers and our liking for hard workers. Because of these, some claim that work should be rewarded not in terms of results but of *effort;* the more effort, the more pay. (It's an interesting fact that we tend to forgive lack of ability in almost every case—except lack of the ability to exert greater effort.)

But would this be fair to those who can't work hard? And what is fair about an employer paying someone a lot who works hard but produces little?

One objection to the idea of more pay for more effort is that it would probably have inhumane consequences, because some people are physically unable to work hard. Another is that there is no fairness to others in rewarding a person for effort instead of results. Where is the fairness to an employer in paying high wages to an employee who works hard but produces little of value? Furthermore, many economists would argue that the best and perhaps only viable economic system must reward *productivity*—at least to some extent. If we reward anything else, the long-run result is bound to be gross economic inefficiency. (Although Marxist doctrine required "From each according to his ability, to each according to his needs," Stalin, faced with the realities of life, changed that doctrine to "From each according to his ability, to each according to his work.")

More Pay for More Odious Work

More odious work deserves more pay.

Finally, there is the idea that more odious (unpleasant) work should earn more pay. If some have to dig coal a mile down in the earth—an extremely nasty job whose odiousness is not appreciated by most white-collar or even factory workers—surely they deserve more pay than those who have much nicer jobs, like working in an office or teaching college students. (In real life, the tendency is for nasty jobs to receive less pay, because those who can get better ones do so and those who are left are in greater need of any job and therefore are more vulnerable. Contrariwise, the jobs most sought after, such as high management positions and most professional jobs, tend to pay the highest salaries.)

But how determine odiousness?

One objection to paying extra for nastiness is that it's hard to determine just how odious a job is; and anyway what seems odious differs greatly from person to person. Most of us would find skyscraper construction work terrifying, even impossible; yet some American Indians have both marvelous balance and absolutely no fear of heights, and they find walking on girders no more nerve-wracking than walking on the ground.

One person's meat is another's poison.

Perhaps the strongest reply to this objection is that the difficulty of deciding in practice is no reason for not coming as close as we can. For example, when a garbage collector's union bargains with a city government for higher wages, it should be relevant in the minds of the public that the job has its literally odious side to it.

The difficulty of judging odiousness is not a sufficient reason for not trying.

Another objection to greater pay for more odious jobs is that it may be economically damaging to employers forced to pay the higher wages, because it puts them at a disadvantage with competitors. This has always been the cry of management when workers demand more pay. And surely management has a point, *unless* competitors are bound by the same rules. If coal miners in the United States were paid salaries reflecting the nastiness, risk, and difficulty of their jobs, U.S. coal might be priced out of the market, either by cheaper labor in foreign coal mines or by cheaper alternative energy sources, such as oil. But if we could get the whole world to agree to pay more for odious jobs, there would be no economic drawback to the idea. Otherwise, justice, if this would be the just thing to do, might have too high an economic cost.

However, paying more for more odious work will be uneconomical unless everyone does.

What Are Fair Taxes?

Governments being necessary, taxes are inevitable. What are the moral aspects of taxation? What would *fair* taxes be like?

Everyone Should Pay the Same Tax

One idea is that equality requires everyone to pay the same amount of taxes. If you work harder or in some other fair way make lots of money, why should you then be punished by a larger burden of government being placed on your shoulders? If those who earn more deserve more (as would be the case in a fair society), taxing them more resembles giving with one hand and taking away with the other.

All should pay the same taxes.

167

Taxes Should Reflect Services Rendered

*More govern-
ment services
should result in
higher taxes.*

Another idea, consistent with a contract theory of government, is that taxes are payments for services rendered by governments. Because everyone receives some benefits from government, everyone ought to pay some taxes (except, perhaps, when governments act as legitimate channels for charity). But some people benefit much more from government than others. Everyone needs police and fire protection, as an example, but protecting the rich costs much more than does protecting the poor. If the rich then pay no more in taxes than the poor, this amounts to the poor subsidizing government services for the rich, which doesn't seem like justice or fairness, at least not according to the idea that the laws of a society are *fair* if they could serve as fair contracts between all the parties in society.

Taxes Should Reflect Ability to Pay

*Those who can
pay more should
pay more in
taxes.*

And then there are those who favor taxes such as a truly graduated income tax, on grounds that the rich should pay more in taxes *because* they're rich and can afford to pay more, whether they receive more services in return or not. A utilitarian might argue this way on grounds that socking the rich is the best way to maximize overall social utility (for one reason, because of the diminishing utility of wealth).

*Objection: If a
rich person gets
few government
services, why
pay high taxes?*

On the other hand, contract theorists may find this idea unsatisfactory. Suppose you fairly earn a large salary but use it in such a way that you need no more government services than ordinary people do (let's say you systematically give part of your income to some charity). Where is the fairness in requiring you to give greater support to government, if government doesn't do any more for you in return?

4. Governments and Individual Morality

*Should govern-
ments legislate
private morality?*

Another difficult question is when, if ever, governments ought to interfere in cases of individual morality. It's clear that governments have to "legislate morality" in cases where great social harm might result—every society, for example, legislates against murder. But what about cases where no direct social harm is in question, as in the case of fornication in private between consenting adults, or the use of birth control devices?

For better or for worse, Karl Marx has had immense influence on the course of history over the past 100 years. Here are excerpts from his The Communist Manifesto *and* Critique of the Gotha Program.

Karl Marx: **THE COMMUNIST MANIFESTO**

The history of all hitherto existing society is the history of class struggles.

Freeman and slave, patrician and plebeian, lord and serf, guildmaster and journeyman, in a word, oppressor and oppressed, stood in constant opposition to one another, carried on an uninterrupted, now hidden, now open fight, a fight that each time ended, either in a revolutionary re-constitution of society at large, or in the common ruin of the contending classes. . . .

All societies so far have been class societies with the classes struggling against each other.

The modern bourgeois society that has sprouted from the ruins of feudal society, has not done away with class antagonisms. It has but established new classes, new conditions of oppression, new forms of struggle in place of the old ones.

Our epoch, the epoch of the bourgeoisie, possesses, however, this distinctive feature; it has simplified the class antagonisms. Society as a whole is more and more splitting up into two great hostile camps, into two great classes directly facing each other: Bourgeoisie and Proletariat. . . .

Now (nineteenth century) society is splitting into two great classes: bourgeoisie and proletariat. The bourgeoisie has engaged in shameless brutal exploitation (of the proletariat).

The bourgeoisie, wherever it has got the upper hand, has put an end to all feudal, patriarchal, idyllic relations. It has pitilessly torn asunder the motley feudal ties that bound man to his "natural superiors," and has left remaining no other nexus between man and man than naked self-interest, than callous "cash payment." It has drowned the most heavenly ecstasies of religious fervor, of chivalrous enthusiasm, of philistine sentimentalism, in the icy water of egotistical calculation. It has resolved personal worth into exchange value, and in place of the numberless indefeasible chartered freedoms, has set up that single, unconscionable freedom—Free Trade. In one word, for exploitation, veiled by religious and political illusions, it has substituted naked, shameless, direct, brutal exploitation.

The bourgeoisie has stripped of its halo every occupation hitherto honored and looked up to with reverent awe. It has converted the physician, the lawyer, the priest, the poet, the man of science, into its paid wage-laborers.

The bourgeoisie has torn away from the family its sentimental veil, and has reduced the family relation to a mere money relation. . . .

The weapons with which the bourgeoisie felled feudalism to the ground are now turned against the bourgeoisie itself. . . .

The bourgeoisie turn the weapons used to defeat feudalism onto themselves.

The essential condition for the existence, and for the sway of the bourgeois class, is the formation and augmentation of capital; the condition for capital

Their own devices lead to their own downfall.

is wage-labor. Wage-labor rests exclusively on competition between the laborers. The advance of industry, whose involuntary promoter is the bourgeoisie, replaces the isolation of the laborers, due to competition, by their revolutionary combination, due to association. The development of Modern Industry, therefore, cuts from under its feet the very foundation on which the bourgeoisie therefore produces, and appropriates products. What the bourgeoisie therefore produces, above all, are its own grave-diggers. Its fall and the victory of the proletariat are equally inevitable.

WHAT IS "A FAIR DISTRIBUTION"?

Isn't the bourgeois distribution of wealth fair?

In the first phase of communism, as it emerges from capitalism, wages are paid in proportion to amount of labor. Laborers thus get back what they contribute (in another form).

Do not the bourgeois assert that the present-day distribution is "fair"? And is it not, in fact, the only "fair" distribution on the basis of the present-day mode of production? . . .

What we have to deal with here is a communist society, not as it has *developed* on its own foundations, but, on the contrary, just as it *emerges* from capitalist society, which is thus in every respect, economically, morally, and intellectually, still stamped with the birthmarks of the old society from whose womb it emerges. Accordingly, the individual producer receives back from society—after the deductions have been made—exactly what he gives to it. What he has given to it is his individual quantum of labor. For example, the social working day consists of the sum of the individual hours of work; the individual labor time of the individual producer is the part of the social working day contributed by him, his share in it. He receives a certificate from society that he has furnished such and such an amount of labor (after deducting his labor for the common funds), and with this certificate he draws from the social stock of means of consumption as much as costs the same amount of labor. The same amount of labor which he has given to society in one form he receives back in another.

Here obviously the same principle prevails as that which regulates the exchange of commodities, as far as this is exchange of equal values. Content and form are changed because under the altered circumstances no one can give anything except his labor, and because, on the other hand, nothing can pass to the ownership of individuals except individual means of consumption. But, as far as the distribution of the latter among the individual producers is concerned, the same principle prevails as in the exchange of commodity equivalents: a given amount of labor in one form is exchanged for an equal amount of labor in another form.

This equal right is still bourgeois right.

Hence *equal right* here is still in principle—*bourgeois right*, although principle and practice are no longer at loggerheads, while the exchange of equivalents in commodity exchange exists only *on the average* and not in the individual case.

In spite of this advance this *equal right* is still constantly stigmatized by a bourgeois limitation. The right of the producers is *proportional* to the labor they supply; the equality consists in the fact that measurement is made with an *equal standard,* labor.

But one man is superior to another physically or mentally, and so supplies more labor in the same time, or can labor for a longer time; and labor, to serve as a measure, must be defined by its duration or intensity, otherwise it ceases to be a standard of measurement. This *equal* right is an unequal right for unequal labor. It recognizes no class differences because everyone is only a worker like everyone else, but it tacitly recognizes unequal individual endowment and thus productive capacity as natural privileges. *It is, therefore, a right of inequality, in its content, like every right.* Right by its very nature can consist only in the application of an equal standard; but unequal individuals (and they would not be different individuals if these were not unequal) are measurable only by an equal point of view, are taken from one *definite* side only, for instance, in the present case, are regarded *only as workers,* and nothing more is seen in them, everything else being ignored. Further, one worker is married, another not; one has more children than another, and so on and so forth. Thus, with an equal performance of labor, and hence an equal share in the social consumption fund, one will in fact receive more than another, one will be richer than another, and so on. To avoid all these defects, right instead of being equal would have to be unequal.

But these defects are inevitable in the first phase of communist society as it is when it has just emerged after prolonged birth pangs from capitalist society. Right can never be higher than the economic structure of society and the cultural development conditioned by it.

In a higher phase of communist society, after the enslaving subordination of the individual to the division of labor, and therewith also the antithesis between mental and physical labor, has vanished; after labor has become not only a means of life but life's prime want; after the productive forces have also increased with the all-round development of the individual, and all the springs of cooperative wealth flow more abundantly—only then can the narrow horizon of bourgeois right be crossed in its entirety and society inscribe on its banners: "From each according to his ability, to each according to his needs!"

But one person may be stronger or smarter than another. So the equal right to wages is an unequal right (as is every such right).

This equal right regards people only as workers; not as parents, etc. To avoid this we need an unequal rule.

In the first phase of communism, we can't expect that.

But under complete communism, the rule will be: "From each according to his ability, to each according to his needs!"

Here is an excerpt from The Republic *by Plato, in which Socrates "defeats" Thrasymachus in a debate concerning the nature and merit of justice.*

Plato: **THE REPUBLIC**

Thrasymachus:
Justice is the interest of the stronger party.

Socrates: *Aren't rulers liable to err and thus to rule against their own interests? And isn't it just for subjects to obey their rulers?*

Thrasymachus:
Doubtless.

Socrates: *Then justice on your view is not only the interests of the stronger but also the reverse. For you've agreed that justice requires subjects to obey even mistaken laws that harm the rulers.*

Socrates: *Is a physician a healer or a money maker?*

I proclaim that justice is nothing else than the interest of the stronger [said Thrasymachus]. And now why do you not praise me? . . . [Socrates] we are both agreed that justice is interest of some sort, but you go on to say 'of the stronger'; about this addition I am not so sure, tell me, Do you not likewise admit that it is just for subjects to obey their rulers? . . . Are the rulers of the various states infallible, or are they sometimes liable to err?

To be sure, he replied, they are liable to err.

Then in making their laws they may sometimes make them rightly, and sometimes not?

When they make them rightly, they make them agreeably to their interest; when they are mistaken, contrary to their interest; you admit that?

And whatever laws they make must be obeyed by their subjects,—and that is what you call justice?

Doubtless.

Then justice, according to your argument, is not only observance of the interest of the stronger but the reverse?

What is that you are saying? he asked.

I am only repeating what you are saying, I believe. But let us consider: Have we not agreed that the rulers, in commanding some actions, may be mistaken about their own interest but that it is just for the subjects to do whatever their rulers command?

I think so.

Then think that you have acknowledged that it is just to do actions which are contrary to the interest of the government or the stronger, when the governors unintentionally command things to be done which are to their own injury, assuming with you that the obedience which the subject renders to their commands, is just.

[Now] . . . let me ask [said Socrates], in what sense do you speak of a ruler or stronger whose interest, as you were saying, he being the superior, it is just that the inferior should execute—is he a ruler in the popular or in the strict sense of the term?

In the strictest of all senses, he said. . . .

[Then] tell me: Is the physician, taken in that strict sense of which you are speaking, a healer of the sick or a maker of money? And remember that I am now speaking of the true physician.

A healer of the sick, he replied.

Now, I said, has not each of these craftsmen an interest? . . .

For which the art has to consider and provide, that being its origin and purpose? . . .

And the interest of any art consists in its being, as far as possible, perfect—this and nothing else?

What do you mean?

I mean what I may illustrate negatively by the example of the body. Suppose you were to ask me whether the body is self-sufficing or wants assistance, I should reply: Certainly it does so; that is why the science, which we call medicine, was invented, because the body is unsound and cannot survive by itself. The art has been established in order to provide it with things which are beneficial to it.

But is the art of medicine or any other art faulty or deficient in any quality in the same way that the eye may be deficient in sight or the ear fail of hearing, and therefore require another art to provide for the interests of seeing and hearing? Or is each of them able to look after its own interest? Or have they no need either of themselves or of another to provide the remedy for their own unsoundness—for there is no such thing as a fault or unsoundness in any art, and the only benefit which an art need consider is that of its subject? For every art remains pure and faultless while remaining true—that is to say, while perfect and unimpaired. Take the words in your precise sense, and tell me whether I am not right.

Yes, clearly.

Then medicine does not consider the interest of medicine, but the interest of the body?

True, he said.

But surely, Thrasymachus, the arts are the superiors and rulers of their own subjects?

To this he assented with a good deal of reluctance.

Then, I said, no science or art considers or enjoins the interest of the stronger [or superior], but only the interest of the subject and weaker?

He made an attempt to contest this proposition also, but finally acquiesced.

Then, I continued, no physician, in so far as he is a physician, considers his own good in what he prescribes, but the good of his patient; for the true physician is also a ruler having the human body as a subject, and is not a mere money-maker; that has been admitted?

Yes. . . .

And such a . . . ruler will provide and prescribe for the interest of the sailor who is under him, and not for his own interest?

He gave a reluctant 'Yes.'

Thrasymachus: A healer.

Socrates: Now our interest in an art consists in its being perfect. Thus, the body needing help, the science of medicine is invented to provide what the body needs. So the art of medicine considers not the interest of medicine but of the body.

Thrasymachus: True.

Socrates: Aren't the arts superior and rulers of their own subjects? And they consider not the interests of the stronger but of the weaker? Then a physician qua physician considers the good of the patient, not himself or financial gain?

Then, I said, Thrasymachus, there is no one in any rule who, in so far as he is ruler, considers or enjoins what is for his own interest. On the contrary, a ruler attends to the subject which he has undertaken to direct; to that he looks, and in everything which he says and does, considers what is suitable or advantageous to it.

When we had got to this point in the argument, and everyone saw that the definition of justice had been completely turned round, Thrasymachus, instead of replying to me, said: Tell me, Socrates, have you got a nurse?

Why do you ask such a question, I said. . . .

Because she leaves you to snivel, and never wipes your nose: she has not even taught you to know the shepherd from the sheep.

What makes you say that? I replied.

Because you fancy that the shepherd or neatherd fattens and tends the sheep or oxen with a view to something other than the good of himself or his master; and you further imagine that the rulers of states, if they are true rulers, never think of their subjects as sheep, and that they are not studying their own advantage day and night. Oh, no; and so entirely astray are you in your ideas about the just and unjust as not even to know that justice and the just are in reality another's good, that is to say, the interest of the ruler and stronger, and the loss of the subject and servant; and injustice, the opposite, for the unjust is lord over the truly simple and just: he is the stronger, and his subjects do what is for his interest, and minister to his happiness, which is very far from being their own. . . . Mankind censure injustice, fearing that they may be the victims of it and not because they shrink from committing it. And thus, as I have shown, Socrates, injustice, when on a sufficient scale, has more strength and freedom and mastery than justice; and, as I said at first, justice is in fact the interest of the stronger, whereas injustice is a man's own profit and interest. . . .

I must remark, Thrasymachus, if you will recall what was previously said [replied Socrates], that although you began by defining the true physician in an exact sense, you did not observe a like exactness when speaking of the shepherd; you thought that the shepherd as a shepherd tends the sheep not with a view to their own good, but like a mere diner or banqueter with a view to the pleasures of the table; or, again, as a trader, for sale in the market, and not as a shepherd. Yet surely the art of the shepherd is concerned only with the good of his subjects; he has only to provide the best for them, since the perfection of the art itself is already ensured whenever the shepherd's work is perfectly performed. And that was what I was saying just now about the ruler. I conceived that the art of the ruler, considered as ruler, whether in a state or in private life, could only have regard to the maximum good

Socrates: *Then a ruler, qua ruler, looks to the interests of those ruled (which turns Thrasym's original statement upside down).*

Thrasymachus: *Socrates, you believe the shepherd fattens sheep for their good, and similarly for rulers. You haven't yet learned the truth is just the opposite. People are against injustice because they fear being its victim, not because they shrink from committing it.*

Socrates: *You've forgotten that you agreed artists act only for the good of their subjects, so that a ruler, as a ruler, acts to benefit his subjects. You seem to think a ruler likes being in authority.*

that is to say, the true rulers, like being in authority.

Think! Nay, I am sure of it.

Then why in the case of lesser offices do men never take them willingly without payment, unless because they assume that their rule is to be advantageous not to themselves but to the governed? Let me ask you a question: Are not the several arts different, by reason of their each having a separate function? . . .

And each art gives us a particular good and not merely a general one—medicine, for example, gives us health; navigation, safety at sea; and so on?

Yes, he said.

And the art of earning has the special function of giving pay: but we do not confuse this with other arts, any more than the art of the pilot is to be confused with the art of medicine, because the health of the pilot may be improved by a sea voyage. . . .

And we have admitted, I said, that the good of each art is specially confined to the art? . . .

Then, if there be any good which all craftsmen have in common, that is to be attributed to something of which they all make common use? . . .

Moreover, we say that if the craftsman is benefited by receiving pay, that comes from his use of the art of earning in addition to his own?

He gave a reluctant assent to this.

Then the benefit, or receipt of pay, is not derived by the several craftsmen from their respective crafts. But it is more accurate to say that while the art of medicine gives health, and the art of the builder builds a house, another art attends them which is the art of earning. The various arts may be doing their own business and benefiting that over which they preside, but would the craftsman receive any benefit from his art unless he were paid as well?

I suppose not.

But does he therefore confer no benefit when he works for nothing?

Then now, Thrasymachus, there is no longer any doubt that neither arts nor governments provide for their own interests; but, as we were before saying, they rule and provide for the interests of their subjects who are the weaker and not the stronger—to their good they attend and not to the good of the superior. And this is the reason, my dear Thrasymachus, why, as I was just now saying, no one is willing to govern; because no one likes to take in hand the reformation of evils which are not his concern without remuneration. For in the execution of his work, and in giving his orders to another, the true artist does not regard his own interest, but always that of his subjects; and therefore in order that rulers may be willing to rule, they must be paid in one of three modes of payment—money, or honour, or a penalty for refusing. . . .

Thrasymachus: *I'm sure of it.*

Socrates: *Why does no one rule without payment? Because their rule benefits others, not themselves?*

And the art of earning has pay as its function, not, say, the art of medicine?

Further, doesn't a craftsman receive pay as a wage earner, not from his other craft?

So payment results from the art of wage earning; a craftsman practicing an art receives no benefit from the practice itself. So neither artists nor rulers provide for their own interests but for the interests of those they serve, which is why rulers must be paid either in money or honor.

Should Governments Legislate Private Morality?

Governments shouldn't legislate private morality, because the purpose of government is social.

But don't all acts have social consequences?

Shouldn't we legislate the social effects of private behavior, not the private acts themselves?

And doesn't social cohesion require being tolerant of others' beliefs?

Some people say that governments have no business legislating private morality, because the purposes of government are completely social. The people on this side generally argue against laws forbidding homosexual (or any private sexual) behavior, abortion, the use or sale of birth control devices, or the use or sale of drugs like marijuana, coffee, tobacco, or alcohol.

One argument on the other side of this issue is that few if any acts are totally private in their consequences. So-called individual morality or private morality, it is claimed, doesn't exist, because all human beings are social animals—what one person does inevitably affects others. For example, the private drinking of alcoholics inevitably affects the people around them, when they fail to support dependents, when they drive while drunk and kill people, and so on.

Although there certainly is some merit in this second argument, still there is a difference between legislating against the harmful *public effects* of private behavior and legislating against the private behavior itself. For example, it makes more sense to punish for driving while drunk than for the drinking in private that preceded the drunk driving. Similarly, it makes sense to punish drunkards who fail to support legal dependents, but not the private drinking that leads to their failure. (Of course, if all private drinking inevitably led to public harm, we might be justified in making it illegal, but in fact most drinkers are able to control their drinking, just as most Valium or Quaalude users control their intake of these drugs.)

In addition, people who oppose the legislation of private morality often appeal to the fact that in modern, diverse societies such as our own, there are great differences of opinion as to the correct principles of morality. Some think birth control devices are immoral; others believe they are perfectly all right. If we are to achieve the social cohesion and cooperation necessary for a society to function well, it is argued, we must be tolerant of each other's moral beliefs, as we are (in the United States) of religious beliefs.

Should We Be Each Other's Keepers?

The dispute concerning the legislation of private morality also concerns the broader question of the help we *owe* to other individuals in our society. Clearly, anyone who is able to should toss a line to a fellow citizen who is drowning. But ought we in general be "our brother's keeper"? Should we interfere in the lives of others "for their own good," even when they don't want us to? We do this with children, of course, because we feel that children aren't able to judge rightly for themselves. Should we similarly interfere when it seems obvious to us that other people are acting against their own interests? If Smith chooses to drink himself into a stupor every day, do we have the obligation, or even the right, to stop him if he harms no one else (or if those harmed don't wish to complain)?

Should we interfere in the private lives of others "for their own good"?

The question is one of freedom versus benevolent interference. Utilitarians must answer it in each case by considering the overall utility of one practice rather than another. Those who believe in natural rights can point to the right of all people to control their private destinies.

Whatever utilitarianism or natural rights theory may seem to imply, we should note that power over others historically has been used to benefit the powerful.

But underlying any discussion of this issue are the sobering facts about how actual, real-life human beings are likely to act in various circumstances, especially those in which one person is given power over another. If history teaches us anything, it teaches us that power tends to be used in the interests of whoever has power. In the case of close relatives or friends, interests may be shared, as they often are between parents and children. But in other cases, where there is often a conflict of interests between those who have power and those over whom they have it, we can't expect true, unbiased benevolence. So a strong argument can be made for the idea that each (adult) person is the best judge of his or her own interests. If this is true, then it would be a mistake to legislate private morality—wrong to make things such as suicide, euthanasia, the use of birth control devices, and private sexual acts illegal. (Of course, those whose moral code consists of a list of hard and fast rules, like the Ten Commandments construed literally, will be inclined to think this is all wrong; suicide, in their view, is the taking of a human life and so should be made illegal.)

Perhaps each person should decide his own private interests.

Summary of Chapter 5

Because human beings are social animals by nature, social and political philosophy are important fields in philosophy.

1. The legitimacy of social institutions, in particular governments and their laws, therefore becomes a basic moral question.

a. *Utilitarianism.* According to *utilitarian* theory, a society is *just* when its laws and customs are designed to produce more benefit (utility) for the whole of society than any other laws or customs.

Although very plausible, this idea suffers from the defects mentioned in Chapter 4 against utilitarianism as a general moral theory, in particular by failing to take account of the common belief that benefits should be distributed according to just desserts, whether that maximizes utility or not. Furthermore, a utilitarian system might well on occasion lead to a system in which the benefits tend to go to a privileged majority, while the harms are inflicted on a "scapegoat" minority.

b. *Natural Rights Theory.* According to some, human beings have *natural rights*—to things such as life, liberty, property, and so on. Governments are legitimate, natural rights advocates argue, when they conform to the natural rights that all human beings possess.

But how do we decide which rights are natural rights? Because different writers champion different rights, rights don't seem to be "self-evident." Nor does there seem to be any factual evidence (facts about the world) or special principles of reasoning that would settle the issue.

c. *Social Contract Theory.* According to social contract advocates, the legitimacy of government stems from the uncoerced consent of the governed—as though everyone in society had gotten together and contracted to form a government. The laws of such a society are *fair,* according to one social contract theory, when they could serve as *fair contracts* among all the people in the society.

2. Although everyone is in favor of social justice and liberty, their actual content is in dispute. Does justice require maximum freedom from government interference? Or should governments force people to act against their will (say, by forbidding acts of racial discrimination)?

3. Economic justice is certainly one of the crucial parts of justice. Is economic justice more likely to be obtained by means of a *free enterprise* or *capitalistic* economic system, or by a *socialistic* one, or perhaps by some combination?

It's difficult to deal with this question, first because it's hard to see what any broad moral theory such as utilitarianism or social contract theory implies for any given society, and second because there is great disagreement over the economic consequences of any economic policy. In practice, the issue in the United States in recent times has centered on government regulation of private industry, not ownership.

A relatively neglected question is that of fair wages for one's time and labor. Some say wages are fair when there is *equal pay for equal work.* Others deny this, arguing for a principle of need—*more pay for greater need.* Still others champion the idea that fairness requires that *those who produce more, or better, goods deserve higher pay* (although this may be unfair if carried to an extreme, because a few great geniuses produce thousands of times more of value than most of us).

Another idea is that fairness requires *more pay for greater effort,* which at least takes account of our distaste for slackers and liking for hard workers. But if some work hard to little effect, where is the fairness to their employers, who must pay them high wages but get little in return?

And then there is the idea that *more odious work merits higher pay.* Whatever its moral merits, this idea makes economic sense only when applied universally—otherwise those employers who don't pay more for odious work will have an economic advantage and drive out employers who do pay more. (This point is relevant to any system of pay that rewards anything but productivity.)

Another difficult question concerns taxes. Are taxes fair when everyone pays the same amount, or when everyone pays the same proportion of income? Or should we tax only for services rendered, so that those who get more expensive government services pay more in taxes? (Requiring all to pay equal taxes inevitably results in the poor subsidizing the rich, because the rich receive more benefits from government than do the poor.)

And then there is the idea that taxes should be in proportion to ability to pay, so that the rich pay more not because they get more in return but just because they're able to pay more. This rule might conform to utilitarian theory, because of the principle of the diminishing utility of money, but not to social contract theory, because it would harm those rich people who for some reason receive fewer benefits of government.

4. There also are questions concerning government interference in private lives. When should governments legislate morality? Obviously, they should in cases where great social harm will result if they don't. But what of other cases—say, cases of private sexual behavior?

Some argue that private morality should not be legislated, for one thing because there isn't any general agreement in this area. Others claim that all private actions have social consequences, therefore all behavior can be legislated.

The issue is in part one of freedom versus benevolent interference. Do governments know what's best for individuals, so that, say, they can rightly forbid suicide? Should we be "our brother's keeper," or should we as much as possible stay off each other's backs? Whatever the answer, it certainly is relevant that in practice those who have obtained power over others have tended to use it more in their own interests than in the interests of the alleged beneficiaries.

179

Questions for Further Thought

1. What do you think of Karl Marx's principle for distributing wealth: From each according to his ability, to each according to his needs?

2. What do you think of the idea that the laws and customs of a society are just only when they could serve as fair contracts between all the parties affected?

3. There are two principles that seem quite plausible to many people; namely, (1) we should be our brother's keeper, and (2) we should get off each other's backs. Yet these principles in practice oppose each other. Which one do you think is right? Or is some in-between principle the correct one?

4. Some social contract theorists have argued that paying some people more than the value of what they produce is unfair to those who therefore have to be paid less than the value of what *they* produce. Does this seem right to you?

5. Let's suppose abortion is in fact murder (whether it really is or not), but that a very large minority in society think it isn't murder. Would the majority be justified in forcing their opinion on the minority by passing laws against abortion?

6. Thomas Hobbes argued that life in a "state of nature" would be "nasty, short, and brutish," and therefore intelligent people in a state of nature would come to see that it's to their advantage to join together and to give up their rights to a sovereign, a king, so as to acquire the resulting benefits of domestic peace and cooperation. Is he right? Can this sort of argument justify having a king rule?

7. How does the following passage strike you:

> We hold these truths to be self-evident, that all men are created equal, that they are endowed by their Creator with certain unalienable Rights, that among these are Life, Liberty and the pursuit of Happiness.

8. And here is another Thomas Jefferson quote:

> . . . Can history produce an instance of rebellion so honorably conducted [as was the Revolutionary War]? . . . God forbid we should ever be twenty years without such a rebellion. . . . What country can preserve its liberties if their rulers are not warned from time to time that their people preserve the spirit of resistance? Let them take arms. . . . The tree of liberty must be refreshed from time to time with the blood of patriots and tyrants. It is its natural manure.

Although we didn't discuss the question of loyalty and rebellion, do you think Jefferson is right? Does your opinion flow from some larger sociopolitical theory?

9. Perhaps Thrasymachus was just being cynical when (in the Plato excerpt in this chapter) he defined justice as "Whatever is in the interest of the stronger parties in society." But what do you think of the objections to this raised by Socrates? And what about the definition Socrates then defends?

10. Utilitarianism seems very plausible to many as a sociopolitical theory because, among other things, it would require legislators to pass only those bills that are believed to maximize overall social welfare. Since the point of government is to obtain the benefits of social cooperation, justice requires the maximization of overall welfare, not special benefits for some at the expense of overall social usefulness. Is this right in your opinion?

A consciousness externally motivated becomes itself pure exteriority and ceases to be consciousness.—JEAN PAUL SARTRE

Reason is substance, as well as infinite power, its own infinite material underlying all the natural and spiritual life; as also the infinite form, that which sets the material in motion. Reason is the substance from which all things derive their being.—G. W. HEGEL

The Absolute Idea. The idea, as unity of the subjective and objective idea, is the notion of the Idea—a notion whose objective is the Idea as such, and for which the objective is Idea— an Object which embraces all characteristics in its unity.—G. W. HEGEL

What is to be investigated is being only and— *nothing* else; being alone and further—*nothing;* solely being, and beyond being—*nothing. What about this Nothing?* . . . Does the nothing exist only because the Not, i.e., the Negation, exists? Or is it the other way around? Does Negation and the Not exist only because the Nothing exists? We assert: the Nothing is prior to the Not and the Negation. . . . Where do we seek the Nothing? How do we find the Nothing? . . . We know the Nothing. . . .

Anxiety reveals the Nothing. . . . That for which and because of which we were anxious was 'really'—nothing. Indeed: the Nothing itself—as such—was present. . . . *What about this Nothing?—The Nothing Itself nothings.*
—MARTIN HEIDEGGER

In dread there is a retreat from something, though it is not so much a flight as a spellbound peace. This "retreat from" has its source in Nothing. The latter does not attract: its nature is to repel. This "repelling from itself" is essentially an "expelling into": a conscious gradual relegation to the vanishing what-is-in-totality. And this total relegation to the vanishing what-is-in-totality—such being the form in which Nothing crowds round us in dread— is the essence of Nothing: nihilation. Nihilation is neither an annihilation of what-is, nor does it spring from negation. Nihilation cannot be reckoned in terms of annihilation or negation at all. Nothing "nihilates" of itself. Nihilation is not a fortuitous event; but understood as the relegation to the vanishing what-is-in-totality, it reveals the latter in all its till now undisclosed strangeness as the pure "Other"—contrasted with Nothing.
—MARTIN HEIDEGGER

The above quotes are examples of the kind of writing some philosophers consider to be confused nonsense (or perhaps obvious platitudes)—anything but profound truths about reality or the human condition. Starting in the late nineteenth century and continuing into the early twentieth century, a revolution occurred in philosophy and generated the broad philosophical position called analytic. A striking belief of some analytic philosophers is that large portions of the well-known writings in the history of philosophy are confused, even nonsense, and should be weeded out wholesale by applying general principles such as the verification theory of meaning (see p. 193) or by some other kind of careful linguistic analysis. They had in mind passages such as the ones just cited from Hegel, Heidegger, and Sartre, which seemed to them to contain gross misuses of language by

means of which unwarranted conclusions are drawn.

In the excerpt in this chapter by the analytic philosopher Moritz Schlick, he explains why he rejects this kind of "metaphysical" philosophy (and explains what he believes the true job of philosophers consists in). In another excerpt in this chapter, Hans Reichenbach (who called himself a logical empiricist) analyzes the first Hegel quote just given and then examines Descartes' famous proof of his own existence (see the Descartes excerpt in Chapter 3), finding both grossly defective. Interestingly, some of the best examples of what analytic philosophers call metaphysical nonsense come out of two other schools in recent philosophy; namely existentialism (see the Sartre excerpt in Chapter 2) and phenomenology (see the Husserl excerpt in this chapter).

6

Some Recent Turns in Philosophy

It's an interesting question whether philosophy makes progress the way the sciences have. Average physicists today know a great deal more than did Isaac Newton, perhaps the greatest of all physicists, precisely because they stand on the shoulders of the great scientific giants of the past, Newton in particular. By way of contrast, many would argue that the average philosopher today is no closer to philosophical truth than was, say, David Hume (to mention the author's particular hero), or Kant. Scientists over the years have come to agree on increasingly subtle theories; philosophers agree on nothing.*

One reason for this difference may be that the moral subjectivists (discussed at the end of Chapter 4) as well as other subjectivists are right and thus that large portions of philosophy rest on subjective principles—unlike the sciences, which deal entirely with objective reality. Every philosopher thus in effect has to start from scratch, guided, of course, by the results of previous philosophers, but always having to match what others have said to his or her own basic starting points (basic intuitions) and experiences. Recall, for example, the differences in basic starting points between an atheist and a theist, or a libertarian and a soft determinist. Having started out differently, it's no surprise that philosophers have failed to reach the kind of

It seems as though there is not progress in philosophy as there is in science.

Perhaps this is so because philosophy rests on subjective principles, so that every philosopher has to start from scratch, and having different starting points, reach different conclusions.

---

*Except, of course, that they don't agree on *nothing* thus Heidegger's famous "The nothing nihilates of itself" (or "The nothing nothings"), called nonsense by logical positivists.

general agreement that characterizes science, no surprise that each philosopher must in a sense start from scratch, even though the paths finally taken are well marked by previous philosophical journeys.

Still, some believe there is philosophical progress, and analytic philosophy is an example.

Even so, there are some (including this writer) who believe that there *is* progress in philosophy, and that the late nineteenth and early twentieth centuries were times of unusually rapid progress, in particular in the flowering of what has come to be called **analytic philosophy,** consisting roughly of three schools: **logical positivism** (or **logical empiricism; pragmatism;** and **ordinary language philosophy**). (Today, the once-dominant analytic school is just one of several enjoying some popularity; many philosophical flowers bloom.)

1. Logical Positivism

Positivists disdain metaphysical talk as virtually meaningless.

Logical positivists are united in their disdain for a certain kind of philosophy they sometimes derisively refer to as **metaphysical** (a term that has very positive emotive overtones for their opponents). When they come across philosophy of this kind, which characterizes a great deal of the philosophical literature, logical positivists are inclined to dismiss it as so vague, ambiguous, or obscure, as to be virtually meaningless, or perhaps, when interpreted or deciphered, either trivial or just plain false, in any case hardly containing profound truths about the nature of reality, knowledge, or the human condition. (Some positivists would say that much of this obscure language is a kind of misplaced poetry—misplaced because they consider clarity to be a requirement of good philosophical discourse.)

The task of philosophy is (1) analysis of concepts, and (2) investigation of the principles of correct reasoning.

In place of the metaphysical talk they so disparage, positivists propose that the task of philosophers is (1) the careful analysis and clarification of key concepts in science and in philosophy itself, and (2) the investigation of the principles of logic or cogent (correct) reasoning, or, in other words, the investigation of the correct method for finding any truths whatsoever.

Science and Methodology

Science is the area of factual inquiry,

Positivists believe that there are essentially two basic areas of inquiry: *science* and *methodology*. Science is the area of factual inquiry. Its realm is every question concerning the nature of the experienceable universe, from the nature of distant galaxies to the composition of human cells to the nature of molecules and atoms.

Methodology is the realm of philosophy. It divides into two different but related tasks: (1) logic, concerned with the questions of valid or cogent reasoning, and (2) conceptual analysis, or meaning analysis, concerned with the analysis of key terms, concepts, or expressions, in particular those used in science and in the pursuit of methodology itself.

philosophy of good reasoning and meaning analysis.

Deductive and Inductive Logic

Logic in turn divides into *deductive* logic and *inductive* logic. To see the difference, consider the following two arguments:

1. All metaphysicians frequently utter nonsense.
2. Hegel is a metaphysician.
∴ 3. Hegel frequently utters nonsense.

1. All diamonds discovered so far have been smaller than 10,000 carats.
∴ 2. (Probably) all diamonds whatsoever are smaller than 10,000 carats.

The first of these arguments is a **deductively valid argument:** *If its premises are true, then its conclusion must be true also,* or to put it another way, if its premises are true, then its conclusion cannot be false. The truth of the premises of a deductively valid argument (in the cases where the premises *are* true) "guarantees" the truth of its conclusion. The reason this is so, at least according to many positivists, is that the conclusion of a valid deductive argument is already "contained in" its premises, either explicitly or implicitly. In the case at hand, the premises say that *all* metaphysicians frequently utter nonsense and then say that Hegel is a metaphysician, thus implicitly saying the conclusion that Hegel frequently utters nonsense (which happens to be just what all good logical positivists believe about Hegel).

The second argument is an **inductively valid argument.*** In contrast

Valid deductive argument: If its premises are true, then its conclusion must be true, because its conclusion is already contained in its premises.

---

*According to some, it could be invalid, for instance, if we have what is called higher-level inductive reasons for assuming that gigantic diamonds will probably be discovered or manufactured someday. Some logicians reserve the term "valid" for deductively valid arguments, referring to inductively valid arguments as *inductively correct,* or *inductively strong.*

Valid inductive argument: Its premises provide good but not conclusive support for its conclusion.

to the first one, the premise of the second argument does not already contain or say what its conclusion says. Its premise asserts something about all diamonds *discovered so far,* while its conclusion makes a claim about all diamonds *whatsoever.* So its premise might be true even though its conclusion turns out to be false (as it will if someday someone discovers a gigantic diamond of over 10,000 carats). So the truth of the premise of this inductively valid argument does *not* guar-

Inductive reasoning infers the continuation of patterns in our experiences.

antee the truth of its conclusion. However, it does provide good evidence for the conclusion, because, as mentioned in Chapter 3 in the discussion of inductive reasoning, an inductively valid argument captures a pattern or connection existing between two or more kinds of things that we've noticed in our experiences of the world. In the case of the second argument, it captures the connection between being a diamond and having a relatively small size that we've noticed in our experience.

Scientific Reasoning Centers on Induction

Positivists believe scientific reasoning must be at least in part inductive.

One point of distinguishing inductive from deductive reasoning is that logical positivists believe scientific reasoning about the world must always contain at least one inductive argument. Deductively valid arguments, as we have seen, already contain their conclusions in their premises; they thus provide us with what may be psychologically new information, but not with anything genuinely new. Inductively valid reasoning, on the other hand, always goes beyond its premises, saying something not said in its premises—which is why some philosophers speak of the "inductive leap" from premises to conclusion. (It's also why the conclusion of an inductively valid argument, although sensible, may turn out to be false even though its premises are true. The new "knowledge" gained by induction thus has a risk attached to it that the knowledge gained via deduction does not—which is why skeptics have been quicker to challenge the legitimacy of induction than of deduction.*)

---

*However, there is an interesting skeptical challenge even to valid deduction, because the proof that an argument *is* deductively valid itself must use at least some of the valid principles of deduction, and thus be circular.

Scientific knowledge, according to the positivists, is thus gained by observing the world and reasoning inductively (and deductively) from statements of patterns observed (or hypothesized) to conclusions about "laws of nature" and how the world seems to work. Philosophers, of course, may use this factual knowledge about how human beings work, but *as philosophers* they don't discover new factual truths. That's why, say the positivists, we can be sure metaphysical philosophy contains no good reasons for believing any facts about the world. For example, dyed-in-the-wool positivists would feel reasonably sure that Immanuel Kant's arguments to prove that every event has a cause are defective somehow or other, even before actually examining his arguments in detail to discover their flaws—they're sure there must be flaws, because Kant doesn't argue to his conclusion inductively from observations of patterns noticed in his (or anyone's) experiences.

So science reasons by induction from past experiences to (hopefully) laws of nature and how the world works. But philosophers don't do this. They don't discover new facts about the world.

The Analytic, Synthetic, A Priori, and A Posteriori

David Hume divided all knowledge into **matters of fact,** discoverable only through observation, or experience, and **relations of ideas,** discoverable just by reasoning—comparing one idea or concept with another. But, following the later language of Immanuel Kant, logical positivists tend to refer to matters of fact as **synthetic,** and to relations of ideas as **analytic.** * So they would say that analytic knowledge can be obtained **a priori,** which means roughly that it can be known prior to or without experience of the thing known. An example is the *a priori* knowledge that two apples plus two apples equals four apples, which can be known without ever checking up on apples. And they say that synthetic knowledge can be obtained only **empirically,** or **a posteriori,** which means that it can be known only through experiences of some kind. An example is the knowledge that sugar sweetens coffee, which we can obtain only by putting sugar into coffee (or into something) and tasting it (or by bringing to bear knowledge of a more general nature obtained by higher-level inductive inferences from other experiences).

Positivists believe analytic knowledge (relations of ideas) can be known a priori, but synthetic knowledge (matters of fact) only empirically, or a posteriori.

---

*Kant defined these terms so that a judgment is *synthetic* if the meaning of its predicate is not part of the meaning of its subject, and *analytic* if it is, a definition positivists tend to reject (for one thing because many statements are not in subject-predicate form).

Scientific Knowledge Is Synthetic, Mathematical Knowledge Analytic

Scientists discover synthetic truths a posteriori, mathematicians and logicians discover analytic truths a priori.

In dividing knowledge into the analytic *a priori* and the synthetic *a posteriori*, logical positivists also divide the labor between scientists and mathematicians. Scientists are trying to discover that which can be known *a posteriori*; science thus deals in synthetic *a posteriori* knowledge. And mathematicians (and deductive logicians—the two are placed in the same category by logical positivists*) attempt to discover that which can be known *a priori*; mathematics thus deals in analytic *a priori* knowledge.

Analytic Truths Have No Factual Content

Analytic truths can be known a priori because they're factually empty. They follow from the meanings of the terms they contain.

The question naturally arises as to why analytic truths, or any truths, can be known *a priori*. How can we know anything, say, about apples without experiencing apples? The positivist's answer is that we can know *a priori* that, say, two plus two equals four, or that something either is red or isn't (the law of the excluded middle, in deductive logic), because statements of this kind are *factually empty*; that is, they don't tell us anything about the way the universe happens to be (in contrast to synthetic propositions such as "Snow melts at 32°F," which tells us a fact about snow). Instead, they tell us about how words and expressions, or concepts, are used. Thus, "Two apples plus two apples equals four apples" tells us nothing about apples, instead telling us how the terms *two, plus, equals,* and *four* are used (because it tells us that two of anything plus two of that thing equals four of that thing). Two apples plus two apples thus equals four apples no matter what apples happen to be like, and even if there aren't any apples.

There Are No Synthetic A Priori Truths

Empiricists believe there can be no synthetic a priori truths.

Logical positivism arises largely within the philosophical tradition of **empiricism.** One basic principle of empiricism is that no synthetic truths can be known *a priori*, whereas other schools in philosophy, in

---

*Starting with Bertrand Russell, several not entirely successful attempts have been made to prove that mathematics is a branch of, or kind of, deductive logic.

In the 1920s and '30s, what was called the Vienna Circle was the center of the logical positivist movement, and Moritz Schlick was the leader of the Vienna Circle. In this excerpt, he expounds on a dominant theme in logical positivism.

Moritz Schlick: **THE METHOD OF PHILOSOPHY**

The philosopher cannot be satisfied to ask, as the historian would ask of all the systems of thought—are they beautiful, are they brilliant, are they historically important? and so on. The only question which will interest him is the question "What truth is there in these systems?" And the moment he asks it he will be discouraged when he looks at the history of philosophy because, as you all know, there is so much contradiction between the various systems—so much quarreling and strife between the different opinions that have been advanced in different periods by different philosophers belonging to different nations—that it seems at first quite impossible to believe that there is anything like a steady advance in the history of philosophy as there seems to be in other pursuits of the human mind. . . .

. . . When we examine the history of philosophy honestly, it seems as if there were no traces of any discovery that might lead to unanimous philosophical opinion.

This skeptical inference, in fact, has been drawn by a good many historians, and even some philosophers have come to the conclusion that there is no such thing as philosophical advancement, and that philosophy itself is nothing but the history of philosophy. . . .

I intend to take an entirely different view of philosophy and it is, of course, my opinion that this view of philosophy will some time in the future be adopted by everybody. In fact, it would seem strange to me if philosophy . . . were nothing at all but one great deception. . . .

There is unquestionably some kind of advance shown in science, but . . . a similar kind of advance cannot be discovered in philosophy.

The same great issues are discussed nowadays that were discussed in the time of Plato. When for a time it seemed as though a certain question were definitely settled, soon the same question comes up again and has to be discussed and reconsidered. It was characteristic of the work of the philosopher that he always had to begin at the beginning again. He never takes anything for granted. He feels that every solution to any philosophical problem is not certain or sure enough, and he feels that he must begin all over again in settling the problem. There is, then, this difference between science and philosophy which makes us very skeptical about any future advance of philosophy. Still we might believe that times may change, and that we might

The philosophers ask about the truth of a system of thought, not its beauty or brilliance. But they have always disagreed as to the truth of the various contradictory theories proposed.

Some say no agreement will be reached. Philosophy is just the history of philosophy.

But surely philosophy is not just one great deception— agreement is possible.

There surely is progress in science, but there has been little in philosophy. The same issues are debated, now as in Plato's time. Each philosopher starts anew. The hope that philosophers will come

189

to agree, like scientists, is a vain hope.

possibly find the true philosophical system. But this hope is in vain, for we can find reasons why philosophy has failed, and must fail, to produce lasting scientific results as science has done. If these reasons are good then we shall be justified in not trusting in any system of philosophy, and in believing that no such system will come forward in the future.

The reason is not the difficulty of the problems or lack of ability. It is that philosophy cannot be a system of truths, like science.

Let me say at once that these reasons do not lie in the difficulty of the problems with which philosophy deals; neither are they to be found in the weakness and incapacity of human understanding. . . . No, the real reason is to be found in a curious misunderstanding and misinterpretation of the nature of philosophy; it lies in the failure to distinguish between the scientific attitude and the philosophical attitude. It lies in the idea that the natures of philosophy and science are more or less the same, that they both consist of systems of true propositions about the world. In reality philosophy is never a system of propositions and is therefore quite different from science.

Philosophy and science were one discipline until the sciences branched off one by one.

In its beginnings . . . philosophy was considered to be simply another name for the "search for truth"—it was identical with science. Men who pursued the truth for its own sake were called philosophers, and there was no distinction made between men of science and philosophers.

Philosophy remained united with the various sciences until gradually the latter branched off from philosophy. In this way, mathematics, astronomy, mechanics and medicine became independent one after the other. . . .

In the 19th century, antagonism developed, because some philosophers claimed a better method than science to discover truth.

It was in the nineteenth century that the real antagonism began, with a certain feeling of unfriendliness developing on the part of the philosopher toward the scientist and the scientist toward the philosopher. This feeling arose when philosophy claimed to possess a nobler and better method of discovering truth than the scientific method of observation and experiment. . . . They thought that they could attain the same truth that the scientist was trying to find but could discover it in a much easier way by taking a short cut that was reserved . . . only for the philosophical genius. . . .

Others say philosophy deals with more general truths than science. Philosophy is thus a science, only the most general one.

There is another view, however, which tried to distinguish between science and philosophy by saying that philosophy dealt with the most general truths that could be known about the world and that science dealt with the more particular truths. . . .

This so-called "synoptic view" of philosophy, holding as it does that philosophy is also a science, only one of a more general character than the special sciences, has, it seems to me, led to terrible confusion. On the one hand it has given to the philosopher the character of the scientist. He sits in his library, he consults innumerable books, he works at his desk and studies various opinions of many philosophers as a historian would compare his different sources, or as a scientist would do while engaged in some particular pursuit in any special domain of knowledge; . . .

On the other hand, with this picture of the philosopher in mind we find a very great contrast when we look at the results that have been really achieved by philosophical work carried on in this manner. There is all the outward appearance of the scientist in the philosopher's mode of work but there is no similarity of results. Scientific results go on developing, combining themselves with other achievements, and receiving general acknowledgment, but there is no such thing to be discovered in the work of the philosopher. . . . Let me just mention that some say that philosophy is the "science of values" because they believe that the most general issues to which all questions finally lead have to do with value in some way or another. Others say that it is epistemology, i.e., the theory of knowledge, because the theory of knowledge is supposed to deal with the most general principles on which all particular truths rest. One of the consequences usually drawn by the adherents of the view we are discussing is that philosophy is either partly or entirely metaphysics. And metaphysics is supposed to be some kind of a structure built over . . . the structure of science but towering into lofty heights which are far beyond the reach of all the sciences and of experience. . . .

Scientific knowledge increases, and general agreement is gained. But not philosophical knowledge.

Some say philosophy is the science of values, or of the theory of knowledge, and so philosophy is (in part) metaphysics, far beyond experiential sciences.

However, you have probably read some of Plato's Dialogues, wherein he pictures Socrates as giving and receiving questions and answers. If you observe what was really done—or what Socrates tried to do—you discover that he usually did not arrive at certain definite truths which would appear at the end of the dialogue but the whole investigation was carried on for the primary purpose of making clear what was meant when certain questions were asked or when certain words were used.

But if you look, say, at Plato's dialogues, you'll see that Socrates didn't arrive at definite truths, but at clarity regarding language.

Socrates' philosophy consists of what we may call "The Pursuit of Meaning." He tried to clarify thought by analyzing the meaning of our expressions and the real sense of our propositions.

Socrates was engaged in the clarification of meaning.

Here then we find a definite contrast between this philosophic method, which has for its object the discovery of meaning, and the method of the sciences, which have for their object the discovery of truth. In fact, let me state shortly and clearly that I believe Science should be defined as the "pursuit of truth" and Philosophy as the "pursuit of meaning."

Science is the pursuit of truth; philosophy of meaning.

When we make a statement about anything we do this by pronouncing a sentence and the sentence stands for the proposition. This proposition is either true or false, but before we can know or decide whether it is true or false we must know what this proposition says. We must know the meaning of the proposition first. After we know its sense we may be able to find out whether it is true or not. . . .

We must know the meaning of a sentence before we can determine its truth.

But how can we be quite sure that we really know and understand what

We know the meaning of a proposition when we know in what circumstances it would be true (or false). Then we can look and see which circumstances obtain and which sentences are true.

However, some philosophers tried to discover the truth of propositions without knowing their meanings.

It might seem that philosophy is the science of meaning.

But there can't be a science of meaning, because there are no true propositions about (particular) meanings.

And what of alleged philosophical problems? (1) Some are not genuine problems, although grammatical form makes us think they are.

(2) Some are real problems answerable by science, not philosophy.

we mean when we make an assertion? What is the ultimate criterion of its sense? The answer is this: We know the meaning of a proposition when we are able to indicate exactly the circumstances under which it would be true (or, what amounts to the same, the circumstances which would make it false). The description of these circumstances is absolutely the only way in which the meaning of a sentence can be made clear. After it has been made clear we can proceed to look for the actual circumstances in the world and decide whether they make our proposition true or false. There is no vital difference between the ways we decide about truth and falsity in science and in every-day life.

It seems evident that a scientist or a philosopher when he propounds a proposition must of necessity know what he is talking about before he proceeds to find out its truth. But it is very remarkable that oftentimes it has happened in the history of human thought that thinkers have tried to find out whether a certain proposition was true or false before being clear about the meaning of it, before really knowing what it was they were desirous of finding out. This has nearly always been the case in traditional philosophy.

From what I have said so far it might seem that philosophy would simply have to be defined as the science of meaning . . . and that philosophy would be a science just as other sciences, only its subject would be "Meaning." . . .

But philosophy is not a science in this sense. There can be no science of meaning, because there cannot be any set of true propositions about meaning. The reason for this is that in order to arrive at the meaning of a sentence or of a proposition we must go beyond propositions. For we cannot hope to explain the meaning of a proposition merely by presenting another proposition. When I ask somebody, "What is the meaning of this or that?" he must answer by a sentence that would try to describe the meaning. But he cannot ultimately succeed in this, for his answering sentence would be but another proposition and I would be perfectly justified in asking "What do you mean by this?" . . .

And what was the matter with those great questions that have been looked upon as specific "philosophical problems" for so many centuries? In the first place, there are a great many questions which look like questions because they are formed according to a certain grammatical order but which nevertheless are not real questions, since it can easily be shown that the words, as they are put together, do not make logical sense. . . .

In the second place, there are some "philosophical" problems which prove to be real questions. But of these it can always be shown by proper analysis that they are capable of being solved by the methods of science although we may not be able to apply these methods . . . for technical reasons.

particular the one usually called **rationalist,** claim that synthetic *a priori* knowledge is possible, and in fact often is obtained. Examples are the truths of geometry, and in particular the metaphysical "truths," such as the statements that time is unreal, or that the Nothing nihilates itself. Positivists argue that these apparently profound propositions are simply obscure (agreeing with Nietzsche's remark "They muddy the water that it may appear deep").

Others believe there is such knowledge, for instance, in geometry and in metaphysics.

But to the extent that they can analyze such statements, positivists find them to be meaningless (or obvious truths, or simple falsehoods, or poetic) instead of philosophical. Take Heidegger's famous statement "Nothing nihilates of itself," or "The Nothing itself nothings" (in German "Das Nichts selbst nichtet"). This statement is doubly non-sensical, on the positivist view, first because it contains an utterly meaningless word, namely, the verb *nothings,* and second because it uses the word *nothing* as a noun and subject of the sentence, leading to the confused idea that perhaps nothing is something, whereas the term *nothing* functions as a *quantifier*—telling us how many of the kind of thing mentioned in a statement are being talked about, in this case none. So the logical positivists see misguided misuse of language where the metaphysicians see profound truths.

But positivists believe alleged synthetic a priori metaphysical statements are meaningless. Example: Heidegger's "The nothing itself nothings," which contains misuses of the idea of nothing.

The Verification Theory of Meaning

To combat metaphysical nonsense on a wholesale basis, positivists have proposed various versions of what may be called the **principle of verification,** or the **verification theory of meaning.** In early versions, this principle said that a statement has meaning only if it can be *verified* as true or false. However, when it was pointed out that scientific theories can't be verified absolutely, but only confirmed by evidence (made more probable by evidence) or disconfirmed by evidence, the principle was modified to say roughly that a statement has meaning only if it is possible to *confirm* or *disconfirm* it by some relevant observation. (The sense of possibility intended differed from one advocate to another, some choosing logical and some physical possibility—that is, some conceiving of a thing as possible if it doesn't violate laws of logic and some if it doesn't violate known laws of nature.) Thus the statement "Water molecules are composed of hydrogen and oxygen atoms" has meaning because there are possible

Verification theory of meaning: A statement has meaning only if it can be confirmed or disconfirmed by observation or experience.

Thus, "Nothing nihilates of

193

itself" is
meaningless
because no
conceivable
observation could
confirm or
disconfirm it.

observations relevant to its confirmation or disconfirmation, and even the statement "There is life in every one of the almost countless galaxies in the universe" has meaning because it is physically possible to check up on every galaxy even though as a practical matter it's impossible to do so. But statements such as "Nothing nihilates of itself" can't be checked up on by means of any conceivable observation, and so are meaningless according to the verification principle.

Does the Principle of Verification Have Meaning?

Some reject the
verification the-
ory of meaning
as meaningless
according to it-
self. But that
principle seems
to be put forth as
a proposal as to
how we can
profitably use
language, hence
it isn't supposed
to have factual
content.

Almost immediately after the verification principle was proposed, the question arose as to the status of that very principle according to itself. Is it itself meaningful? What observations would help confirm or disconfirm it? It isn't like a principle of logic (say, the principle that nothing can both be and not be in the same way). Nor is it like a meaningful statement of fact confirmable through observation (such as "Copper conducts electricity"). Although no general agreement has been reached on the question, the principle seems to function as a *proposal* or *recommendation* as to how to profitably use language or concepts, especially the key term *meaning*. It *itself* is a philosophical statement, and thus tells us nothing about the nature of the world, or any part of it, but rather gives us a tool to use in analyzing language, an important task of philosophy, according to positivists. If it states a fact at all, the fact is just that a proposal or announcement to use language in a certain way has been made.

Value Statements Are Cognitively Meaningless

In addition to
factual or cogni-
tive meaning,
there is also
emotive
meaning.

The principle of verification was intended to concern only a particular kind of meaning, namely **factual** or **cognitive meaning.** Scientific and everyday factual statements have this kind of meaning—metaphysical ones don't. But there is another sort of meaning, **emotive meaning,** that lots of other statements have, including some metaphysical statements. (Factual statements may also have emotive meaning.) And some sentences function in an entirely different manner; for example, commands and questions.

Positivists think
of moral state-
ments as stating

All this has crucial bearing on the question discussed in Chapter 4 whether moral or esthetic "truths" are objective or subjective. For the hard-core positivist, statements of moral or esthetic value have no

194

cognitive or factual meaning, but function in some other way. Take the statement "It's wrong to kill." This seems to be a factual statement, just like "It's half past eight." But in fact it's one of those statements whose grammatical structure masks its logical structure. One thing we can mean to do in uttering this sentence is to utter a command: "Don't kill!" Another is to express or state a negative attitude toward killing: "Killing, ugh!" or "I intensely hate killing." By saying "It's wrong to kill," we mislead people into thinking there is some objective property—moral wrongness—and killing has that property, just as when we say "It's raining in Chicago" we indicate an objective property of the weather in Chicago. But according to positivists, there are no objective moral properties. (There aren't any objective esthetic properties, such as beauty or unity, either.)

or expressing emotive meaning, not cognitive or factual meaning.

They believe there are no objective moral properties.

This approach has led to the theory called **emotivism,** which says that value statements such as "X is good" either express or state *attitudes* or *emotions*—in the case of "X is good," a pro attitude—of the speaker, and definitely don't state objective facts about the nature of the world. They are, according to the principle of verification, cognitively meaningless.

Emotivism: *Value statements express or state attitudes or emotions, not objective facts.*

Positivists Aren't against Morality

Of course, positivists are not less moral than other people. They have their attitudes toward things in the moral realm just like the rest of us. They simply see moral discourse as the expression of subjective feelings or attitudes, so that they would reject appeals to an alleged objective authority, such as God, or the nature of reality, and insist that moral disputes arise for the most part because attitudes and interests differ, not because some of us don't "see" the objective moral reality.

Positivists aren't less moral. They just think of morality differently than some other philosophers.

Positivists Aren't Emotionless or Unpoetic

The charge is sometimes heard that positivists are somehow devoid of the usual emotions, or at least don't believe they're very important compared to facts and to reason, since they intend to banish emotive language from philosophy. Some see them as crass materialists. But this is a mistake. The difference between the positivists and some other philosophers is in their insistence that philosophy and poetry

Nor do they lack emotions. They just think certain kinds of language, fine for poetry, are deadly for philosophy.

195

The philosopher Hans Reichenbach, was typical of many analytic philosophers in insisting that philosophers pay close attention to science and in his belief that a good deal of "speculative" philosophy is radically mistaken.

Hans Reichenbach: **THE RISE OF SCIENTIFIC PHILOSOPHY***

Here is a passage taken from the writings of a famous philosopher [Hegel]: "Reason is substance, as well as infinite power, it's own infinite material underlying all the natural and spiritual life; as also the infinite form, that which sets the material in motion. Reason is the substance from which all things derive their being."

Many have no patience with philosophy.

Many a reader has no patience with linguistic products of this brand. Failing to see any meaning in them, he may feel inclined to throw the book into the fire. . . .

Students of philosophy often puzzle over metaphysical works and finally believe they understand them.

The student of philosophy usually is not irritated by obscure formulations. On the contrary, reading the quoted passage he would presumably be convinced that it must be his fault if he does not understand it. He therefore would read it again and again and thus would eventually reach a stage in which he thinks he has understood it. At this point it would appear quite obvious to him that reason consists of an infinite material which underlies all natural and spiritual life and is therefore the substance of all things. He has been so conditioned to this way of talking as to forget all criticisms which a less "educated" man would make.

What would scientists think of metaphysical language?

Now consider a scientist trained to use his words in such a way that every sentence has a meaning. His statements are so phrased that he is always able to prove their truth. He does not mind if long chains of thought are involved in the proof; he is not afraid of abstract reasoning. But he demands that somehow the abstract thought be connected with what his eyes see and his ears hear and his fingers feel. . . .

They understand "material" and "substance." But how can reason be a substance?

The words "material" and "substance" are no strangers to him. He has applied them in his description of many an experiment; he has learned to measure the weight and the solidity of a material or a substance. He knows that a material may consist of several substances, each of which may look very different from the material. So these words do not offer any difficulty in themselves.

But what kind of material is that which underlies life? One would like to assume that it is the substance of which our bodies are made. How then can

*Hans Reichenbach, *The Rise of Scientific Philosophy.* Copyright 1951 by University of California Press. Reprinted by permission.

it be identical with reason? Reason is an abstract capacity of human beings, manifesting itself in their behavior, or to be modest, in parts of their behavior. Does the philosopher quoted wish to say that our bodies are made of an abstract capacity of themselves?

Does Hegel mean we're made of an abstract capacity?

Even a philosopher cannot mean such an absurdity. What then does he mean? Presumably he means to say that all happenings in the universe are so arranged that they serve a reasonable purpose. That is a questionable assumption, but at least a comprehensible one. Yet if it is all the philosopher wants to say, why must he say it in a cryptic way?

Presumably, Hegel doesn't mean that. Does he mean all events serve a purpose? If so, why be so cryptic?

That is the question I wish to answer before I can say what philosophy is, and what it should be. . . .

The essence of knowledge is *generalization*. That fire can be produced by rubbing wood in a certain way is a knowledge derived by generalization from individual experiences; the statement means that rubbing wood in this way will *always* produce fire. The art of discovery is therefore the art of correct generalization. . . . Generalization, therefore, is the origin of science.

The art of (factual) discovery is the art of correct generalization.

Generalization, furthermore, is the very nature of explanation. What we mean by explaining an observed fact is incorporating that fact into a general law. We observe that as the day progresses a wind begins to blow from the sea to the land; we explain this fact by incorporating it into the general law that heated bodies expand and thus become lighter with respect to equal volumes. We then see how this law applies in the example considered: the sun heats the land more strongly than the water so that the air over the land becomes warm and rises, thus leaving its place to an air current from the sea. . . . There are two kinds of false generalization, which can be classified as innocuous and pernicious forms of error. . . .

Generalization is the guts of explanation. To explain is to incorporate into a general law.

As an instance of a pernicious generalization, which uses a superficial analogy with the intention of constructing a universal law, consider the philosophic passage quoted in the introduction. The observation on which the statement is based is the fact that reason in large measure controls human actions and thus determines, at least partly, social developments. Looking for an explanation the philosopher regards reason as analogous to a substance that determines the properties of the objects which are composed of it. For instance, the substance iron determines the properties of a bridge built of it. Obviously, the analogy is pretty bad. Iron is the same kind of stuff as the bridge; but reason is not a stuff like human bodies and cannot be the material carrier of human actions. When Thales, who about 600 B.C. acquired fame as the "sage of Miletus," put forth the theory that water is the substance of all things, he made a false generalization; the observation that water is contained in many materials, as in the soil, or in living organisms, was falsely

Hegel's passage contains an analogy between reason, which causes us to act, and material substances, which determine the properties of things. This is a poor analogy, because reason is not a "stuff" like a human body.

extrapolated to the assumption that water is contained in every object. Thales' theory, however, is sensible in so far as it makes one physical substance the building block for all the others; it is at least a generalization, though a false one, and not an analogy. . . . The trouble with loose language is that it creates false ideas, and the comparison of reason with a substance offers a good illustration for this fact. The philosopher who wrote this passage would strongly object to the interpretation of his statement as a mere analogy. He would claim that he had found the real substance of all things and would ridicule an insistence on physical substance. He would maintain that there is a "deeper" meaning of substance, of which physical substance is but a special case. Translated into comprehensible language this would mean that the relation between the happenings in the universe and reason is the same as the relation between the bridge and the iron out of which it is made. But this comparison is obviously untenable, and the translation shows that any serious interpretation of the analogy would lead to logical blunder. Calling reason a substance may produce some images in the listener; but in further application such word combinations mislead the philosopher to jump to conclusions which logic cannot warrant. Pernicious errors through false analogies have been the philosopher's disease at all times. . . .

Hegel's loose language creates false ideas in us. He would no doubt claim he has found a deeper meaning of substance. But his analogy still is a logical blunder.

The fallacy committed in this analogy is an example of a kind of mistake called the *substantialization of abstracta*. An abstract noun, like "reason," is treated as though it refers to some thing-like entity. There is a classic illustration of this kind of fallacy in the philosophy of Aristotle (384–322 B.C.), where he treats of form and matter.

Hegel's "reification" of reason is sometimes called the "substantialization of abstracta." Aristotle was also guilty of this. His treatment of form and matter makes form—an abstraction—into something substantial.

Geometrical objects present the aspect of a form as distinct from the matter of which they are built; the form can change while the matter remains the same. This simple daily experience has become the source of a chapter of philosophy which is as obscure as it is influential and which is made possible only by the misuse of an analogy. The form of the future statue, Aristotle argues, must be in the block of wood before it is carved, otherwise it would not be there later; all becoming, likewise, consists in the process of matter taking on form. Form, therefore, must be a something. It is obvious that this inference can only be made by the help of a vague usage of words. To say that the form of the statue is in the wood before the sculptor has shaped it, means that it is possible for us to define inside the block of wood, or "see" into it, a surface which is identical with the later surface of the statue. Reading Aristotle, one sometimes has the feeling that he really means only this trivial fact. But clear and reasonable passages in his writings are followed by obscure language; he says such things as that one makes a brazen sphere out of bronze and sphere by putting the form into this material, and arrives at regarding form as a substance which exists perpetually without change. . . .

A figure of speech has thus become the root of a philosophical discipline, which is called *ontology*, and which is supposed to deal with the ultimate grounds of being. The phrase "ultimate grounds of being" is itself a figure of speech; . . . for Aristotle form and matter are such ultimate grounds of being. Form is actual reality and matter is potential reality, because matter is capable of taking on many different forms. Furthermore, the relation of form and matter is regarded as lurking behind many other relations. In the scheme of the universe, the upper and the lower spheres and elements, the soul and the body, the male and the female, stand to one another in the same relation as form and matter. Aristotle evidently believes that these other relations are explained by the strained comparison with the fundamental relation of form and matter. A literal interpretation of analogy thus supplies a pseudo explanation, which by the uncritical use of a picture brings many different phenomena together under one label. . . .

A figure of speech thus became (part of) the roots of ontology, a study of the "ultimate grounds of being," itself a metaphysical figure of speech.

Descartes' proof for absolute certainty is constructed by means of a logical trick. I can doubt everything, he argues, except one thing: that is the fact that I doubt. But when I doubt I think; and when I think I must exist. He thus claims to have proved the existence of the ego by logical reasoning; I think, therefore, I am, so goes his magical formula. When I call this inference a logical trick, I do not wish to say that Descartes intended to deceive his readers; I would rather say that he was himself deceived by this tricky form of reasoning. But logically speaking, the step from doubt to certainty performed in Descartes' inference resembles a sleight of hand—from doubting he proceeds to considering doubt as an action of an *ego*, and thus believes that he has found some fact which cannot be doubted.

Descartes proved he exists by means of an unintentional logical trick.

Later analysis has shown the fallacy in Descartes' argument. The concept of the ego is not of so simple a nature as Descartes believed. We do not see our own selves in the way we see houses and people around us. We may perhaps speak of an observation of our acts of thought, or of doubt; they are not perceived, however, as the products of an ego, but as separate objects, as images accompanied by feelings. To say "I think" goes beyond the immediate experience in that the sentence employs the word "I." The statement "I think" represents not an observational datum, but the end of long chains of thought which uncover the existence of an ego distinct from the ego of other persons. Descartes should have said "there is thought," thus indicating the sort of detached occurrence of the contents of thought, their emergence independent of acts of volition or other attitudes involving the ego. But then Descartes' inference could no longer be made. . . .

Against Descartes: We can experience thoughts, but not ourselves. When Descartes said, "I think," he went beyond what he experienced—that there is thought—and begged the question by placing the "I" to be proved into his premise.

(or literature in general) are two different sorts of enterprises. Although positivists differ on the exact role of literature, they agree in believing that the use of poetic language when doing philosophy results in obscure or ambiguous language instead of the clear language necessary to avoid the pitfalls into which the metaphysical philosophers have fallen.

2. Pragmatism

Pragmatism tries to relate the theoretical with the practical.

Historically prior to logical positivism, **pragmatism** is the only widely accepted school of philosophy to originate in America. Pragmatism is sometimes confused with *practicalism,* with the attempt to replace the theoretical, especially as it occurs in earlier Western philosophy, with the practical. Instead, the core of pragmatism is the attempt to relate theory to practice and to give significance to theory in the practical affairs of our lives.

The Pragmatic Theory of Meaning

Pragmatic theory of meaning: Statements have meaning for us only when we know how their truth would bear on our lives.

The theory of meaning is key for pragmatists, just as for positivists, and their meaning principle is very similar to the verification principle. According to the **pragmatic theory of meaning,** a statement has meaning for us only when we can specify at least some conceivable bearing its truth might have on our lives. And two statements have the *same* meaning, are *synonymous,* if their truths would have identical bearings on our lives. (This is the import of William James's statement "A difference that makes no difference *is* no difference." It's just a difference in words.) For example, the sentences "More rain falls in Seattle than in Los Angeles" and "Coca Cola contains caffeine but not cocaine" have obvious relevance to everyday life and its problems. The same is true for esoteric scientific formulas such as $E = mc^2$, as the atom bomb dramatically illustrates. But Sartre's statement "a consciousness externally motivated becomes itself pure exteriority and ceases to be consciousness" would appear to have no relevance to life's problems, and thus to have no genuine meaning. (Of course, Sartre and other existentialists think otherwise.)

Much philosophy fails to satisfy this criterion.

Language originates in purposive

For the pragmatist, statements have meaning only because *people mean something by them.* There aren't free-floating meanings wafting about. Language originates in *purposive human behavior*, which is why meaning is connected to human activities and problems. Every declarative statement believed is a *rule of action*. Thus, "This bowl is full of sugar" means something like "If you want to sweeten your coffee or tea, use some of the contents of this bowl." (More precisely, a statement is a whole set of rules of action. "This bowl is full of sugar" means also "If you're diabetic, don't use the contents of this bowl," and "This bowl contains a CHO compound," and so on.)

behavior. Statements are rules of action.

The Pragmatic Theory of Truth

For pragmatists, the truth of a sentence lies in the fulfillment of the purposes that belief in the sentence makes possible. The truth is what works in the everyday world of problems. Thus, the statement "This bowl is full of sugar" is true (assuming it is full of sugar) because if we believe it and pour some of its contents into coffee it makes the coffee taste sweet, and so on. The truth is what works, what is expedient in our thinking. Of course truth is what works in the long run, not just in the short run.

For pragmatists, the truth is what works in everyday life in the long run.

We ordinarily think of true statements as true because they correctly describe some feature of the world. But pragmatists look on true statements as rules of action, and thus as *predictions* about the outcomes of possible human actions. They don't deny that true statements correctly describe the world; rather, they insist that description necessarily involves prediction. We're justified in believing they correctly describe because they correctly predict, not the other way around. Thus, "This bowl is full of sugar" is true because it correctly predicts that if you put its contents into tea, the tea will be sweetened.

Statements are predictions about the outcome of human actions. "This is sugar" predicts that if we put this substance in coffee, it will taste sweet.

This is even true of historical truths, according to some pragmatists. Take the statement that modern horses evolved from a much smaller variety. This means, among lots of other things, that if we look in certain places in the earth, our chances are good that we'll eventually find fossils of horselike animals ranging down in size from present-day horses to much smaller ones. Discovering such fossils, as we have, thus gives us reason to think that the original statement is true, because it's been a good rule of action.

Even statements about the past are predictions about the future.

Of course, such examples are simplifications. No one statement predicts anything all by itself, and so no one sentence is true all by itself. Statements yield predictions only in conjunction with theories.

More precisely, one statement alone yields no

201

predictions. Only whole theories do; so only whole theories are true or false.

And so, strictly speaking, only whole theories are meaningful, or true or false. We often fail to realize this because, for example, when an experiment results in negative (disconfirming) evidence, we usually conclude that only a small part of the overall theory has been disconfirmed; if we can, we hang on to the rest of the theory by revising it to take account of the negative observations.

For example, the statement that the earth is flat yields no predictions. We need to add the idea, say, that light travels in straight lines.

Take the old idea that the earth is flat. One implication of this theory is that if we go down to the sea and watch a ship arrive, we should see the hull as soon as the mast. But when we check up, we find that the mast of a ship comes into view over the horizon before the hull, confirming the idea that the earth is a sphere and disconfirming the belief that it's flat. At least that's the way we usually reason. Yet it's possible for the earth to be flat and for us to see a ship's top coming over the horizon before its hull. The flat earth theory by itself makes no predictions on the matter. We need to add the usual theory that light travels in straight lines, which, when combined with the flat earth theory, yields the conclusion that all of the ship will come into view at the same time. (If light traveled in certain kinds of curved lines, the earth could be flat and we'd still see the top of a ship before the rest when it came into port.) So when it turns out that we see the top first, this disconfirms the whole package

Faced with negative evidence, we reject the weakest link in our theory.

of theories that yielded the incorrect prediction. But we reject just that part of the package about the earth being flat, because the theory that light travels in straight lines enters into countless other packages that have yielded many successful predictions (for instance, about the distance to the moon or the heights of distant buildings). In other words, in the face of negative evidence, we hang on to the most useful and discard the least needed so as to bring our overall theory into conformity with actual observations.

Logic Is the Theory of Rational Inquiry or Problem Solving

Logic, for pragmatists, is the whole theory of rational problem solving.

For pragmatists, logic is the general method for solving concrete as well as abstract problems. It thus is the theory of scientific problem solving as well as everyday problem solving, because engaging in science is just a systematic way to solve real-life problems. (By *logic*, pragmatists mean what we've called inductive as well as deductive logic, although some pragmatists refuse to make that distinction.)

When we examine actual problem situations, we find that some of

202

the ideas appealed to are not problematic, at least not in that context. A genuine problem can't even be formulated without assuming something that isn't problematic. At least some goals, desires, or interests must be taken for granted in a given problematic situation; otherwise, there is no conflict of goals and nothing with which to evaluate the possible courses of action to resolve the conflict. Take a person torn between the choice of going to a college close to home and one far away. The first may be attractive precisely because of the security felt by being close to helping parents, while the second is attractive because of the greater freedom distance from parents is expected to bring. The *problem* arises only because there is a clash of values—someone who no longer needs parental attention can't have this problem, which *is* a problem only because both the desirability of parental aid and also of freedom from parental hovering are taken for granted to have value. The problem is solved by finding out which need is stronger, or by challenging the need for one of them—say, by concluding that close parental attention is no longer as valued as it once was. (One reason we often go wrong in problem solving is that we fail to realize that some value or other has changed.) But we can't give up all our desires, goals, and needs and still have a problem or be able to get a solution. In the case at hand, the problem is solved either by giving up one desire in favor of another or by realizing that one desire has faded. Giving up every desire and need would result not in solving the problem but in not having it.

Problems arise from conflicting goals or desires. We can't challenge all of our goals at once, because then there is no problem.

Adoption of the Cartesian method of trying to doubt, all at once, everything that can be doubted (see the Descartes excerpt in Chapter 3) simply leads to the denial of everything, to complete doubt, to complete skepticism, as should have become apparent from going through part of such a complete program of doubt in Chapter 3. (Descartes himself came to a different conclusion, but no pragmatist would accept his reasoning.) Having nothing left to evaluate a given thing, nothing can be justified. But in actual problematic situations in real life (as opposed to the theoretical speculations of skeptical philosophers), some values are always accepted without challenge in that situation. This is true even in philosophical problem-solving situations, unless we pretend to adopt the skeptic's program—pretend, because none of us are genuine skeptics (and even the skeptic holds on to at least one value, namely in accepting only what can be justified by something else). In philosophy, as anywhere else, we always ap-

Descartes' method of doubt leads only to complete doubt of everything, not to necessary truth. In real life, some values always remain undoubted at any time.

Nothing is exempt from

203

doubt, but we can't doubt everything all at once.

proach a particular problem with at least some other unchallenged beliefs, which in fact generate the problem. Not, of course, *never* challenged beliefs, for that amounts to dogmatism, but rather beliefs not challenged at the time. Nothing is exempt from doubt. Everything can be challenged. But not all at once.

Even the Rules of Logic Are Not Unchallengeable

Even the rules of logic can be challenged. The right rules of logic are right because they have worked, not because they're built in heaven.

When pragmatists say nothing is exempt from doubt, they mean *nothing*. Even the principles of logic can be challenged. Logic consists of rules of proof. But the rules were not made in heaven; they aren't eternal rules to be discovered by the sweet light of reason. The warranted nature of the rules of logic is the same as for anything else—they are warranted because of the successful results they yield in science and other problematic situations. Warranted principles of logic have stood the test of success when actually used. (This approach is one important way in which pragmatism differs from logical positivism.)

Logic is not *how* we think but how we *ought* to think. However, the reason why is not founded in any metaphysical necessity, but rather in the success of logical principles in doing the job they're supposed to do, which is to help us solve our problems. We ought to think one way rather than some other because that way has been most successful over the long run. (All sorts of crazy methods, even including crystal ball gazing, are sometimes successful for a while, but that doesn't make them warranted methods for solving problems.)

The Truth Is Connected with Successful Prediction

The truth is what helps us to solve life's problems, to correctly anticipate the future.

The connection between logical inquiry and truth is clear. Logical inquiry results not in absolute or eternal truth but rather in theories that enable us to be more and more successful in solving life's problems. This is true in particular of scientific truths, which *are* truths simply because they have so often led us to anticipate a future that really arrived, and so helped us to cope successfully with everyday problems.

Facts and Values Are Intertwined and Inseparable

Pragmatists don't divide between facts and values.

Finally, it should be noted that pragmatists reject David Hume's sharp distinction between facts and values, another important way in which they differ from logical positivists. On their view, what we call a fact is simply what we have taken *to be* a fact. The world just *is*. When we divide it into facts, *we* choose those aspects of reality to honor with our choice; *we* choose the divisions and categories, and we do so because of their usefulness in problem solving, their usefulness in our attempts to satisfy our values. We categorize according to *our* problems and interests. Thus, a wristwatch is just a timepiece to most of us, but is jewelry to a socialite, a commodity to a merchant, an intricate mechanism to a watch repairer, and so on. (Contrast this categorization with Sartre's account of the essence of a papercutter being to cut paper, and of a hammer to drive nails; in fact papercutters make excellent torture devices, and hammers crack skulls just as well as they drive nails. What we say these objects *are* is determined by our needs, desires, and goals.) There are an infinite number of ways to slice the pie of reality—not that every division is equally good. We choose those of value to us. And merely to slice the pie at all, merely to engage in scientific investigation at all, results from a value judgment on our part.

There are many ways to divide the pie of reality. We choose those of value to us.

Just as facts thus have their value aspect, so also values have their factual tinge. Science is as important in the determination of values as it is of facts. We tend to overlook this because when we think of values, we think of *old* values, safe (right now), not problematic now, overlooking the time when they too were problematic, under challenge, and overlooking the fact that the same method was used to accept them as genuine. But the intelligent person does not forever accept old values unchallenged. We test them to see how they work in practice, and if they fail try to replace them with new values more likely to do the job. Thus, intelligent liberals have challenged the value of certain government regulations and agencies they previously valued, because experience has shown that these previously valued institutions and policies probably will not get us the values they were designed to reach. And some socialists have challenged the value of state-owned industry in favor of other devices, such as greater worker control and ownership of large corporations. If these new turns work in solving the problems they are intended to, they'll be accepted by intelligent people as valued new methods and institutions, taking the place of the discarded old. In like manner, all values, moral, esthetic, or whatever, are subject to recall in favor of new values that better further our overall interests.

Facts have their value tinge and values have their factual side.

A valued institution may be rejected (revalued) because it fails to work in practice, and may be replaced by others designed to further our overall purposes.

205

Reason and Emotion Don't Oppose Each Other

Pragmatists reject the division between reason and emotion in favor of the idea of rational and irrational emotions.

In the history of ethics, there are many disputes over what is central to ethical choice: reason or emotion, knowledge or feeling, reason or sentiment. Some take one side, some the other. But pragmatists refuse to make the very distinctions that generate these issues. For them, the distinction isn't between reason and emotion, but rather between rational and irrational emotions. Emotions are attitudes toward things or situations. To the extent that they fail to take account of what reason tells us about ourselves and our surroundings, instead stemming from factual ignorance, or from lethargy or appeals to hidebound authorities, they are irrational. Only those attitudes that take account of what reason tells us about ourselves and about the causes and consequences of acting out our attitudes, can be considered rational.

There are no absolute ends in life. Every end is in turn a means to something else. And no end is desirable no matter what means are needed to get it. What counts are means-ends packages.

It should be obvious, then, that pragmatists deny the usual distinction between *means* and *ends*. There are no absolute or ultimate ends. Every end is in its turn a means to something else. (The paradigm case, perhaps, is the earning of money.) And nothing is desirable as an end without regard for the means to that end. Thus, according to political libertarians, the end of getting people to not do some sort of action (such as engage in prostitution) or not use some sort of item (such as marijuana or cocaine) fails to be a rational end even for those who would value the disappearance of these things from society, because the means necessary to truly eliminate these things from our lives would be so ghastly as to make the whole *means-end package* lack any true value for us (as, libertarians would point out, we should have learned from the "Great Experiment" of Prohibition in the 1920s). Pragmatists thus speak of a *means-end continuum*, instead of means, or ends, alone.

Pragmatism and Some Philosophical Dualities

Pragmatists "solve" many philosophic problems by denying they arise. For example, they deny there is a problem of choosing realism

In general, pragmatists try to solve many of the age-old philosophical problems by denying the framework in which they arise. Some examples are problems about free will versus determinism, the existence of a mental and a physical realm, the mind-body problem (not discussed in this text), and so on.

Take the dispute between realists and phenomenalists over the existence of material substance (or any nonmental entities). This dispute clearly doesn't matter one whit with respect to any real-life everyday problem. But it doesn't even matter for any conceivable problem, however unlikely it may be to arise. To see this, imagine that a realist and a phenomenalist are standing in front of us and we ask each in turn if there is some experience they would expect to have, even in some unlikely situation, that they'd expect to be different were they to change sides in the dispute. The answer each must give is no, for reasons discussed in Chapter 3, so that the experiential content of each theory must be the same. It follows, then, on the pragmatic theory of meaning that if the theories of realism and phenomenalism have any meaning at all, they must have the same meaning. (Recall that on the pragmatist's theory of meaning, two theories have the same meaning if it makes no difference in our expectations under any circumstances which one we accept.) In fact, statements such as "Everything in the world is mental" would appear to be meaningless, because believing them can have no conceivable bearing on how we conduct our lives and try to solve life's problems. (Anyone who thinks otherwise, say pragmatists, should point out the practical difference this theoretical difference might make in the conduct of anyone's life.)

or idealism because it can't possibly make a real-life difference which we choose, so that on their theory of meaning, they mean the same thing.

3. Ordinary Language Philosophy

Logical positivists want to purge philosophy of metaphysical nonsense by pointing out the misuses of language that generate such nonsense. In place of metaphysical talk, they propose "logically perfect" artificial notations (of the kind studied in symbolic logic classes) whose grammatical rules would forbid ambiguity and vagueness and assure the clarity and precision they believe is necessary in the sciences and logic.

By way of contrast, a later group of analytic philosophers, sprung from the same general sources, espouses what has come to be called **ordinary language philosophy** (which divides into several camps lumped all together here for simplicity). They have turned away from the idea that we need to construct precise logic languages to get the needed clarification and to avoid the worst of the metaphysical confusion. Instead, they believe the most profitable way to avoid linguistic confusion and error is by the careful analysis of everyday and philosophical language.

Ordinary language philosophers believe we should analyze everyday language, not construct logically perfect languages.

207

Charles Peirce (1839–1914) is the father of Pragmatism, the only important philosophical position to originate in the United States. The following is from his 1877 article "The Fixation of Belief."

Charles Peirce: THE FIXATION OF BELIEF

We all think we, but not others, know how to think correctly.

Few persons care to study logic, because everybody conceives himself to be proficient enough in the art of reasoning already. But I observe that this satisfaction is limited to one's own ratiocination, and does not extend to that of other men. . . .

We try to change the uneasy state of doubt for the calm state of belief.

Doubt is an uneasy and dissatisfied state from which we struggle to free ourselves and pass into the state of belief; while the latter is a calm and satisfactory state which we do not wish to avoid, or to change to a belief in anything else. On the contrary, we cling tenaciously, not merely to believing, but to believing just what we do believe. . . .

Some settle doubt by taking any answer and then holding fast to it no matter what, deliberately ignoring contrary evidence. This yields peace of mind.

If the settlement of opinion is the sole object of inquiry, and if belief is of the nature of a habit, why should we not attain the desired end, by taking any answer to a question, which we may fancy, and constantly reiterating it to ourselves, dwelling on all which may conduce to that belief, and learning to turn with contempt and hatred from anything which might disturb it? This simple and direct method is really pursued by many men. I remember once being entreated not to read a certain newspaper lest it might change my opinion upon free-trade. . . . A similar consideration seems to have weight with many persons in religious topics, for we frequently hear it said, "Oh, I could not believe so-and-so, because I should be wretched if I did."

But this method of tenacity fails in practice, because others believe differently, shaking one's faith.

But this method of fixing belief, which may be called the method of tenacity, will be unable to hold its ground in practice. The social impulse is against it. The man who adopts it will find that other men think differently from him, and it will be apt to occur to him in some saner moment that their opinions are quite as good as his own, and this will shake his confidence in his belief. This conception, that another man's thought or sentiment may be equivalent to one's own, is a distinctly new step, and a highly important one. It arises from an impulse too strong in man to be suppressed, without danger of destroying the human species; so that the problem becomes how to fix belief, not in the individual merely, but in the community.

So let society decide and teach the young.

Let the will of the state act, then, instead of that of the individual. Let an institution be created which shall have for its object to keep correct doctrines before the attention of the people, to reiterate them perpetually, and to teach them to the young; having at the same time power to prevent contrary doctrines from being taught, advocated, or expressed. . . .

This method has, from the earliest times, been one of the chief means of upholding correct theological and political doctrines, and of preserving their universal or catholic character. . . .

For the mass of mankind, then, there is perhaps no better method than this. If it is their highest impulse to be intellectual slaves, then slaves they ought to remain.

But in the most priest-ridden states some individuals will be found who are raised above that condition. These men possess a wider sort of social feeling; they see that men in other countries and in other ages have held to very different doctrines from those which they themselves have been brought up to believe; and they cannot help seeing that it is the mere accident of their having been taught as they have . . . that has caused them to believe as they do and not far differently. Nor can their candour resist the reflection that there is no reason to rate their own views at a higher value than those of other nations and other centuries; thus giving rise to doubts in their minds.

A different method of settling opinions must be adopted, that shall not only produce an impulse to believe, but shall also decide what proposition it is which is to be believed. Let the action of natural preferences be unimpeded, then, and under their influence let men, conversing together and regarding matters in different lights, gradually develop beliefs in harmony with natural causes. This method resembles that by which conceptions of art have been brought to maturity. The most perfect example of it is to be found in the history of metaphysical philosophy. Systems of this sort have not usually rested upon any observed facts, at least not in any great degree. They have been chiefly adopted because their fundamental propositions seemed "agreeable to reason." This is an apt expression; it does not mean that which agrees with experience, but that which we find ourselves inclined to believe. Plato, for example, finds it agreeable to reason that the distances of the celestial spheres from one another should be proportional to the different lengths of strings which produce harmonious chords. Many philosophers have been led to their main conclusions by considerations like this.

This method is far more intellectual and respectable from the point of view of reason than either of the others which we have noticed. But its failure has been the most manifest. It makes of inquiry something similar to the development of taste; but taste, unfortunately, is always more or less a matter of fashion, and accordingly metaphysicians have never come to any fixed agreement, but the pendulum has swung backward and forward between a more material and a more spiritual philosophy, from the earliest times to the latest. And so from this, which has been called the *a priori* method, we are driven, in Lord Bacon's phrase, to a true induction. . . . [For] some

This is the method of theology and politics.

Perhaps it's best for most of us—intellectual slaves.

But even in the most priest-ridden state some will notice that in other places opinions differ, shaking their faith.

So a new method must be developed, like the one used in metaphysical philosophy. These systems rest not primarily on observed fact, but on beliefs "agreeable to reason."

This a priori method fails because it makes inquiry a matter of taste, fashion, so that general agreement can't be reached.

But some will become doubtful. A new method is needed, relating beliefs to external reality.

Mystics think they use this method, but theirs is really tenacity, not a public method.

We need a method that gets the same answer for all. Science believes in an external reality independent of us which we can discover by experience. This is the only method that is self testing or self correcting.

Better than any particular belief is integrity of belief. He who agrees there is truth, and then avoids it, is in a sorry state.

people, among whom I must suppose that my reader is to be found, who, when they see that any belief of theirs is determined by any circumstance extraneous to the facts, will from that moment not merely admit in words that that belief is doubtful, but will experience a real doubt of it, so that it ceases in some degree to be a belief. . . . To satisfy our doubts, therefore, it is necessary that a method should be found by which our beliefs may be caused by nothing human, but by some external permanency—by something upon which our thinking has no effect. Some mystics imagine that they have such a method in a private inspiration from on high. But that is only a form of the method of tenacity, in which the conception of truth as something public is not yet developed. Our external permanency would not be external, in our sense, if it was restricted in its influence to one individual. It must be something which affects, or might affect, every man. And, though these affections are necessarily as various as are individual conditions, yet the method must be such that the ultimate conclusion of every man shall be the same. Such is the method of science. Its fundamental hypothesis, restated in more familiar language, is this: There are Real things, whose characters are entirely independent of our opinions about them; those realities affect our senses according to regular laws, and, though our sensations are as different as are our relations to the objects, yet, by taking advantage of the laws of perception, we can ascertain by reasoning how things really are; and any man, if he have sufficient experience and he reason enough about it, will be led to the one True conclusion. . . .

This is the only one of the four methods which presents any distinction of a right and a wrong way. If I adopt the method of tenacity, and shut myself out from all influences, whatever I think necessary to doing this, is necessary according to that method. So with the method of authority: the state may try to put down heresy by means which, from a scientific point of view, seem very ill-calculated to accomplish its purposes; but the only test *on that method* is what the state thinks; so that it cannot pursue the method wrongly. So with the *a priori* method. The every essence of it is to think as one is inclined to think. All metaphysicians will be sure to do that, however they may be inclined to judge each other to be perversely wrong. . . . above all, let it be considered that what is more wholesome than any particular belief is integrity of belief, and that to avoid looking into the support of any belief from a fear that it may turn out rotten is quite as immoral as it is disadvantageous. The person who confesses that there is such a thing as truth, which is distinguished from falsehood simply by this, that if acted on it will carry us to the point we aim at and not astray, and then, though convinced of this, dares not know the truth and seeks to avoid it, is in a sorry state of mind indeed.

Philosophical Problems Arise from Confused Uses of Language

A key idea of ordinary language philosophy is that philosophical problems arise when we use language in a peculiar or confused way or in odd contexts. We become confused into thinking we have a problem because we've used a sensible feature of everyday language in an inappropriate context or manner.

Philosophical problems arise from using everyday language in an inappropriate way.

A person with a philosophical problem is suffering from a kind of linguistic psychological cramp. Psychiatrists try to remove ordinary psychological problems by getting patients to see the perhaps unconscious motives, past history, and so on, that generated them in the first place. These problems are generally not solved in the way the patient perhaps expects them to be, but rather are *dissolved*. In like manner, ordinary language philosophers claim, philosophical problems are not solved the way we solve ordinary everyday problems, but rather are dissolved the way psychological problems are, in particular by getting the "patient" to see the odd uses of language that generate the "problem" (or, as we shall see, by getting the patient to see what tempted the use of odd language in the first place).

Philosophical problems are not solved, but dissolved, by seeing the odd use of language that generates them, like the shrink who dissolves a sex problem.

Suppose a patient goes to an analyst (of the psychological, not philosophical, variety—but the use of the same term is not an accident!) with a problem of controlling his sexual urges. The analyst doesn't tell the patient to do so and so and thus control his urges; so the problem isn't solved in the usual sense. What the analyst does instead is try to arrange matters so that sex no longer has compulsive power over the person and thus no longer is bothersome. In this way the problem is dissolved, not solved. (Compare this approach with the old idea that we solve such a problem by willpower, or by getting involved in other problems so that we don't have any time to worry about sex.)

In like manner, the philosophical task is not to try to solve the ancient "problems" that have divided philosophers for centuries (realism versus phenomenalism, free will versus determinism, and so on) but to show how misusing language, that in everyday contexts is perfectly useful and sensible, itself *generates* these problems rather than solving them. Once we see how we've generated our own confusion, and see what led us to do this, we no longer will be puzzled and our problems will fade away, not because we've solved them (as we solve

211

the problem, say, of icy streets by putting sand on them) but because they've dissolved in the clarification process.

We need to get the philosopher to see the oddity of his questions, and the peculiarity of his language "answering" it.

The traditional philosopher is like the person who asks "How high is up?" and then is puzzled by the "answers" the question generates and is unable to decide between them. In this case, it's obvious that the way to get rid of the problem is to get the person to see the oddity of the question, the misuse of ordinary locutions that generates it, and the peculiar uses of language employed in attempting to "answer" it. It would be pointless to continue searching for more adequate answers to a question such as how high is up—all such answers are bound to be unsatisfactory, and indeed may generate new and perhaps even more confused questions in their turn.

For example, the problem of free will versus determinism is dissolved by seeing that libertarians and hard determinists have changed the notion of freedom from its everyday sense. Returning to that sense (as soft determinists do) gets rid of the problem.

Take the hard determinists' statement that no one is free, that no one has a free will. This sounds like a perfectly meaningful sort of thing to say, whether true or false, and indeed seems to have much evidence in its favor (namely, the evidence in favor of determinism). Hard determinists, in fact, argue that it is both meaningful and true, and go on to draw the astounding conclusion that we're never justified in holding people morally accountable for what they do (as noted in Chapter 2). And libertarians, also finding it perfectly meaningful, argue that it must be false, because we obviously are responsible for what we do.

But all this is a mistake, according to some ordinary language philosophers. The problem is not to decide between libertarians and hard determinists, but to see what misuses of language produced the issue in the first place, so that once we see this the puzzle about which way to go on the issue will fade away. And that's more or less what soft determinists have done, by pointing out, you may recall, that in everyday life the freedom required to hold people morally or legally accountable for their misdeeds is not the freedom from cause fought over by hard determinists and libertarians, but is rather freedom from compulsion. For in daily life it is absence of this kind of freedom that counts as a legitimate excuse—sometimes exonerating, sometimes just mitigating—for most kinds of wrongdoing. In daily life, the question of freedom from cause never arises;* no one would take proof that an action was caused as an excuse for doing wrong.

---

*Well, it hardly ever arises. A famous exception was Clarence Darrow's brilliant defense of Loeb and Leopold. His hard determinist arguments convinced the judge to sentence the two admitted

But Metaphysical Talk Is Not a Complete Waste of Time

There is, however, another aspect to the philosopher's traditional misuses of language, somewhat like the language uses of poets. A good poet tends to be an extremely perceptive person who notices aspects and connections of things, in particular subtle emotional responses, that the rest of us either fail to notice or only glimpse vaguely. Becoming aware of these subtleties of human experience, the poet stretches everyday language so as to give us the esthetic charge we all seek and to help us see the subtleties in our own experiences (if we would only look at them). There may be no way, at least none readily available to the ordinary literate person, to say these things in anything like so succinct and forceful a manner (as we discover when we try to translate poetry into ordinary prose).

The poet uses poetic language to express what is at least hard to express in everyday prose.

According to some ordinary language philosophers, there is something similar in metaphysical talk. (However, they don't want this comparison to be carried too far.) Sometimes philosophers are trying to point out features of experience or knowledge for which they find no ready-made linguistic devices. So they use inappropriate devices and become confused, and confuse others, even though they believe they're being enlightening.

Philosophers sometimes use this kind of poetic language, inappropriately, causing confusion.

In such cases, we must get philosophers to see how their misuses of language are confusing us—this is the negative part of the job. At the same time, we want to grasp the elusive insight being reached for by the philosopher in the first place—this is the positive part of the job. Philosophy is thus not just a waste of time, or a getting ourselves back to Square One; the point, one hopes, is to learn something about the philosopher's insights, however confused, which generated all that metaphysical language in the first place, without ourselves becoming confused.

We should get the philosopher to see how misuses of language are confusing us, and yet grasp the insight in the poetic language.

Here are two quotes from an ordinary language philosopher on this point. * The first is in the overall context of an attempt to show both

---

murderers to life imprisonment instead of giving them the death penalty public opinion demanded. On the view espoused here, the judge fell for a metaphysical and confused argument (so apparently did Darrow himself). The example is interesting because ordinary language philosophers see the role of philosophy to be the analysis of everyday language and concepts, not just those of the metaphysician.

*John Wisdom. The first quote is from his book *Other Minds*, the second from his *Philosophy and Psychoanalysis*.

the misleadingness and instructiveness of skeptical claims that we can't have knowledge of such things as "other minds," the future, whether there's a sound when a tree falls in a forest with no one to hear, and so on:

> . . . A philosophical difficulty such as "What then, do you say that philosophical questions are meaningless?", "Do we know that dogs hear whistles too high for us to hear?" may be removed by getting the patient to describe himself. He must then describe fully the sort of question or statement he is considering. By the time he has described this, e.g., has described a philosophical question, he has set it in its place on the language map with regard to all other questions. And thus he has answered his own question. He is like the man who first saw a zebra and came back and said, "I saw an animal with hoofs like a donkey but in shape rather more like a pony than a donkey. What sort of animal was it? Would you say it was a kind of a donkey?" His friend said, "Tell me, what sort of coat had it? Like a pony or a donkey? Like a pony you say. Well I should say it was sort of a pony. But what sort of ears had it? Long ears? Oh! well then . . . But neighs like a horse?" And so on. It appears that the man who asked the question was best placed for answering it.
>
> In the same way *every philosophical question,* when it isn't half asked, answers itself; when it is fully asked, answers itself.

Here is the second quote:

> . . . the metaphysical dispute is resolved by explaining what induces each disputant to say what he does. This is done as follows: First explain the nature of the question or request: (a) Negatively—remove the wrong idea that it is a question of fact whether natural *or logical;* (b) Positively—give the right idea by showing how, as in other disputes of this unanswerable sort, the questions are really requests for a description of (1) those features of the use of the expression involved in the questions which incline one to answer "Yes," and of (2) those features of their use which incline one to answer "No." . . . Second provide the descriptions that are really wanted. . . . Fortunately when the nature of the questions has been explained, then the nature of the 'answers,' 'theories,' and 'reasons' which they have been 'offering' and 'advancing' becomes clear to the disputants. And then it becomes clear how much of the work of providing the descriptions has been already done, though under the disguise of a logical dispute. (At one time under the disguise of a contingent or natural dispute.) Thus the metaphysical paradoxes appear no longer as crude falsehoods about how language is actually

used, but as penetrating suggestions as to how it might be used so as to reveal what, by the actual use of language is hidden. . . .

Thus it appears how it is that, to give metaphysicians what they want, we have to do little more than remove the spectacles through which they look at their own work.

4. Existentialism

In the twentieth century, various waves have swept over the philosophic scene, leaving their residue (some more, some less). In addition to the analytic waves just discussed, there have been several concerned with Asian philosophy (chiefly Indian, Chinese, and Japanese), Marxism, and in particular existentialism and its cousin phenomenology.

Existentialism is so broad a grouping that there isn't any agreed-on way to characterize it, or to divide it into types. One plausible division is into religious and atheistic existentialism. (In the United States, in particular in the 1950s and 1960s, atheistic existentialism had the greater impact in coffee houses and on the philosophical scene—as opposed to the theological scene.)

Perhaps one reason for the immense popularity achieved by existentialism then was that it was seen to be more directly concerned with the fundamental philosophical question of how we should live our lives, while analytic and more traditional philosophy was seen to be doing dreary things like analyzing argument validity or constructing systems of abstract metaphysical propositions. For most of us, the ultimate and most fascinating question is *what should we do*, not what grand abstract pronouncements are true, and existentialism directly addresses itself to that fascinating question.

Perhaps existentialism was so popular because it seemed more directly concerned with what we should do with our lives.

Let's briefly discuss a few of the chiefly atheistic existentialist ideas, especially as popularized by Sartre, and contrast these ideas with those of the analytic philosophers.

Existentialism as Rebellion against Traditional Theology-Based Philosophy

An important point to bear in mind is that existentialism is largely a rebellion against traditional (chiefly) theistically bound philosophies, in which God or some other objective feature of the world defines our

Atheistic existentialism is a rebellion against

traditional theistic philosophy. essence and our place in a unified system of reality. (The very language employed is often that of the rejected theology-philosophy, an example being the key term *essence*.)

Humanity and Choice

Choice is central for humans. But there are no reasons for choosing x over y, and no causes forcing choices.

Perhaps the central theme of recent existentialism is that *choice* is the central fact of our existence. In the first place, choices are the basic stuff of our everyday lives; every action involves choice of one thing rather than another. Second, there are no purely rational or objective grounds for choosing one thing rather than another. And, third, no causal explanations or predictions of human choices can be given (as should be apparent from the Sartre excerpt in Chapter 2).

Human Existence Precedes Human Essence

To grasp the significance of these three points, consider the famous slogan that for human beings *existence precedes essence*. What does this mean? Think of a circle or a cup. A circle is a closed plane figure bounded by a single curved line every point of which is equidistant from its center. And a cup is a relatively small beverage container, usually bowl-shaped and with a handle. In giving these definitions,

For most things, essence precedes existence.

we give the essence of what it is to be a circle or to be a cup. Knowing this, but having never seen a circle or a cup, we know what it would be like for these essences to have *existence*; that is, for circles and cups to exist. The nature of a circle or cup is fixed by its essence; nothing lacking that exact essence can be a circle, or a cup. For a circle or a cup, and in fact for every item except a human being, *its essence precedes its existence*. In fact, if there were no circles or cups, there would still be the essence of circle and of cup.

But for humans, existence precedes essence.

But for human beings alone, according to existentialists, *existence precedes essence*. Human beings don't have fixed natures, like a circle (or the papercutter mentioned by Sartre). Whatever nature a person has is brought into existence—created—by that person's choices, by his or her choosing this rather than that, choices that aren't caused by some outside forces or laws of nature. (Existentialists thus tend to be libertarians of a sort.)

We first exist,

Human beings first *are*, we *exist*, and then we make choices that establish *what* we are, our *essences*. Only human beings stand in this *and then decide* "openness of being." We therefore can't be defined beforehand, unlike *on our essence.* circles, cups, and everything else whose essence precedes its existence.

Human Beings Create Their Own Values

The central fact, the thing most truly human, is our choosing this or *There are no* that, unguided by external objective values or by commands from *external values;* God. ("If God is dead, everything is possible.") But our humanity *we choose our* doesn't consist in choosing good over evil; there is no good or evil *own values.* independent of our choices. It is our choices that *create* or *invent* good *And our choices* and evil; indeed, create all values. The point is important: We don't *create values.* choose wisely when we learn what is good and then choose it. Our choosing it creates its goodness—the only kind of goodness a thing or action can have. And in making choices we can't appeal to reason, or to anything objective.

Life on its own makes no sense, has no plan. There is no cohe- *There are no* siveness or other feature we can look to for guidance in choosing. We *external answers* make our own sense out of our own lives by our own choices. A person *to questions such* who made no choices, were that possible, would not *be* a person, he *as "What is the* wouldn't have existence. Thus, in answer to questions such as "What *purpose of life?"* is the meaning or purpose of life?" "What value is there in existing?" *We invent our* or "Why go on living?" the existentialist replies that there is no *own purposes.* independent meaning or value to existence built into the nature of reality. Humanity invents its own values for human existence. "Man *is freedom"*; what matters for us is that we choose for ourselves, not that we choose the predetermined right.

Morality is thus in some ways like art, says Sartre. What counts in art is the act of creativity, unbounded by precise rules of the kind limiting, say, the mathematician (who can't just choose to make two plus two equal five).

We're Responsible for Ourselves and for All Humanity

It is our freedom to choose independently of outside forces or values *We create our* that generates our responsibilities. Because we choose our own es- *own essences,* sences, create our own values, we're responsible for our own individ- *we're responsible* uality. We make ourselves. But in choosing this or that for ourselves, *for our choices.*

217

While the analytic schools were becoming dominant in America and England earlier in this century, existentialism and then phenomenology were triumphant on the Continent, as in a sense they still are today. Here is the founder of phenomenology, Edmund Husserl, explaining the basic phenomenological starting point of inquiry.

Edmund Husserl: IDEAS: GENERAL INTRODUCTION TO PURE PHENOMENOLOGY*

Our first outlook on life is from the natural standpoint; through our senses things are simply there.

Our first outlook upon life is that of natural human beings, imaging, judging, feeling, willing, *"from the natural standpoint."* Let us make clear to ourselves what this means. . . .

I am aware of a world, spread out in space endlessly, and in time becoming and become, without end. I am aware of it, that means, first of all, I discover it immediately, intuitively, I experience it. Through sight, touch, hearing, etc., in the different ways of sensory perception, corporeal things somehow spatially distributed are *for me simply there*, in verbal or figurative sense "present," whether or not I pay them special attention by busying myself with them, considering, thinking, feeling, willing.

It's there not just as a world of facts, but as a practical world of goods, of values.

In this way, when consciously awake, I find myself at all times, and without my ever being able to change this, set in relation to a world which, through its constant changes, remains one and ever the same. It is continually "present" for me, and I myself am a member of it. Therefore this world is not there for me as a mere *world of facts and affairs*, but, with the same immediacy, as a *world of values*, a *world of goods*, a *practical world*. Without further effort on my part I find things before me furnished not only with the qualities that befit their positive nature, but with value-characters such as beautiful or ugly, agreeable or disagreeable, pleasant or unpleasant, and so forth. Things in their immediacy stand there as objects to be used, the "table" with its "books," the "glass to drink from," the "vase," the "piano," and so forth. These values and practicalities, they too belong to *the constitution of* the *"actually present" objects as such*, irrespective of my turning or not turning to consider them or indeed any other objects. . . .

That which is given to us from the natural standpoint is prior to all theory.

That which we have submitted towards the characterization of what is given to us from the natural standpoint, and thereby of the natural standpoint itself, was a piece of pure description *prior to all "theory."* In these studies we stand bodily aloof from all theories, and by 'theories' we here mean antici-

*Reprinted with permission of Macmillan Publishing Co., Inc. from *Ideas: General Introduction to Pure Phenomenology*, by Edmund Husserl, trans. W. R. Boyce Gibson (New York: Macmillan, 1931). Permission also granted by George Allen & Unwin Publishers Ltd.

patory ideas of every kind. Only as facts of our environment, not as agencies for uniting facts validly together, do theories concern us at all. . . .

We emphasize a most important point once again: I find continually present and standing over against me the one spatio-temporal fact-world to which I myself belong, as do all other men found in it and related in the same way to it. This "fact-world," as the word already tells us, I find to *be out there,* and also *take it just as it gives itself to me as something that exists out there.* All doubting and rejecting of the data of the natural world leaves standing the *general thesis of the natural standpoint.*

Instead now of remaining at this standpoint, we propose to alter it radically. Our aim must be to convince ourselves of the possibility of this alteration on grounds of principle. . . .

Consider the attempt to doubt everything which *Descartes,* with an entirely different end in view, with the purpose of setting up an absolutely indubitable sphere of Being, undertook to carry through. We link on here, but add directly and emphatically that this attempt to doubt everything should serve us *only as a device of method,* helping us to stress certain points which by its means, as though secluded in its essence, must be brought clearly to light.

The attempt to doubt everything has its place in the realm of our *perfect freedom.* We can *attempt to doubt* anything and everything, however convinced we may be concerning what we doubt, even though the evidence which seals our assurance is completely adequate.

Let us consider what is essentially involved in an act of this kind. He who attempts to doubt is attempting to doubt "Being" of some form or other, or it may be Being expanded into such predicative forms as "It is," "It is this or thus," and the like. The attempt does not affect the form of Being itself. He who doubts, for instance, whether an object, whose Being he does not doubt, is constituted in such and such a way, doubts *the way it is constituted.* We can obviously transfer this way of speaking from the doubting to the *attempt* at doubting. It is clear that we cannot doubt the Being of anything, and in the same act of consciousness (under the unifying form of simultaneity) bring what is substantive to this Being under the terms of the Natural Thesis, and so confer upon it the character of "being actually there" (*vorhanden*). Or to put the same in another way: we cannot at once doubt and hold for certain one and the same quality of Being. It is likewise clear that the *attempt* to doubt any object of awareness in respect of its *being actually there necessarily conditions a certain suspension (Aufhebung) of the thesis;* and it is precisely this that interests us. It is not a transformation of the thesis into antithesis, of positive into negative; it is also not a transformation into presumption, suggestion, indecision, doubt (in one or another sense of the word); such

All doubts about the natural world leave standing the general thesis of the natural standpoint.

We now propose to alter the natural standpoint.

We can use Descartes' method of complete doubt, but only as a helpful device.

We're free to try to doubt everything.

To doubt is to doubt Being. Not the Being itself of a thing, but the way it is constituted.

Attempts to doubt that an object is really there require a suspension of the thesis of the

natural standpoint. But we don't abandon it, we set it "out of action," "disconnect it," "bracket it."

We "transvalue" the original simple thesis, which is a concern of our full freedom, and is opposed to all cognitive attitudes.

Trying to doubt what is certain, the disconnection takes place with a change in the antithesis—with the supposition of Non-Being.

We use this epoché, a refraining from judgment compatible with the self evident Truth.

We now let the universal epoché replace Cartesian doubt, limiting its universality, otherwise nothing, not even

shifting indeed is not at our free pleasure. *Rather is it something quite unique. We do not abandon the thesis we have adopted, we make no change in our conviction,* which remains in itself what it is so long as we do not introduce new motives of judgment, which we precisely refrain from doing. And yet the thesis undergoes a modification—whilst remaining in itself what it is, *we set it as it were "out of action,"* we *"disconnect it," "bracket it."* It still remains there like the bracketed in the bracket, like the disconnected outside the connexional system. We can also say: The thesis is experience as lived (*Erlebnis*), *but we make "no use" of it,* and by that, of course, we do not indicate privation (as when we say of the ignorant that he makes no use of a certain thesis); in this case rather, as with all parallel expressions, we are dealing with indicators that point to a definite but *unique form of consciousness,* which clamps on to the original simple thesis (whether it actually or even predicatively *posits* existence or not), and transvalues it in a quite peculiar way. *This transvaluing is a concern of our full freedom, and is opposed to all cognitive attitudes* that would set themselves up as co-ordinate with *the thesis,* and yet within the unity of "simultaneity" remain incompatible with it . . .

In *the attempt to doubt* applied to a thesis which, as we presuppose, is certain and tenaciously held, the "disconnexion" takes place in and with a modification of the antithesis, namely, with the *"supposition" (Ansetzung) of Non-Being,* which is thus the partial basis of the attempt to doubt. With Descartes this is so markedly the case that one can say that his universal attempt at doubt is just an attempt at universal denial. We disregard this possibility here, we are not interested in every analytic component of the attempt to doubt, nor therefore in its exact and completely sufficing analysis. *We extract only the phenomenon of "bracketing" or "disconnecting,"* which is obviously not limited to that of the attempt to doubt, although it can be detached from it with special ease, but can appear *in other contexts also,* and with no less ease *independently.* In relation to *every* thesis and wholly uncoerced we can use this *peculiar ἐποχή (epoché), a certain refraining from judgment which is compatible with the unshaken and unshakable because self-evidencing conviction of Truth.* The thesis is "put out of action," bracketed, it passes off into the modified status of a "bracketed thesis," and the judgment *simpliciter* into *"bracketed judgment."*

We can now let the universal *ἐποχή* in the sharply defined and novel sense we have given to it step into the place of the Cartesian attempt at universal doubt. But on good grounds we *limit* the universality of this *ἐποχή.* For were it as inclusive as it is in general capable of being, then since every thesis and every judgment can be modified freely to any extent, and every objectivity that we can judge or criticize can be bracketed, no field would be left over for unmodified judgments, to say nothing of a science. But our design is just to discover a new scientific domain, such as might be won precisely *through the method of bracketing*, though only through a definitely limited form of it.

The limiting consideration can be indicated in a word.

We put out of action the general thesis which belongs to the essence of the natural standpoint, we place in brackets whatever it includes respecting the nature of Being: *this entire natural world therefore* which is continually "there for us," "present to our hand," and will ever remain there, is a "fact-world" of which we continue to be conscious, even though it pleases us to put it in brackets.

If I do this, as I am fully free to do, I do *not* then *deny* this "world," as though I were a sophist, *I do not doubt that it is there* as though I were a sceptic; but I use the "phenomenological" ἐποχή, which *completely bars* me *from using any judgment that concerns spatio-temporal existence (Dasein).*

Thus *all sciences which relate to this natural world,* though they stand never so firm to me, though they fill me with wondering admiration, though I am far from any thought of objecting to them in the least degree, *I disconnect them all, I make absolutely no use of their standards, I do not appropriate a single one of the propositions that enter into their systems, even though their evidential value is perfect, I take none of them, no one of them serves me for a foundation*— so long, that is, as it is understood, in the way these sciences themselves understand it, as a truth *concerning the realities of this world. I may accept it only after I have placed it in the bracket.* That means: only in the modified consciousness of the judgment as it appears in disconnexion, and *not as it figures within the science as its proposition, a proposition which claims to be valid and whose validity I recognize and make use of.*

The ἐποχή here in question will not be confused with that which positivism demands, and against which, as we were compelled to admit, it is itself an offender. We are not concerned at present with removing the preconceptions which trouble the pure positivity (*Sachlichkeit*) of research, with the constituting of a science "free from theory" and "free from metaphysics" by bringing all the grounding back to the immediate data, nor with the means of reaching such ends, concerning whose value there is indeed no question. What *we* demand lies along another line. The whole world as placed within the nature-setting and presented in experience as real, taken completely "free from all theory," just as it is in reality experienced, and made clearly manifest in and through the linkings of our experiences, has now no validity for us, it must be set in brackets, untested indeed but also uncontested. Similarly all theories and sciences, positivistic or otherwise, which relate to this world, however good they may be, succumb to the same fate.

science, would be left. Our aim is a new science won by this method.

Limiting places in brackets all in the natural standpoint re Being.

We don't deny the world but bar ourselves from using judgments about existence.

Thus, we disconnect all natural sciences, make no use of them as a foundation.

We shouldn't confuse this epoché with what positivism demands. We aren't concerned to free science from metaphysics by returning to the given in experience but freeing the world from all theory, just as it is experienced.

And in choosing for ourselves, we choose for all humanity.

we choose for everyone, and thus take responsibility for all mankind. In the act of choosing, we say not just "I've chosen *this*," but also "This is *to be* chosen," "This is *choosable*."*

We Are Condemned to Be Free

Existentialists see the absence of outside guides as being condemned to freedom, creating anguish.

The absence of outside guidance for our choices coupled with the enormous responsibility to choose both for ourselves and for all humanity, and without any guidance, leads to the idea that we are *condemned* to freedom. This is why Kierkegaard, for instance, says we choose only "in fear and trembling," and why existentialists speak of the "anguish" of the human condition. They see this unguided freedom of choice as a dreadful responsibility.

We Choose to Be Individuals

They can't say what we *should choose, but they do choose to be self-aware individuals, not self-deceived, but "identical with themselves," thus, authentic.*

What then precisely *should* we choose? Existentialists, of course, can't say, because that would violate a basic tenet of their position; namely, that there aren't any outside values for us to fasten on. Still, there is a kind of value they opt for; namely, to be an *individual*, which entails knowing oneself. The supreme value is to be as we have chosen, which involves a kind of *integrity*. The opposite of this, *self-deception*, is the great vice. A person who is *"identical with himself"* is "authentic"; the self-deceived person lacks authenticity. Such a person is not "himself," doesn't any longer have a self to deceive.

We're All Alone and Life Is Absurd

Each of us is alone. We choose our own values, so life is absurd—there are no external

Existentialists therefore conceive of each of us as a self-contained entity, *alone*, and *lonely*. We must choose our own essences; no one else can do it for us, nor can we find rules of guidance written somewhere. We thus live by values of our own invention, which they say makes life *absurd* because there aren't any criteria by means of which

---

*So our actions define not just our own essences, but the essence of humanity. According to some interpretations, existentialism thus comes close to Kant's categorical imperative [presented in the Kant excerpt in Chapter 4], the existentialist version being: Don't choose that which can't be consistently chosen by all other human beings. Thus, it's wrong to lie, as Kant argued, because that would make it impossible for everyone to lie successfully. The maxim of our action could not be universalized.

to choose. We live in an ambiguous world, "in a seething cauldron of possibilities," with no prior essences to guide us, and with "no exit."

guiding values, and "no exit."

A Quick Critique of Existentialism

It should be obvious that the very language of the existentialist is the kind positivists rail against as perhaps appropriate for literature but not for philosophy. Take the concept of *essence*. Sartre says the essence of a papercutter, which exists prior to the papercutter itself, is to cut paper. But what does this mean other than that human beings make and use certain objects in order to cut paper? If *that* is all it means, then the famous existentialist slogan turns out to be obvious and trivial. To say of a papercutter that its essence preceded its existence would mean just that its maker made it according to a plan in order to fulfill the purpose of cutting paper. (A not very enlightening truth.)

Positivists reject the existentialist language. Sartre's use of "existence" and "essence" yields either nonsense or trivial truths.

Worse, suppose a piece of flint just happened to be shaped so as to have a sharp edge, thus making an excellent papercutter. *Its* paper-cutting essence would not precede its existence, thus contradicting existentialist doctrine.

And what about human beings? An intelligent creature from Alpha Centauri might well conceive of a carbon-based life system (suppose the system on Alpha Centauri is based on other sorts of chemical compounds) that would generate an animal like a human being, and in fact might then set about successfully creating such a being, or might then find us by means of space explorations. In such a case, it would seem that our essence would exist in the minds of Alpha Centaurians without their ever having experienced our existence; in fact, perhaps before there were any existing human beings to experience. So human essences could exist equally well before human existence, just as the papercutter's essence does.

A papercutter's existence might precede its essence. And a person's essence might precede his existence.

Furthermore, how does it follow from or remain consistent with the existentialist ideas about freedom and the absence of external values that human beings choose for all humanity? What can this consistently mean? If each person freely chooses, and does so in the absence of objective rules, what sense is there in saying we choose for all people, other than, perhaps, the simple truism that we usually want others to have and further our values and often try to get them to do so?

How does it follow that we choose for all people?

223

Here is a rather sophisticated pragmatic analysis by the contemporary philosopher, Abraham Kaplan of how words function and meanings are specified.

Abraham Kaplan: **DEFINITION AND SPECIFICATION OF MEANING***

Definition is not always the best way to specify meanings.

The process by which a term is introduced into discourse or by which the meaning of a term already in use is more exactly specified, may be called *specification of meaning.* This process is ordinarily explicated by the concept of definition—a logical equivalence between the term defined and an expression whose meaning has already been specified. However, this procedure is not always a satisfactory treatment of specification of meaning. . . .

Definitions give the outcomes of processes at a given stage. Specifying meanings is processive, hypothetical, provisional. There is no "the" meaning of a concept as definitions imply.

Definitions construe science and its language not as processes of inquiry and communication, but only as the outcome of these processes at some particular stage. In fact specification of meaning is processive; it is hypothetical and provisional, and undergoes modification as inquiry proceeds. The concept of definition does not in itself provide a logical account of this modification. Moreover, "the" process of inquiry is an abstraction from particular inquiries, so that a given concept has various meanings in different contexts—meanings not related to one another as logical equivalents, but empirically coinciding to a greater or lesser degree. It follows that one can not speak of "the" meaning of a concept as it actually functions in inquiry. But just such a determinate reference is assigned to it in the definitional representation of the language of science. Every concept is purported to be defined in one particular way and no other. . . .

It's hard to give definitions in a field of inquiry that all accept, because of the requirements the various contexts in which it is used.

So long as the representation is in abstract and general terms, the procedure seems to be satisfactory. But serious problems arise when the attempt is made to give the representation specific content from some particular field of inquiry. The formulation of a definition for any empirical concept satisfactory to all investigators employing the concept is notoriously difficult. And this difficulty . . . is due, not to a psychology of captiousness, but to the logical requirements of the varying contexts in which the concept functions.

Let us take a single example, the biological concept of species. J. S. Huxley, in a book on . . . biology, observes:

> There is no single criterion of species. Morphological differences; failure to interbreed; infertility of offspring; ecological, geographical, or genetical distinct-

---

*Abraham Kaplan, "Definition and Specification of Meaning," from *The Journal of Philosophy.* Reprinted by permission.

ness—all these must be taken into account, but none of them singly is decisive. . . . A combination of criteria is needed, together with some sort of flair. With the aid of these, it is remarkable how the variety of organic life falls apart into biologically discontinuous groups.

The biological concept of a species is an example.

Clearly, the function of the concept does not depend on its having been *defined,* if there has been a specification of its meaning in some other form.

Whenever a term is introduced into a context of inquiry—whether *de novo* or extended from some other context—situations (pertaining to the new context) are described in which the term may be applied. Any such description may be called an *indicator* for the term. But the term is not in general logically equivalent to any or all of its indicators; they assign to the application of the term under the described conditions, not a logical certainty, but only a specified weight. Thus, failure to interbreed is an indicator for distinctness of species; but that two animals do in fact interbreed does not logically entail that they belong to the same species, but only adds some weight to the assumption.

When a term is introduced situations are described where the term applies. These are indications of the term, and have different weights. Thus, interbreeding is a reliable indication of sameness of species.

Such weights are not specified quantitatively, but they are ordered, at least with regard to other indicators for the same term. The weight which an indicator assigns to the application of a term is often called the *reliability* of the indicator. In the example, infertility of offspring is a more reliable indicator of distinct species than differences in phenotypic characteristics; geographical distinctness is perhaps less reliable, and so on. In general, one indicator may be said to be more or less reliable than another for the same term, even though it be impossible to compare the reliability of indicators for different terms. . . . Thus, just as semantical rules of the familiar sort specify the meaning of a sentence by giving the conditions under which the sentence would be true, the indicators specify a more or less indefinite meaning by giving conditions under which the term is likely to apply.

Weights are ordered but not quantitative. A weight gives the reliability of an indicator.

There may, of course, be negative indicators specifying situations to which the term is likely not to apply. In general, the negation of a positive indicator is a negative indicator but of different weight than the positive. A test may be highly sensitive to the presence of a particular property, but may sometimes react even in its absence; it would then be a highly reliable negative indicator, but not as good a positive indicator. Or, to take an example of the converse, two animals that closely resemble one another phenotypically (as do, say, two dachshunds) may reliably be presumed to belong to the same species; but that two animals belong to *distinct* species is less reliably indicated by phenotypical *differences.*

There are negative as well as positive indicators. And the negation of a positive indicator is usually a negative indicator, but of a different weight.

The specification of indicators for a term is not in itself sufficient for the use of the term. The indicators describe situations to which the term probably applies, but given a sentence in which the term occurs, we can not *deduce* characteristics of the situation described: a *reverse* weight for these indicators must be separately specified. Such reverse specifications may be called *references* of the term. Thus, a proposition about species can be interpreted as making reference to morphological differences, to genetic or geographical distinctness, to phenotypic differences, and so on. All these references are involved in varying weights (degrees of relevance). The weights of the references will obviously differ in different contexts of inquiry, and need not correspond to the weights of the indicators. . . . In Darwin's investigation of the distribution of species, geographical distinctness had perhaps a high weight as an indicator, but the reference of "species" in the resultant hypotheses was more to genetic and morphological distinctness.

The weight of a reference depends, not just on the weight of the corresponding indicator, but on the weights of the entire set of indicators. A particular indicator may be more reliable than others but occur less frequently or under more limited conditions, so that its weight as a reference will be correspondingly less as compared with other references. The set of references and the set of indicators thus coincide, but the corresponding weights in general differ from one another. It is this difference, indeed, which requires the distinction between indicators and references. The distinction can not be made in the case of definition because logical equivalence is symmetrical. The specification of a meaning consists, therefore, of weighted indicators and references both.

The references can not be *substituted* for the term whose meaning is specified, any more than could the term for its indicators. The transition from a proposition containing the term to one containing only its references is not, as in the case of definition, an immediate deduction, but one in which the premise gives the conclusion only some weight or other. But the term is useful even though (perhaps one should say *because*) it can not be eliminated with strictness and certitude. It provides a linkage among its set of indicators (or references) as a whole. It embodies, in fact, a propositional content: that the members of this set are positively correlated with one another. The term is applied and refers to a variety of situations which do not necessarily all exhibit some single common character, but a number of distinct characters empirically related to one another. From this standpoint, the term "species"— to pursue the example—is not eliminable from the language of biology. Its introduction does not constitute merely a convenient shorthand for more cumbersome locutions, but marks an advance in biological theory—that the various characteristics serving as indicators and references of the concept have an empirically significant relatedness: problems of biology can be formulated and solved in terms of this relatedness. . . .

Thus the specification [of meaning] at any stage is a provisional one, both as to the indicators included, and the weights associated with them. We begin with indicators by which the initial partial extension of the term is selected, and in terms of which the initial context of application can be confirmed. As the context of application grows, the specified meaning grows—and changes—with it. The stipulation of new indicators affects the weights of the old ones, while they in turn limit the range of choice in the stipulation. The adequacy of a particular indicator is not judged by its accordance with a pre-determined concept; the new and old indicators are appraised conjointly.

Specification of meaning is always provisional. As we learn more and the context of application grows, meaning specifications change, and indicators are reappraised.

An explicatum of specification of meaning along the lines discussed would take the acknowledged vagueness of all terms directly into account. The designation of a term would not in general be represented as a well-defined area, but as an open set of regions overlapping to a greater or lesser degree, each indicator determining one such region. The meaning of this term would correspond neither to the logical sum nor product of these regions, but to the pattern as a whole. The designatum, to paraphrase Claude Bernard's famous dictum about disease, is not an entity but a complex of symptoms. It is made clear, not by a precise definition, but by a specification of the characteristic syndrome. . . .

Specifications of meaning must take account of the vagueness of all terms, and specify a "complex of symptoms," not a specific set of criteria (as in definition).

The "sameness" of a concept employed in different contexts of inquiry (or communication) would thus be explicated, not by the constancy of a single reference, but by the patterns of its references. It is like the "same face" in the members of a family; the familial resemblance is constituted, not by similarity in some one feature, but in the general cast of features. Every term designates in this sense a "family of meanings." The inevitable vagueness of the term results from this dispersion of its reference. This dispersion is reduced, and the meaning of the term brought into sharper focus, as the reliability of the indicators is improved and the degree of their overlapping increased. This degree of overlapping may be called the *congruence* of the indicator set. At each stage the attempt is to specify the meaning in a way which will maximize both reliability and congruence. The addition of more and more reliable indicators may necessitate rejection of some old ones to preserve congruence; indicators which lower congruence may nevertheless be adopted to increase reliability. In a limiting case, indicators are subdivided into two or more groups, each of higher congruence and reliability than the original set. We say that the term was ambiguous, and specify distinct meanings.

Sameness of concepts is like family resemblance, a pattern of features. The vagueness of a term can be reduced by increasing the congruence of its indicators. We may adopt indicators with lower congruence to increase reliability, and (sometimes) divide them into two groups—the term has become ambiguous.

It seems, therefore, that analyzing some of the basics of existentialism leads to the conclusion that existentialism is a compendium of simple truths (for instance, that there are no objective values) and of fairly obvious falsehoods, or at least unjustified claims to truth (for example, that we choose for and are thus responsible for all humanity).

Is existentialism new and of value chiefly for those coming from certain traditions and old news to many others?

Finally, let this analytically inclined person point out the unanalytic thought that existentialists seem to fixate on only part of the human story—the anxiety-producing lack of external support or sense to our lives, while neglecting the vibrant aspects of the human situation. They appear to do so, let it be suggested, because for them these are new truths in need of emphasis, given that existentialists tend to come from a philosophical background that claims an objective coherence to the universe and an objective source of values outside of humanity itself. Existentialists see this traditional objectification of values as a denial of true human freedom and *individuality*. But the absence of such an external objective moral reality is old stuff to many who are attracted to the analytic way of doing philosophy, whether they agree with this idea or not. Perhaps in philosophy we get what we need more than is generally supposed, and needing different things, we turn to different philosophies.

Summary of Chapter 6

There have been several interesting turns in philosophy in the past hundred years or so.

1. *Logical positivism* is one of essentially three different schools within the *analytic* tradition. Logical positivists reject a good deal of the classical literature in philosophy as *metaphysical* (so vague or ambiguous as to be virtually meaningless), or disguised platitudes. For them, philosophy consists of (1) analysis and clarification of language, and (2) investigation of the correct principles of reasoning. The area of facts or theories about the nature of the universe, no matter how general, is the domain of science, not philosophy.

Logic divides into the *deductive*, where conclusions follow necessarily from premises, and *inductive*, where premises only make conclusions probable. According to positivists, at least some reasoning of scientists must be inductive, since deductively obtained conclusions only repeat (perhaps in different words) part of what was already contained in their premises, while scientific theories go beyond the evidence or experiences on which they are based.

(Roughly, scientists project patterns they've gleaned in experience onto all future experiences.)

Analytic knowledge, positivists say, can be derived *a priori* (prior to experience of the thing known), while *synthetic* knowledge of a thing or event can be known only *a posteriori*, or empirically, through experiences with things like that kind of thing or event. Scientific knowledge, then, always has a synthetic part, unlike mathematical knowledge, which is completely analytic and can be known *a priori*.

The reason analytic truths can be known *a priori* is that they contain no factual content—they don't tell us about the nature of this universe.

According to *empiricists* in general, and logical positivists in particular, no synthetic truths can be known *a priori*. *Rationalists*, on the other hand, tend to accept the existence of synthetic *a priori* truths in mathematics, logic, and metaphysics.

Positivists try to eliminate the alleged metaphysical nonsense on a wholesale basis by introducing the *verification theory of meaning* which states roughly that a sentence or proposition has meaning only to the extent that it's possible to confirm or refute it by relevant observations. Metaphysical statements, such as "The Nothing nothings," have no meaning according to this criterion because no observation or experience could possibly confirm or refute them.

Does the verification theory itself have meaning according to its own standards? Some positivists, agreeing with their opponents, say *no*; the principle is really a proposal as to how to use language.

In addition to the factual or *cognitive* meaning tested for by the verification theory of meaning, there is also *emotive* meaning. Positivists tend to believe that value statements, whether aesthetic or moral, have emotive meaning but not factual meaning. Thus, they often opt for some version of emotivism, the theory that moral judgments simply state or express emotive responses to things. Positivists adopt what we called the *subjectivist* view (in Chapter 4) that values are not part of the objective world but are just our responses or attitudes to what is in the world.

Of course, this doesn't mean that positivists are anti-moral any more than anyone else, they just analyze morality differently. Similarly, in rejecting metaphysics positivists are not revealing some lack of emotion or bias against poetry or literature. They just believe that philosophy is not poetry.

2. The position in the analytic tradition called *pragmatism* attempts to relate theory to everyday practice. According to the *pragmatic theory of meaning* we know the meaning of a statement only to the extent we can specify the bearing its truth might have on our lives, so that two statements have the same meaning (are synonymous) if they have identical bearings on our lives. A statement believed is a rule of action, as belief that sugar sweetens coffee

contains the rule to put sugar in coffee when you want coffee to taste sweet.

Pragmatists believe the *truth* is what works in our lives. Statements are predictions, and true statements are accurate predictions. "This bowl contains sugar" is true because it correctly predicts that the bowl's contents will sweeten drinks, burn when lit, etc. Of course, no statements alone predict much of anything, but they do in conjunction with other statements. Thus, "This is a match" alone doesn't predict that if struck it will light; we need to add that oxygen is present, the match is dry, etc.

For pragmatists, *logic* is just the general method for solving problems, the general theory of rational inquiry (and thus the theory of scientific inquiry). To have a problem, we must have goals, desires, etc. We can't just decide to doubt everything—in any case such doubt would just lead to the denial of everything. In real life, some values, some beliefs, always remain undoubted at any particular moment. Of course, later we may doubt them, no beliefs are forever exempt from doubt. Even the rules of logic can be challenged. The right rules of logic are just the ones that have worked.

Pragmatists deny the positivist's division of facts and values, into statements having cognitive or emotive meanings. There are many ways to divide the pie of reality, we choose that which is of value to us. It isn't that some statements are both of facts and values, both cognitive and emotive. It's that facts have their value, and values their facts. Values need to be tested just as facts. A valued institution may be rejected (revalued) because it fails to work in practice and replaced by a newly valued institution that better serves our overall values or purposes.

Pragmatists tend to reject the dualities that generate many philosophical problems. For instance, is morality concerned with reason or emotion? Pragmatists reject the very division into reason and emotion that generates this question, thinking instead of rational emotions and irrational emotions.

Pragmatists also deny the sharp distinction between *means* and *ends*. Life has no absolute ends. Every end is in turn a means to something else, nor are there ends desirable no matter what means are needed to get them. What counts are *means-ends* packages.

Similarly, pragmatists solve the phenomenalism versus realism dispute by denying there is a difference between the two theories, thus denying there is a real issue at stake, because it makes no difference, they say, to any real-life problems which side is right, so that on the pragmatic theory of meaning the two apparently different theories are one and the same.

3. According to *ordinary language* philosophy, philosophical problems arise in large part because of confused unordinary uses of terms and locutions that in everyday life have a perfectly sensible ordinary meaning. Thus, philosophical problems are not solved by showing which solution is correct, but

are dissolved by showing how inappropriate language generated them. So we "solve" the problem of free will versus determinism by showing how the metaphysical use of concepts like the free choice of actions is different from their everyday usages.

But metaphysical uses of language need not be a complete waste. Somewhat like a poet, the metaphysician attempts to use language to express things that are hard to say retaining everyday usage exactly. The trouble is that philosophers become confused by their own odd uses of language. The trick, then, is to become aware of how the misused language has confused us while still grasping the philosopher's insights.

4. While analytic schools swept the boards in the English-speaking universities, *existentialism* and *phenomenology* were dominant on the European continent. Existentialism also became quite popular in some circles in the United States, perhaps because it seemed more concerned than the analytic schools with questions about what we should be doing with our lives.

Atheistic existentialism is partly a rebellion against traditional theistic philosophy in which God defines our essence. The central fact of human existence, say existentialists, is choice, yet there are no purely rational grounds for choosing one thing over another, and no causes forcing our choices.

For human beings, unlike everything else, *existence precedes essence*, which means that we don't have natures fixed by causal forces but we freely choose our own essences. By choosing this rather than that, we create our own values. There are no external rights and wrongs. ("If God is dead, everything is possible.") Our choosing makes what we choose valuable.

Life on its own makes no sense, has no plan. We invent our own purposes, and our own essences. Since we create our own essences, we're responsible for our own choices. But in choosing for ourselves, we choose for all mankind by declaring, in effect, that what we choose is *choosable*. (Some give this a Kantian twist: Choose only what can be chosen by all humanity.)

The freedom to choose, divorced from outside guidance, is seen by existentialists as an enormous responsibility. We are *condemned* to freedom, and choose "in fear and trembling." But existentialists don't tell us what we should choose, since there aren't any values independent of our choices. Yet they do choose a certain value, namely, to be an individual, to know oneself, to have the integrity of one's choices, to be "identical with oneself," "authentic," and definitely not self-deceived. Life is *absurd* (makes no external sense) and there is "no exit."

Analytic philosophers reject the existentialist's language and thus his theories. In particular, they find his key terms like "essence" and "existence" confused. On a sensible use of these terms, anything's existence might precede

231

its essence and vice versa. Further, how does it follow that in choosing for ourselves we choose for all humanity? And why fasten on the anxiety of some choices? Is it because existentialism stresses what is new for the reformed Christian theist but stale news for atheists and agnostics?

Questions for Further Thought

1. How would you describe what it is that unites analytic philosophers into one school of philosophical thought?

2. What do you think of the claim many make that analytic philosophy has gotten too far away from the basic philosophical question of how we should lead our lives (or the question of what is the meaning or purpose of life)?

3. *Are* true beliefs just beliefs that work in everyday life, as some pragmatists claim? What makes you think so?

4. What do you think of the "solution" some pragmatists offer to the issue of realism versus phenomenalism or idealism?

5. Is Sartre right in claiming that human existence precedes human essence? What are the implications of this (or of its falsehood, if you think it's false) for moral right and wrong?

6. Having looked over the various excerpts from the famous philosophers, does it appear to you that philosophy has made progress since the days of Plato and Aristotle? If so, what sort of progress? If not, why not?

7. While much has been said, especially in this last chapter, about metaphysics, no definition or careful description of metaphysics has been provided. (The name stems from a book of Aristotle's that came after *The Physics.*) In your opinion, what *is* the difference between the metaphysics that analytic philosophers tend to condemn (which others extol as the key to philosophy) and the rest of philosophy (if any)?

8. What do you think of Hans Reichenbach's refutation of Descartes' proof of his own existence?

9. What is it that John Wisdom is trying to tell us in the excerpt in this chapter? Does it make good sense to you?

10. What do you think of the logical positivists' claim that discovering facts and theories about the nature of the world, however general, is the job of

scientists, not philosophers? What about their claim that scientific knowledge never can be obtained *a priori*?

11. Most analytic philosophers, and empiricists in general, deny that there are any synthetic *a priori* truths. But don't we learn such truths in geometry when we prove the theorems of geometry *a priori*; for instance, proving that the angles of a triangle equal 180°? And don't scientists assume, *a priori*, that every event has a cause? And what about Kant's *a priori* proof (in the excerpts in Chapter 4) of the synthetic proposition he calls the *categorical imperative?*

12. The verification theory of meaning has been objected to on grounds that it is itself meaningless according to itself. Positivists reply that the verification theory is indeed factually meaningless. But they point out that they intend it as a proposal concerning what it is useful to mean by "meaning" (some say it's also a declaration of their intended use of that term). Does this satisfactorily answer the objection?

13. Kant says that the truths of arithmetic are synthetic, as well as *a priori*. Consider that 7 + 5 = 12. Kant believes that expression synthetic, because try as he will, when he examines the addition of 7 and 5 he doesn't find 12 in it. Is he right about this? How would a logical positivist reply?

14. Do you agree with Sartre's argument that in choosing our own values we choose for all humanity?

15. What do you think of Reichenbach's analysis (in the excerpt in this chapter) of the excerpt from Hegel's writings? Opponents of the analytic philosophers have argued that analyses such as Reichenbach's (that lift passages out of context) are foolish, since Hegel wrote lengthy books explaining what he is talking about. To come to any firm convictions on the issue, we clearly have to read lots of Hegel and then return to the passage in question. But life is short, and Hegel fiendishly difficult (as are many of the famous philosophical tracts). Can we make a sensible *provisional* judgment without reading a great deal of Hegel, at least as to whether Hegel is *worth* pursuing, given that reading one thing precludes reading something else?

Index